PRAISE FOR

Save-My-Life

My work as a member of Parliament advocating for ... military, veterans, and first responders with post-traumatic str... ...er and operational stress injuries has been largely influenced by Natalie's story and the friendship we have built over the past several years. She is an inspiration to me, and I am so glad she found the even greater courage needed to tell her story. I know her story will reassure those suffering from PTSD and OSI that they are not alone and that it is OK to talk about it and seek the help they need. I am proud to call Natalie a friend and proud of the work she is doing to help others.

~ JOHN BRASSARD, MP Barrie-Innisfil

Written from the heart and exposing the pure vulnerability paramedics struggle with while in the community looking after our loved ones, Natalie's story plants the question: While they are providing skilled and compassionate care to us, how well are we giving back to them?

~ RANDI MCDERMOTT, Program Coordinator, Georgian College

Natalie Harris is a passionate and dedicated professional with a huge heart. She speaks about her personal journey to educate and show others that they are not alone in what they are feeling. Natalie has been a huge proponent of creating awareness about first responders and their battles with PTSD. Anyone who has the privilege of knowing Natalie and reading her story will have their spirits lifted and find a sense of peacefulness.

~ SHAUN TAYLOR, Co-founder of Ivegotyourback911

This masterful work, full of courage, honesty, and healing, is invaluable for all first responders on their own personal mental health journey.

~ JILL FOSTER, Co-founder of Ivegotyourback911

Natalie's raw honesty and thoughtful proclamations have been a source of inspiration and calm for many first responders. To say that "you are not alone" is the greatest gift she could give to her colleagues.

~ VINCE SAVOIA, Founder of Tema Conter Memorial Trust

I first learned of Natalie's struggle with PTSD through social media. What caught my attention was her openness and strength in talking about her life and what she was going through. I now know Natalie personally, and I can see that she is changing lives by telling her story. I am so proud of her.

~ NAME WITHHELD, Police Officer

Natalie Harris's willingness to share her journey is a source of inspiration. She goes beyond honestly talking about her personal struggles—she speaks about solutions. "You are not alone."

~ RANDY PAPPLE, County of Brant Ambulance Service

Showing us all how not only to survive but to thrive, Nat unselfishly shares her journey through her writings and leads us all down the path to positive constructive attitudes, self-reflection, and wellness. Her heart has been the greatest gift to the first responder community, and words cannot express the positive impact she is making.

~ BRAD MCKAY, CTSS, Mood Disorders Society of Canada

Perhaps the butterfly is evidence that we all can go through a great deal of darkness yet become something beautiful. Natalie Harris is living proof of this remarkable journey, and she is a true testament to survival and healing. This book gives the reader an in-depth look at and understanding of the struggles she faced, and of her courage and determination not to give up. Many who read her book will be touched by her strength and will be inspired to follow her example.

~ STACEY FERLAND, MPCC National Practice Lead, Homewood Health

By telling her story, Natalie has provided a voice for all first responders, helped shatter the silence associated with PTSD, and initiated efforts to make meaningful changes to support the women and men who serve our communities.

~ JIM HARRIS, Canadian Mental Health Association, Simcoe County Branch

Through her blog, and now her book, Save-My-Life School, "Paramedic Nat" has given us the opportunity to bear witness to the extreme pain, grief, and shame that those who suffer from mental health challenges—including PTSD, OSI and depression—deal with on a daily basis. Natalie is a true hero who advocates tirelessly to ensure that no one suffers in silence. There is no doubt in my mind that the courage she has shown, and continues to show, will save the lives of those who so bravely put on their uniforms each day in the face of unfathomable danger.

~ TODD DOHERTY, MP Cariboo-Prince George

Natalie has quickly recognized the value of empathy and the healing merits of sharing common feelings and thoughts among peers. Her founding and development of Wings of Change is part of the beginning of a change in culture among first responders. Few of us of the old guard succeeded in accomplishing that work in all the years that we had to make peer support a common standard within these paramilitary organizations. There is nothing more important to many who suffer than to hear someone say, "I understand because I have been there too."

~ SYLVIO GRAVEL, Author of 56 Seconds

To: Jessica

Save-My-Life School

A first responder's mental health journey

All the very best!

NATALIE HARRIS

with select excerpts written by

AMANDA BARROWCLIFFE

CAROLINE HARRIS ~ ADAM HUNWICKS ~ MANDY JOHNSON ~ ROB THERIAULT

PUBLISHED BY WINTERTICKLE PRESS

echo
BOOKS

Save-My-Life School
A first responder's mental health journey

"Save-My-Life School" credit: Amanda Barrowcliffe
Cover photo credit: Natalie Harris
Cover and book design credit: Heather Down
Acquisition credit: Kim Forster
Font credit for *Save-My-Life School*: Hesster Moffett font, licensed from joebobgraphics.com

Library and Archives Canada Cataloguing in Publication

Harris, Natalie M., author
    Save-my-life school : a first responder's mental health journey / Natalie
Harris.

Based on the Paramedic Nat blog.
ISBN 978-1-894813-91-4 (softcover)

    1. Harris, Natalie M. 2. Harris, Natalie M--Mental health. 3. Allied
health personnel--Ontario--Barrie--Biography. 4. Post-traumatic stress
disorder--Patients--Ontario--Barrie--Biography. 5. Post-traumatic stress
disorder. 6. Autobiographies. I. Title. II. Title: Paramedic Nat (Blog)

RC552.P67H35 2017   616.85'210092   C2016-907855-8 ISBN

Publisher's Note: *Save-My-Life School: A first responder's mental health journey* is a memoir based on the blog written by Natalie Harris. It is told from the perspective of the author. Some details, events, and names may have been altered in the interest of the flow of the book, cohesiveness, privacy, or simple courtesy. The opinions expressed in this book are solely those of the author and not necessarily those of the publisher. This book was written for entertainment and general education purposes only. The author is not a mental health professional or therapist. This book is not a substitute for medical care. If you think you or someone you know may be experiencing a mental health issue, please seek the help of qualified healthcare professionals. If you are in crises, please go directly to the nearest hospital or call emergency services.

Printed in Canada

Published by Wintertickle Press
132 Commerce Park Drive, Unit K, Suite 155, Barrie, ON, L4N 0Z7 | wintticklepress.com

~ AUTHOR ACKNOWLEDGEMENTS

I want to thank my beautiful children, Caroline and Adam, for inspiring me to be a better person every day and for braving this journey beside me.

To my friends and family, thank you for your love and support even when I'm sure I had brought you to your wits' end, and thank you for believing in me.

To the doctors, nurses, and other healthcare professionals who treated me with dignity, saw past stigma, and never treated me as a weak human being—thank you.

To my teachers at the Buddhist centre, thank you for teaching me so many lessons; but above all, thank you for the lessons about love.

To the politicians who allowed my voice to be heard, thank you.

To my fur babies who have been the best medicine I have ever known; I love you.

~ PUBLISHER ACKNOWLEDGEMENTS

The publisher would like to formally thank Kim Forster for early development of this project.

The publisher also wishes to acknowledge Amanda Barrowcliffe for her graciousness and willingness to contribute to this work.

The publisher appreciates the help and stories freely contributed to this book by Rob Theriault.

The publisher would like to acknowledge the many individuals and the focus groups who provided feedback during the development of this book.

CONTENTS

~

FOREWORD

~

Natalie Harris offers a deeply personal, meaningful, and raw glimpse into the very real struggle with mental illness. Illness that is typically and tragically steeped in silence. She breaks the stigma by breaking the silence. She articulates so deeply what it means to live with PTSD, depression, and anxiety. I've had the great gift of knowing Natalie through her writings. After meeting her, I can say she is as she writes: through struggle and joy, she is a shining and clear light that's focused on making sure the silence is ended for those living with or loving someone with similar struggles. There is no one audience for Natalie's writings; I truly feel she writes for us all.

-Clara Hughes, O.C., O.M.
Author of *Open Heart, Open Mind*
Six-Time Olympic Medallist

PART I

~

Save-My-Life School

*Do what you feel in
your heart to be right—for you'll
be criticized anyway.*

–Eleanor Roosevelt

Hi everyone. This is a big deal for me. This first entry may be small, but to me it is *huge*. I've been battling a mental illness, and I feel it's time to talk about it—but it's not easy. Let me start by saying today is the first day of my partial hospitalization mental health program. I have a long road ahead of me, which started years ago. I want to share it with you and possibly help anyone who has been battling a mental illness. Sometimes the stigma is so big, it keeps our minds closed to the pain these illnesses cause.

Stay tuned if you would like. I will be posting often.

Well, here it is loud and very clear—today is *not* my first trip to the mental health wing of the hospital. But today is different because it has one thing all the other trips didn't have—hope.

Making sure I make it on time to the intensive out-patient program now nicknamed "Save-My-Life School," I set my alarm slightly early to allow me enough time to colour my hair, run out the door, and grab a quick coffee. I have no idea what to expect; I just know that I am going to the mental health wing—a wing I could find with my eyes closed.

As I walk into the program meeting room, I feel like the new kid in class—probably because I am.

"I hope you brought Starbucks for everyone," some guy yells from the corner. I find an empty seat and scan the room. "Everyone looks pretty normal," I think to myself. How ironic of me! I came here to end the stigma of my mental illnesses, but my very first thoughts scream stigma through and through.

"What's your deal?" asks Starbucks Guy.

"Pardon?" I say, not immediately knowing what he means. Then I catch on. "Oh, why am I here?"

"Yeah…and you look really familiar."

Where do I begin? And how do I summarize this in a sentence? "I overdosed on September 21." I realize this will take more than one sentence, so I continue, "I've been diagnosed with major depressive disorder, anxiety, and I'm pretty sure PTSD is in there somewhere."

"I have post-traumatic stress disorder as well," he replies. "I was in the military, but I know you from somewhere!"

"I'm a paramedic," I say, as this is usually the link between me and anyone who recognizes me.

Slight pause. Suddenly his eyes widen, and I can tell he has made the connection. He blurts, "I was your patient!"

Talk about a full-circle smack in the face! Not only have I met Starbucks Guy before, I took care of him. I feel incredibly awkward and self-conscious at first. How did this come to be? *I had been the one helping others such as Starbucks Guy for eleven years as a paramedic. I* was the one who spoke in front of classes filled with students eager to learn everything I could teach, but I am sick—just like Starbucks Guy. I belong here with him, and I am ready to get better. The awkwardness dissolves quickly as I remind myself I am here because I have the courage to realize it is *my* turn to be helped.

~ PATIENCE, NATALIE, PATIENCE

This morning starts off really well. I am on time. I walk my dog, Walter, through the fall leaves. I remember my binder for class. I have all the hope in the world that today will be a fairly straightforward Save-My-Life School day (I am shaking my head right now. You just can't see it.) In reality, most of today is crap.

The teacher hands me a booklet when we all sit down. It is titled *Identifying and Expressing Your Feelings.* It is nine double-sided pages of *just* text. There are no illustrations at all. *Please, dear God, make this homework.* She can't be reading this word for word, right? WRONG! She reads every…single…word! The booklet is about dealing with anxiety. How ironic. Each paragraph she reads (and re-reads because she constantly loses her place) *gives* me anxiety.

"Patience, Natalie, patience," I say to myself repeatedly, but my inner dialogue doesn't seem to help. *Deep breathing.* That helps a bit, but not enough. All I can do is scan the room for a "don't worry this is driving me crazy too" wink or nod. Nope. Nothing. Everyone seems pretty in tune with the reading. This intensifies my anxiety even more. My chest tightens. I fidget. I can't concentrate. I find myself getting mad. Doodles in my booklet include: "Boring, blah blah blah, so tired, YAWN!," "I get it...move on," "daydreaming... dumb," "get through this faster," and "POKE MY EYES OUT!"

Why is this happening to me? "It's only Day 2. Cut yourself some slack," I think over and over. I decide to hold off on my "Have *you* ever had anxiety?" question directed at the teacher. I bet she hasn't. This makes me even *more* anxious. "Stop making assumptions," I tell myself for the forty-third time.

Then suddenly someone grabs my attention. A girl, maybe in her late twenties, puts her hand up and barely gargles the words through her tears as she tells the class that *this* session and *this* booklet just enlightened her to what she suffered from. She hadn't been able to connect with a counsellor. She felt terribly lost and alone. She didn't know what was wrong with her and lived in constant confusion. Everyone told her she should simply "just stop feeling the way she did," and she would miraculously get better. Her family had slowly distanced themselves from her. But this session was her light bulb moment, and I was present for it—an amazing thing to witness.

I feel my anxiety clear as I find myself naturally focusing on her words without effort. I recognize myself in her. I don't know what circumstances brought her to the class, but that doesn't matter. What matters is that I know *exactly* how she feels. I know *precisely* how it feels to finally have something make sense. So that's why I'm here! Not every class will be made for me, but I can provide the support someone else may desperately need. I am good at doing that anyway—this is *my* light bulb moment.

I feel sad and selfish about walking into class this morning not even noticing how entitled I felt to learn something more about *my* mental illnesses. That isn't what these weeks will always be about. My time here is equally about how the group supports one another. Maybe others were also bored with the word-by-word play-by-play that I wrestled my way through (which I am assured isn't always the daily routine), but everyone managed their anxiety well. We take solace in just being here and not being alone, and I am extremely lucky to be a part of this.

I give the girl my cell number at break and tell her that if she wants to chat, I am here for her. We are *all* here for her.

It is the end of Day 2, and I still have a lot to learn.

~

OK, so in the spirit of being honest, I need to add that I failed to mention I did not attend the afternoon class, and I got in trouble (in a loving way) by my best friend. Why? Because she wants me to be one hundred percent accountable for my actions. Yes, all the above did occur, but I should have let you know I bailed. I was judgey of the teacher, and my daughter was not feeling well. My daughter said she would be fine without me, but I jumped at the opportunity to not return to class. As I mentioned, I was feeling very anxious in the morning and resorted to my old habits of just wanting to have a nap and take an anti-anxiety pill (but I didn't take one—*big* step for me!) So, that is the full truth about today's journey. Tomorrow is a new day. I'm not going to lie—I am skipping the afternoon again, but I have a permission slip this time. All I can say is that each day I will try harder to stick around and be grateful.

~ THINK VERSUS FEEL

Thankfully today is a better day! Different teacher. (*Natalie, stop being judgey*…baby steps.) The theme of the day is "Thinking and

Feeling," both at Save-My-Life School and at "the reason why I have a permission slip to skip the afternoon." I will start with the latter.

I have been *thinking* a lot about getting a particular tattoo, so I *felt* a tattoo needle for seven hours today. It's a tattoo that has been a lifetime in the making. Each image carries so much meaning to me. I have other tattoos, but they are much smaller. I've always *felt* that when the time was right, I would get this specific one. (OK, enough with the *think* and *felt* italics. I am annoying myself.) Anyway, I am by no means recommending that people go out and get a three-quarter sleeve because they have a mental illness (obviously), but I know I will cherish this work of art forever.

I had so much support over the course of the seven hours! I received visitors on a regular basis and constant texts. It made the time fly, and I love you all for being there for me. My tattoo artist now knows quite a bit of paramedic lingo.

OK, on to my day at school. Our main topic is "Codependency." This lesson teaches me that…well…I am. I'm a people pleaser and a perfectionist. I have a hard time saying no and feel that a lot of my happiness depends on whether or not I make the people around me happy. I am frustrated by how many check marks are on my page after I take the codependency quiz. I'd rather be doing a *Cosmo* "Who's Your Perfect Guy?" quiz.

So how am I supposed to use this new information? I *enjoy* making people happy and always avoid conflict. Am I supposed to turn into a selfish, argumentative person in order to heal? Apparently not. I learn that my thoughts dictate how I feel. Unfortunately, my thoughts are not always right! *So, wait a minute. Are you telling me my judgment could be wrong?* Whoa, whoa, whoa—I've been right for so long! WRONG.

Today is a perfect example of this. When I am sitting with my friend waiting to start my tattoo, I tell her how much I appreciate all the support people are giving me. However, I feel bad for not being able to reply to everyone because I am so tired. I am sure this is hurting people's feelings! I am positive people think I am rude for not answering. My friend's immediate response: "Nat, people aren't expecting you to reply. They just want to show that they are proud of you and love you." *Stop the train—this can't be.* But I realize it is true. Thinking that people are upset with me makes me sad; hence my thoughts are totally dictating my feelings. If I change my outlook even slightly, it doesn't mean I am rude and selfish; it means I am not forgetting to take care of me.

OK, I'm super tired and off to bed. I am mentally preparing to tell you all about September 7, 2013, and September 21, 2014. But that's for another day. We have lots of days.

P.S. Remember Starbucks Guy? As I left the hospital, he came up to me and gave me a high-five. He's off to a private treatment centre tomorrow. I'm going to cheers a latte to him.

~ HAPPINESS DAY—OH LORD!

OK, I'm not going to lie—I do like discovering a great example of true irony, but I've had enough for one week! "Welcome to Happiness Day!" is announced in the saddest class I've ever been a part of. *Are you kidding me?*

Don't get me wrong; I understand it's a topic we *should* cover, but I am sure the look on almost everyone's face when we get the Happiness Alphabet handout is similar to the look the *Titanic* passengers had just before the ship went down. People are already passing around the tissues, and we haven't even put the handout into our binders. This isn't going to go well.

I am pretty worried. The room is filled with people who can barely get out of bed and have a shower, people who cry all day and don't even know why, people who have suffered horrible abuse and loss—and you want us to sing the Happiness Alphabet? OK, we don't literally have to *sing*, but it is close enough in our eyes.

Cue the music.

A: Accept others for who they are and for the choices they've made even if you have difficulty understanding their beliefs, motives, or actions. Well, that one's not too bad I guess.

B: Break away from everything that stands in the way of what you hope to accomplish with your life. OK, I can deal with this one too, but we're getting into murky water here.

C: Create a family of friends with whom you can share your hopes, dreams, sorrows, and happiness. This alphabet may not be too bad. I do have this family of friends. I never take that for granted. And now I'm also part of a new family of friends here at Save-My-Life School.

D, E, F: Forgive and forget. Yikes! People are already crying. It continues on to say that we should soar above grudges and remember that everyone makes mistakes. I feel like most of the class is about to walk out. And I also feel that this is a concept most people have difficulty with, not just the people in the room. Everyone has been hurt—*everyone!* But apparently, some are much better equipped at practising this forgive-and-forget business than people with mental illnesses are. Evidently, many people can allow for a normal progression of emotions. They have the ingredients to nurture their spirit. *Vomit.* So why did I get the shitty ingredients? Why do I have to be here and learn to "choose" happiness instead of happiness simply choosing me? How do I know whether or not it's just the meds that are allowing me to have better days? Ugh. All I want is my pillow and to sleep this day off. I need my comfort zone.

These thoughts bring me to the next topic of today, "How Comfortable Is Your Comfort Zone?" I suppose it's only temporarily comfortable when I think about it. My alcohol abuse was only temporarily comfortable (none since September 23, may I add!).

The days lost from hours of sleep were only temporarily comfortable. The pills I took to sleep were only temporarily comfortable.

The teacher continues on, saying, "You need to move out of your comfort zone, and you will see it wasn't actually comfortable at all." Hmm, interesting. "And if you don't try, you won't know." Once again she's right. Damn it. I know she's right because I was supposed to be in a similar program last year when I overdosed the first time. I didn't try the program, so I didn't know. Back then I completely believed it was a waste of my time, and look where that got me—back to the mental health wing. Last year when I snuggled back into my comfort zone, I missed out on singing the Happiness Alphabet. I'm sure if I would have tried then, the tune would still have been horribly off-key at first (like it is today). But when I was a kid, after I practised my alphabet really hard, I learned it cold. So I'm trying really hard to learn this new one now: "A, B, C, D, E, F, G..."

~ HOW DID I GET HERE?

Stumbling, I get through my first week of Save-My-Life School, sober and all! I'm very proud of myself, and apparently many of you are proud of me too. Thank you. I have received at least two hundred texts and messages showing me so much love and support.

So, in the spirit of brutal truth (and because some of you have asked a bit about my past), I think I will share how I landed here. Life so far has been a journey almost beyond words, but let's skip right to the "Are you kidding me?" stuff.

At the age of eighteen, I became pregnant while in high school. My mom was devastated, and in turn she picked me up from work one day with my bags packed and dropped me off at a home for unwed mothers run by nuns. I believe it still exists to this day. I cried every day and didn't talk to anyone. The girls there were rough, and I didn't belong. I spent my time sewing a baby blanket in the basement and had twenty minutes a day on a pay phone. After begging to return home, I managed to complete high school, have a baby shower in my English class, and go to my prom nine months pregnant.

When my daughter was one year old, my mom suffered a ruptured brain aneurysm that required hours of surgery. The doctors told us she would likely not survive. Luckily she did survive, but the injury had turned her into a very different mom from the one my three brothers, one sister, and I knew. Her memory was gone, and her speech was almost non-existent. After managing to balance scheduling her cognitive, speech, and physiotherapy appointments, I was still a single mom to my daughter and now had my five-year-old brother to take care of—my dad was a long-distance truck driver and rarely home. That same brother (who is now twenty-three) still remembers that I taught him how to read and hold a pencil.

My mom had so many seizures on a regular basis that paramedics came to know our family well. They knew where to find my little brother who would hide, terrified, either behind the couch or in the bathroom. My mom had developed such severe psychosis that she would barely leave her room. This also caused her to resent me because I became the household mom by default. After another year of struggling to take care of her, she once again packed my bags (a garbage bag this time around) and kicked my two-year-old daughter and me out onto the street with nowhere to go. I lived in a family friend's bedroom for a month until I was able to find an apartment.

I desperately needed to find a paying job—taking care of my mom had been my full-time job for the past year. I was soon successful, but the money I made each month was still not enough to pay for the car I purchased with my dad. I tried to sell it but couldn't. It was repossessed, causing me a horrible spiral of depression. Even with my car gone, collection agencies called every day looking for the money I still owed them. It didn't matter what my story was. I tried to explain that I was excellent with budgeting my money but had not anticipated being kicked out of my home. They wanted what was rightfully theirs. Soon after, I had no choice but to file for bankruptcy for the eight thousand dollars I owed.

At that point I began to see how much of a toll the depression (clinical or situational? I was unsure back then) had taken on me, and I made a pivotal decision to go back to school. As a single mom, I fought hard to become a paramedic. The program was not an easy one to get into. I didn't even make it onto the waiting list the first time I applied. But I was determined to succeed and spent the next year stacking my resumé by volunteering, and I was finally accepted into the program.

I put myself through school by waitressing, and I bought a beat-up car. As I made the hour-long drive back and forth on the highway every day, I wondered if the bottom of the car would fall out. Fortunately, my grades were at the top of the class, and this enabled me to receive an outside scholarship, which helped me out immensely. After two years of late nights studying while my daughter was in bed, scheduling 450 hours of ambulance ride-outs, in-class school, waitressing, and being a mom, I graduated and was chosen to receive the college's Health Science Department's Board of Governors Award. I felt I had finally made it! And during the next eleven years, I grew as a paramedic and developed an EMS family I love very much.

I felt so lucky to actually enjoy going to work. Not very many people can say that about their careers. I learned something new every day, was financially stable, and made such a difference in people's lives. I was in my glory. But no matter how much I loved it, each year became a bit tougher for me to cope with. I wasn't going to let this amazing career slip away from me. I had fought too hard for it. At the time I was sure how I felt was totally normal. I only saw tiny changes in myself in the early years. Days just seemed to go by and calls just happened to add up. I could let most calls move through my mind in a healthy way. But looking back now over all the years, I see how life as a paramedic has changed me—some changes for the good, and sadly some for the bad. This makes me very sad—and mad! I was a good paramedic. I loved helping people. I loved teaching. And I absolutely loved my co-workers. But somewhere along the way, all those good things were no longer enough. I slowly began to drink on a regular basis to quiet the bad calls that haunted my mind. I stopped talking about these calls with my family—it didn't seem to help me anymore. I developed a bad-call pattern—it would take three days before I would feel better. So the three-day depression seemed to be my new normal.

First responders see things they should never see—sights, sounds, and smells stay with them long past the high they feel after a call well done. For me, my inability to cope with some very stressful calls wasn't an overnight change, but for some it is. I feel a lot of my work-related depression was cumulative, and over the years I successfully masked it with alcohol. But sadly, I inevitably got that "big bad call" that pushed me over the edge.

I will never forget May 2, 2012. It was the date of a double murder at a hotel in my hometown. Two women were brutally killed, almost decapitated, allegedly part of a Satanic murder-suicide pact. The details of the call are too gruesome to replay—it still disturbs me so much. As a seasoned paramedic, I managed to push my feelings surrounding this call to the back of my brain (for two years) until I had to testify and see my patient, the murderer (he pled guilty), again. I had support from my work and fellow paramedics who had to testify that day, and for that I am so grateful. However, no one could have prepared me for how I would feel in that courtroom.

Oddly, I wasn't that nervous about testifying—I'd spoken in front of groups for years. I was confident in my knowledge of the call and was ready to go in, say what I needed to say, and leave—*without* looking at him. But as soon as I was sworn in and took a seat on the stand, the Crown attorney promptly asked me to "Please stand up and move to your left so the accused [my patient] can see you... You're very little."

Can I what? Are you kidding me? You are ruining my precise plan to not look at him! Why should he get to see me? I stood up and moved to my left, but not knowing if that was a big enough step for him to see me, I instinctively turned to look at him to make sure. There he was, behind a huge piece of bulletproof glass. Uncontrollably, the call rushed back to me, washing me with that horrific feeling I experienced when we walked into the hotel room. It was as vivid, clear, and intense as it was in 2012. I felt sick. In the courtroom, I had just learned of new, gruesome details of the call. It was all too much. It felt very surreal. I couldn't even believe I was there.

After testifying, I went home and pushed the knot in my stomach as far down as it could go; I needed to gather myself to go to a memorial for a good friend and co-worker who had recently died because of a mental illness. He had taken his own life only weeks prior, and the loss hit our EMS family very hard. Anxiety was racing through my body, but there was no way I was missing this memorial. Even though I didn't know the details of the circumstances surrounding his death, I felt I could relate to his pain—even if in the smallest way. I missed him. And I wanted to say goodbye.

When I got home I drank two bottles of wine in a matter of hours, but that wasn't enough. I needed to turn my racing thoughts off! It was all way too much for one day. Seeing a patient who brutally murdered two women and appeared remorseless for the lives he took, and then going to a memorial for a friend who suffered in silence and didn't deserve to die because of his mental illness was all…just… too…much. I had a bottle of allergy pills in my nightstand. I knew it would put me to sleep. I ate them like jellybeans and listened to music. I was in another world now, and it was perfect. I forgot the day—my depression was gone. But I also couldn't remember how many pills I had taken. I eventually learned it was almost the whole bottle.

Thankfully I was texting my best friend, and she could tell I was off. I wasn't making sense. She is an ambulance communications officer, and she called 911 (her work number) to request help. The paramedics were sent, and my best friend saved my life that night. Wearing only my underwear and a sweatshirt, I somehow made it outside to the porch and drifted out of consciousness. I was taken to the hospital as a Level 1 on the Canadian Triage and Acuity Scale— this is the most critical level. I stopped breathing several times on the way, didn't respond to pain, and was almost intubated. If a patient gets to the hospital quickly enough after overdosing, charcoal can sometimes be administered to help neutralize the effect of the drugs. I was well beyond the "charcoal window," so my poor family and best friend just had to wait and see.

The remainder of the night and the following days at the hospital led me to where I am today. I think you've gotten enough info about little ol' me tonight. And I'm sort of done with talking about it for now anyway. I will let you know about Day 5 of school tomorrow. Chat soon.

~ WHERE DOES BRAVERY BELONG IN ALL OF THIS?

Let's put bravery where it belongs!

Bravery is there when we climb mountains or swim to the depths of the ocean. It's there when a baby takes its first step or a child waves goodbye on the school bus for the first day. It's there when we stand up to a bully or leave an abusive relationship. It's there when we ask our crush out on a date or lean in for the first kiss. It's there when we jump out of airplanes or walk across volcanoes. It's there when paramedics pull up to a crash not knowing what horrific things they will see. It's there when firefighters rescue a person from a burning house. It's there when police officers pull their guns and know they may need to fire them. It's there when dispatchers answer a call not knowing what they will hear on the line. It's there when people tell themselves they can make it through the next chemotherapy treatment or when a person is put under before their open-heart surgery. It's there when soldiers crawl through the trenches and when protestors stand up for human rights. Bravery is when the fighter enters the ring.

For me, bravery is there when I fight depression and get out of bed every day. It's there when I drive past the liquor store and get a coffee instead. It's there when I fight the urge to sleep all day or the urge to self-medicate my reality. It's there when I accept the help I am offered and walk into Save-My-Life School. It's there when I pick myself back up when I stumble and when I trust my friends. It's there when I focus on making sure my anxiety doesn't turn into a panic attack and forgiving myself if it does.

Bravery is all these things to me and more, but the bravery it took to post my first entry shouldn't have needed to be there. We shouldn't need bravery to talk about mental illnesses—this belief is killing us. Let's save bravery for the challenges in our lives and for the *actual* fight!

~ WHAT IS A FRIEND?

Today is a short Save-My-Life School day, but we cover a lot of ground. Our main topic is "Friendship," and immediately I feel a bit out of place. I'm so lucky to have lots of amazing friends, and I know that many people here only have each other. That must make them sad. As we work through the module, we ask ourselves questions such as, "Do you have a best friend?" and "Is it better to have a lot of friends or just a few friends and why?" I notice from everyone's answers that I certainly have (once again) made the wrong assumption by thinking I am any luckier than they are. How many reality checks can one girl take in a week? Numbers don't matter, and friends come in all forms. For example, one person is grieving over the loss of his best friend—a service dog. He has three of them (they are beautiful). In his own words: "I rescued them, and they rescued me." Cue tears!

So, in the spirit of friendship, I have a very special entry to share with you tonight, written by my best friend, Amanda. She has seen the world my depression takes me to, and she has put her pain aside when I am in that world—to hold my hand no matter what. She wants to let families and friends of mental illness sufferers know they are not alone. For every person battling a mental illness, I'm sure there are five family members who watch their loved ones go through what to them is an invisible darkness. They may feel helpless and confused as to why this is even happening to their loved one. When I read Amanda's thoughts, I feel so many emotions: love, sadness, guilt—and I am so sure it will give everyone (sufferer or not) a glimpse into the cold, dark world of depression. Because Amanda is my family, she has been brave enough to share my world through her eyes. I love you, Amanda!

From Amanda: I know Natalie loves sushi (it's more like an out-of-control obsession). She has a sensitivity to clarithromycin. I know when she farts because she giggles right after. Her eyebrows are serious business. We've literally laughed until our stomachs hurt. She loves school and furthering her education. She has a brilliant medical mind. When she has an anxiety attack, her body seizes up so tightly that sometimes she needs the bottoms of her legs rubbed. She uses the phrase "dingle dork," and it drives me nuts. She always says she'll be on time, but that usually means fifteen minutes late. She would do anything for me! I know she can't lose her battle with mental illness. She just can't. I love her beyond measure, and I need her. You know that saying about friends being the family you get to choose—she's part of my family! This is an entry from the heart of her best friend. I'm Amanda, affectionately known as "AB."

I remember the day I met Natalie. Up until that day, she had been just the voice of one of the medics I dispatched. I knew her to be polite and always thought she sounded like a little pixie on the air. We talked on the phone many times, as medics and dispatchers do, but that was about it. I knew of her through mutual friends, and it was when those mutual friends and I came together to plan a baby shower that I met her in person. We all agreed to meet at a local restaurant. When Natalie introduced herself, it wasn't just your regular "Oh hi, nice to meet you." It was a hug, a kiss on the cheek, and an "OMG, I love you" in the softest, most high-pitched pixie voice! I think somewhere in there she said she liked my hair colour and then BAM—instant friends! If our mobile provider ever tallied up our text messages, it'd be in the millions; I'm sure of it. Oh, I should mention—if you've ever received a text from Nat, it usually includes a kissy face emoticon, which is how she earned her nickname, "Kissy."

I didn't know at the beginning that Kissy suffered from depression or anxiety. As hard as she worked to be a kick-ass medic, she worked equally as hard to hide that side of her. She used to live seconds away from me. After we worked a day shift, if she had a bad call, sometimes I'd stop by and see how she was doing. The day came where she had the kind of call that hurts her heart the most—a kid call. She was so sad, and it was that day that she started to open up. She told me about her childhood and about her three-day bounce-back cycle (where it takes her three days to get the sad feeling out of her). We talked for hours. She didn't trust easily. It was like she assumed if people knew she suffered from mental health issues, then they'd leave her. Slowly but surely, she started to learn that she could tell me anything and I'd never judge her—that I'd always be there for her, that I'd never leave her. It wasn't always easy, though. When I knew she was down and things could go sideways, she would still try to hide behind the facade that everything was fine, "I'm OK, AB. I just need to sleep."

~

Fast forward years later. It is September 7, 2013. Happy birthday, AB—or not. Nat is having some rough days but managing. In the afternoon, Nat and I are messaging back and forth. I can tell she is off just by the way she is texting. But this isn't uncommon. She sends me a picture of a sink full of hair—her hair. She tells me she's taken a pill to help calm her and she needed a "trim." Good lord of all, it is more than a trim. Now, you need to understand, it's a tricky road to navigate. I don't want to treat Natalie like a child, and I want to trust her. Our rule is that she always has to tell me the truth (re: taking pills, drinking, where she is on the anxiety 1–10 scale, etc.). Earlier, she told me she was doing OK and just needed to have a gumball (our word for nap). I trusted her words. So, I told her I would check in on her later when I headed out to dinner. Fine. Not fine. Now, when I check my cell, I have fifteen missed calls and too many texts to count. Without reading all the texts or even seeing who the missed calls are from, I know it is Natalie.

I feel sick. I need to see her. The memories of that night still bring tears to my eyes. The guilt I feel for not doing something earlier in the day haunts me. What if I could have stopped her? What if I could have gotten her help earlier? I finally get the details of what has happened, and I can't breathe. She has taken a cocktail of pills in hopes of sleeping it off. Her boyfriend and brother find her basically unresponsive and call an ambulance. At the hospital Natalie is placed in the mental health unit of the Emergency Department; then later she is transferred to a bed on the mental health wing—where she stays for a week. She even lands herself in the lockdown unit.

One of Kissy's patterns is that when she starts to feel better, she wants to put it all behind her. She promises to never do *it again, and vows to drink less or to stop altogether (which she does for a period of time). She likes to pretend she's fine and can manage it all on her own. And from her perspective, she's been managing it her whole life—and survived. It's all she knows. The hospital staff want her to join an out-patient program, but the start date is months away. What? We need her to have help now. What is wrong with our healthcare system? So frustrating. After getting home, after time passing, after life moving along and getting back to normal—Nat never follows through with the out-patient program.*

~

Fast forward again to September 23, 2014 (she keeps saying it was September 21, but it was September 23). Well, you've read Nat's version. You all know it happens again. But this time it is worse. Kissy and I have been texting all day. She is telling me about the trial. She tells me how surreal it is to see her patient (the murderer). The patient she treated. She is sick to her stomach. Then she attends a memorial service for her friend and colleague. Heartbreaking. Not an easy day for anyone! That night she starts texting me, honouring our rule of always being honest. Her texts are scrambled. I know she has done something. I call her. Her voice is empty, and she can't put a sentence together. I tell her to stay on the phone with me and that I am going to have someone come help her. I try calling Nat's ex-boyfriend, Leo, who is currently sleeping in her basement, but there is no answer. I call 911 and speak to my colleagues. I ask them to dispatch a unit to Natalie's address and tell them why, but they already know why. The first responder assigned is Dave, a friend of ours and a truly amazing paramedic. I get in touch with him and give him Natalie's full history. Knowing help is on the way, I get in the car and meet the ambulance at the Emergency Department. The ambulance and I arrive at the same time, as does Leo. We park and go in together. Did I forget to mention Leo woke up once Dave arrived? When we get to the Emergency Department, there she is, covered from head to toe with a white sheet. I recoil in unbelievable panic, nooo—don't tell me she died? Thankfully my fear is temporary—nope, she is just covered up to help maintain her privacy so other medics and staff that may recognize her don't see her. At this point she still hasn't (fully) come out about her mental health issues. She is paranoid about people knowing, so maintaining her privacy is important. They get her into a trauma room. I watch them as they do sternal rubs followed by, "Come on, Natalie, breathe." Not OK. I stand there beside her, and through tiny slits she gazes over at me with the most vacant stare and reaches for my hand. She is so cold! I'm not sure how I don't break her hand as I am holding on so tightly! The strangest things go through your brain when you're in a crisis. Between words from nurses, "We have to monitor for toxicity," and "Her blood pressure is high," I'm looking at her thinking, "What if this time she took one pill too many? Would I have to do a eulogy? What? AB, stop—she didn't die! Could I deliver a eulogy? No, of course not. I'd cry the whole time. What would I tell her daughter, Caroline? OMG, she'll break into a million pieces. Stop it, AB, she didn't die—this time. How do you support an eighteen-year-old who just lost her mom? I'll definitely need to be with her on her wedding day. That's what Natalie would want! AB, that's enough! Shit, I have to make sure Nat's eyebrows look perfect (it's a pact we have—don't ask)."

As time ticks by in the ER, bag after bag of IV fluids pass through Nat, and let me tell you they pass through like the

Hoover Dam breaking, with her catheter bag almost spilling over. Is that too much information?

Nat slowly starts to make words again. Her words are mumbled and so faint you can barely hear them. There are no sentences, although in her world it probably feels like she is talking for hours. Her mouth moves as though she is quietly reading aloud, but there is no sound. You can tell when she thinks she says something interesting because she darts her eyes over to me and raises her eyebrows as if to say, "You know what I'm saying, AB." I engage in her "conversation" the whole time, hoping to make sense of a word or two, and sure enough, I do! She says things like "the knife," "it was right there," and "he's guilty." Are you kidding me? Here she is in a state of delirium post-overdose and this is what is at the forefront of her brain.

My heart is breaking for her. I am angry and sad. That man has no idea how fortunate he was to have Natalie as the attending paramedic. I can't help thinking that because of him (at least in part), we may have lost her. No, no—that's not OK with me! She doesn't deserve to be left with the horror from that scene and the details of that disgusting event. It is etched in her brain like a vivid nightmare. She has, on multiple occasions, told me about that call and what she walked into. I can't even wrap my brain around it. I can't imagine what it was like for all the medics, police, fire, and the ER staff. Horror beyond horror.

More faint whispers, garbled words: "I won't get to see him get married" and "I won't get to see his kids." Oh heavens— now she's thinking about her friend and colleague who had taken his life only days prior. The heavy thoughts that swirl around in her head collide with her heavy heart—which aches because of her recent breakup with Leo. It's too much! Kissy is on overload, and she does the only thing she knows how to—numb it all. Nat self-medicates with pills and alcohol. She always says she never does it to kill herself, but I firmly believe that if death was a side effect during those terrible lows, she'd be OK with it. So, perhaps now you see why I'm as serious as a pantsuit about her not skipping Save-My-Life School. I called it Save-My-Life School for a reason—it very literally is helping her to save her own life. She doesn't have enough tools in her tool box (OMG, that's something Dr. Phil would say—sorry) to help her navigate the lows, and I—we all—need Natalie to get help, so she never secretly wishes for side effects.

The story doesn't end here. Natalie is released the next day (Thursday, September 25). There is no plan or follow-up appointments. Leo and I are beside ourselves. (The breakup may be in progress, but Leo and Natalie care for each other. His unconditional support for her is incredible.) We believe she needs to be in the hospital. She requires help like people need oxygen. Leo is trying to arrange for Natalie to go to a private facility, but that takes time. We need her to be safe until she has a program willing to accept her. All the options require time to coordinate—referrals, available beds, etc.

Well, brutal honesty, Natalie doesn't always tell the whole truth. The doctors only spoke with Natalie—not once did they come to Leo and me to fill in some blanks. So, Natalie goes home, has a nice refreshing shower, and meets with her counsellor. Fine, right? Wrong! She wants to come home and have a magic plan, a checklist of things to do that once completed means she is cured. She wants to prove to everyone she is fine, and you guessed it—it will never happen again.

I'm on my way to Kissy's to spend some time with her now that she's home, and my phone rings. It's Leo's number. I pick up, and all I can hear is Natalie sobbing in the background. He simply asks, "Where are you?"

I am parking the car outside the house. I get upstairs to find Natalie sitting on the floor, balled up between her bed and the wall (about a two-foot space). I sit down in front of her and reassure her that I am here. I hold her tear-soaked face in my hands and softly encourage her to breathe. She is cracking into a million pieces. She is going back to the hospital. She begs me not to make her go. She holds my hand tightly as she sobs and cries, "AB, pleeease no, I don't want to go back."

She wants to sleep it off. Sorry, Kissy, I'd rather you are mad at me for going against your wishes than have you dead. Simple as that. When the ambulance arrives, it's Dave. Our dear friend handles the situation perfectly. Again. I don't care how she gets to the hospital. I don't care if she is talking to me or not. I just care that she gets there. She doesn't want to see anyone—me included. I'm not hurt or offended. I am too busy being relieved that she is going back to the hospital. Selfishly, I am also grateful I can get some sleep tonight knowing she is safe. Natalie wants to go to the hospital alone, but we need someone there to keep her accountable and to be with her when she talks to the ER staff.

We get Nat to the Emergency Department. Dave follows her there and steps in to help. When Natalie is finished telling the nurses and doctors what is happening, I meet Dave in the hospital and he fills me in. She is safe. She finally admits to the nurses that she is suicidal—and it is documented. And she is safe. Did I mention that?

Dave asks me how I am holding up. "WHAT?" I say, "Oh, I'm fine. I've been dealing with this for years." He looks at me again and says, "Enough with the bullshit—how are you really holding up?"

That's when my tough-chick exterior cracks. I bite my lip and look away in hopes of fighting off the tears, but no luck. I start to cry. He just stands there and hugs me. I never really stopped to think about how it had weighed on me. It seemed selfish to think about me when she was the one going through it. I had thought about Leo and how hard it was on him. I had thought about Natalie's two children— Caroline and her eight-year-old brother, Adam—but I never had thought about the impact on me.

I drive home in the wee hours of the morning, plunk myself on my couch, and think, "OMG, I need a cream soda, and I wouldn't say no to a bag of Miss Vickie's sea salt and malt vinegar chips." I am spent. There are so many details woven into the whole story—way too much to share in its entirety.

~

But now, here we are in present-day. Kissy is getting help and encouraging others. She is allowing people to support her, and she is writing her story. Not only is she helping herself heal, but she is helping others. How amazing is that?

I have learned that being a part of the frontline support team for someone battling mental illness can be exhausting. It can rob you of sleep, make you sick with worry, and make you angry (and it's OK to be angry). I have learned that taking time to nurture yourself doesn't mean you love them any less. It just means you have enough wisdom to know you need a break. You're no good to them if you're no good to yourself. I have learned that I have the potential to unleash nasty fury towards anyone who judges depression, anxiety, PTSD, or any branch of mental health. I have learned that it's important to educate myself—for Natalie and everyone

else who is suffering, so I can better understand this disease.
Frontline supporters, don't be afraid to tap out of the ring
for a bit.
   AB XOXO

~ GIVING THANKS

As it's Thanksgiving, I think I will share the journal entry I wrote on
the day I returned home from the hospital in 2013, after a week in
the mental health wing. Why, you may ask. Well, you will see I was
very thankful that day:

~

Awake all night. Tossing and turning. Not in a bad way. It's like
Christmas Eve. I finally succumb to the fact that sleep and I are not
friends, so I sit up and open my curtains to a dark hospital parking
lot and look. I have time—more time—to just be, to just sit, to just
accept, to just breathe. I notice the spiders are gone. In every room
I've stayed in, there is always one spinning a web in the corner of
the window. Maybe they are gone because it looks chilly outside (I
can tell by the steam leaving the rooftop pipes), but I don't know for
sure. I haven't felt the temperature outside for a week. Or maybe they
are gone because they don't need to be there anymore. I am going
home, and the home I watched them spin for days doesn't need to be
watched anymore.

After a while of just looking outside, I get up and walk down the
quiet nighttime hall in my sock feet to find the clock at the nursing
station. Careful not to wake up a fellow patient who is asleep in a
chair (I am afraid she may begin her sad, relentless pay-phone calls
too early), I look at the time, which was so hard for me to keep track
of during the last seven days: 5:45 a.m. OK, more time to go. Getting
a bit restless, I take down the poster on my wall by carefully peeling
off the hospital stickers I used as an adhesive. I roll it up and wonder
if I will ever look at it again. Probably not—too many memories.

Then I walk back and forth in my room, a place that, in a matter of days, went from feeling like a jail cell to feeling like freedom. I appreciate every step; I appreciate *everything*—my bed, my washroom, my window, and a few books. I don't need much to be OK.

With my mind too busy, I decide to read for a while, but I still can't focus. Is the sun finally starting to rise, or is it still the streetlight's glow? Finally, I hear a knock at the door. A smiling face introduces himself as my nurse. This is wonderful! In my clock-less room, I now know that it is almost eight o'clock. Time for my medications and almost time to go home.

The nurse asks me, "Do you have anything in the hospital safe?" I reply, "I don't know." Then, "Do you have belongings at the nursing station?" Once again I reply, "I don't know." This is a loud reminder that I am unable to recall my first two days here. It stings a bit. I'm not going to lie. But as time goes by, I get used to saying why I am here. The word "overdose" now rolls off my tongue with a strange ease.

I brush my teeth and decide to treat myself to one last fresh face cloth that is waiting for me in the hall—all my face cloths at home are waiting to be washed. I start to pack. It doesn't take long. One grocery bag and I am done. I can finally trade in my pyjamas for jeans!

My nurse peeks his head in the door, "Do you want to have your breakfast?" The residents of the floor are slowly waking. I walk down the hall to lots of "good mornings" from now-familiar faces. I find my tray on the table in the dining room, which is odd. I usually find it on the tall rack with everyone else's. Hmm, maybe this is what they do on the day you are going home—like a special celebration. Probably not. More likely my place on the rack has been taken, replaced by another new face who will most likely be scared and wary to walk into the dining room, just as I was at first. Days ago, I didn't want anyone to recognize me. I thought, "I'm a professional. I don't belong here! They've made a horrible mistake." But now the room is so easy for me to enter because after a lot of soul-searching (and slowly swallowing my pride), I realize with all my heart and soul that I *do* belong here.

I contemplate high-fiving or hugging every patient when I leave, but I decide that action might land me another week in Hotel Mental Health, so I don't. But I hope they can feel my gratitude for their non-judgmental acceptance of me in my farewells—for becoming my intriguing, entertaining, and caring family for the past week. I wonder when they will be going home. Or if they ever will. Or if they even have a home to go to.

So, while waiting for Leo to walk through the door, I look out the window, enjoying my cereal and shot of apple juice. I am grateful. The web that was so beautifully woven for me caught me—and I love it.

P.S. I am leaving this pen on the side table as it was given to me by a fellow patient. This is an object that was once viewed as dangerous and not allowed to be in my possession only days ago. How's that for a reality check?

~ MY LAYERS OF DEPRESSION

When I was quite young, I remember feeling "off" or weird. That may seem like an odd statement to many, but it's the best way I can describe it. I would use those exact words when talking to my mom. "I don't know why, Mom, but I just feel weird."

The response I often got was, "It's your hormones," or "Just go play and you'll feel better." So, I would cry a lot, alone in my room. I don't think my mom was necessarily being mean. Looking back now, I think she just didn't understand. The feelings would sometimes get so bad I would literally run around my room, ripping everything off my shelves and screaming at the top of my lungs. I was so frustrated! I just wanted to feel better, and I would—*eventually*. However, I never knew when. After these events, I usually got in trouble for making such a mess of my room, felt unbelievably guilty and embarrassed, and then forced myself to put my stuff back—perfectly. I needed my room to look a certain way at all times. I could tell if my little sister had been playing with my Barbie dolls because one wouldn't be sitting exactly the way I had left it. In my out-of-control world, the way my room looked was the only thing I could control, so I kept it perfect. My stuff was tangible, easy to fix. I thought if my outside was perfect, my inside would be too, but that belief would only last for so long.

I now believe that those younger years were likely displaying my first layer of depression. Yes, it's reasonable to think that my hormones also contributed to the feelings and outbursts. But now that I am much older, I can recall those feelings perfectly, and they duplicate the feelings I get when my depression starts to descend on me, even to this day—it's very weird.

People who know I suffer from depression (and who are comfortable enough to ask) often inquire what it feels like. *Sigh*. Where do I begin? First of all, there are very few symptom words I can use from the English language to describe it. It starts off more like a heaviness and a sixth sense. Now don't start thinking I'm an alien or something. Bear with me. It's taken me thirty-odd years to publicly talk about my depression, putting it into words is going to be tricky. The first layer feels like what I had mentioned earlier—off. I still function throughout my day, but the world starts to feel very different to me. It doesn't seem real. I'm more conscious of my actions. I *really* notice every move I make. On a normal day, I can go grocery shopping and just feel my usual frustration when people park their carts in the middle of the aisle or when they stand too close to me in the lineup, but when I start to feel this off feeling, my brain becomes very attentive to everything I do. I pick up items, put them in my cart, and feel like I'm in slow motion. I hate this feeling. It just lingers there, taunting me, and I always try to will it away! I don't want it to turn into another layer, so I ignore it with all my might. I'm just grocery shopping like everyone else. I'm just like everyone here, right? Well, I suppose theoretically I may have been walking past a person experiencing the same off feeling, but the horrible part about depression is that you can't see it. It would be greatly appreciated if everyone feeling the same way could wear their "I have depression today" T-shirt to the store, but oh wait—no one has that shirt—nor would they want to wear it. It's a secret life, a secret feeling, and it's very, very lonely.

I never know when or *if* that feeling will just go away—or if it will progress to the next layer. I dread it. Many people who don't suffer from depression believe that if I just go do something fun or take a walk outside on a beautiful day, the feeling will vanish. Wrong! Goodness, I *wish* it were that easy. I would never have depression again. Nor would anyone for that matter. Getting out to do something can sometimes lessen this layer, but the depression seems to be an entity of its own that does what it wants to do. If it does progress, the world becomes very dark. My senses are heightened even more. I feel uncomfortable in my own skin, which is probably part of the reason why I just want to sleep it off or drink it away. I just feel gross. When I do get to this layer, I'm pretty certain there's no turning back. My depression cloud will be with me for days. How I deal with it depends on what I need to do that day. For example, the kids need to go to school. OK, smile on, try not to be irritable. Lunches need to get made and teeth need to be brushed, so I manage. But all I can think about is getting home. I have anxiety in the car because I can't drive to school and back fast enough. But I hide it, hide it, hide it—that's just what I have to do. I don't want to ruin my kids' day by making them worry about me. As soon as I get home, I go to bed. No housework will get done, and I definitely don't care. On a good day, I will sleep this layer away, but that's rare.

When the next layer appears, I am at the point of barely functioning. I rely on other people's help to get stuff done. I will say, "I have a migraine" or "I'm sure I have the flu," so that people don't worry—so that it seems like I just have a "normal" sickness. I wish depression could be normal. People can relate to a migraine or the flu, which by default makes me not a crazy person. But as soon as I'm alone I feel frustrated, sad, mad, sorry for myself, and nauseated all at the same time. I *want* to go outside and rake the leaves, but I simply can't will myself to do anything but breathe. I don't eat. I forget to drink, and I sleep, sleep, sleep.

As I've gotten older, this specific layer of depression doesn't appear out of nowhere as often—maybe once or twice a year. But over the years, I have unfortunately developed triggers that can drag me to this layer instead. This may sound confusing, but when it's a trigger that causes my depression, I don't mind it as much. I feel more so like a normal person who just feels really sad. I think, "I know for sure that all my co-workers feel horrible after doing a bad kid-call." When I do one, and it causes me to sink into my depression, I feel like the bad-call trigger set it off. I couldn't control the trigger, so therefore I couldn't control the depression. I muscle my way through three horrible days of uncontrollable crying, sad thoughts, and exhaustion—because it was all the trigger's fault. I don't know how long my co-workers feel sad. Does the sadness interrupt their daily lives? Do they just feel a normal level of sadness (whatever that is) rather than my debilitating kind? I more readily accept my inevitable dark world because I can blame my feelings on the trigger.

The bad part that I am just realizing lately is that my triggered-depression is easier for me to bury in the back of my mind (apparently not a good coping mechanism). I can usually stop it in its tracks if I don't think about what is causing it. Is this healthy? Clearly not, but I just don't care. If I can trade a depression day for a relatively normal day, I grab on tightly to that option—healthy or not. Maybe I'm able to bury these thoughts caused by a trigger because of the necessary work rhythm—attend bad call; talk about it for a few minutes while doing our paperwork; get called out again right away; repeat. There's simply no time to process the emotions associated with these calls. The likelihood of getting consecutive bad calls is low, so I go on with my day, occupied and numb.

The last layer is where I find the stigma line is truly drawn. People either understand how this cold, haunted world filled with demons feels, or they don't. Furthermore, people either accept others who experience this layer, or they leave them because they don't understand—or worse, they don't even believe it exists. "They're just looking for attention," "It can't be that bad!" "If they wanted to kill themselves they would have done it right the first time," "They are just crazy," and "Just get on the stretcher; let's go," are all things I have heard as a paramedic many times over the past eleven years. And to be honest, before I got really sick, I went along with these comments most of the time because, you guessed it, it was easier, making me equally as guilty for allowing the stigma to flourish.

The depression at this layer is so elaborate, deep and complicated. That's probably why it's taken so long for us as a society to even start to unravel it. Through the centuries, if someone didn't experience depression personally, it was easy not to worry about the condition on a wider scale. People couldn't see the feelings that others with a major depressive disorder felt, so ignoring their pain just made sense. It's not tangible. As human beings, if we can't see it, we often don't believe it. We can see cancer, fractures, and kidney stones. We have sympathy for these people. We just want to help them, and we hate it when we can't. We may never have experienced those things before and therefore can't empathize, but sympathy is automatically there. So, as I announce that I have a major depressive disorder, well—you just have to believe me. I have no X-rays, blood work, or MRIs to prove it. Yes, there are recent studies documenting physiological changes in patients with such mental illnesses, and that is very exciting progress. But generally speaking, our society is accustomed to turning a blind eye to the presence of mental illness unless they've experienced it themselves.

My darkest depression layer goes far beyond fear. The whole world doesn't make sense anymore. I constantly battle thoughts in my mind telling me I shouldn't be here. Logic is non-existent. Trust me, I'm usually an intelligent, logical person. But when my mind is in this layer, distorted thinking prevails every time. I completely retreat from the outside world because I feel like I don't belong there. I don't want to hurt the people that I love. I'm afraid I exhaust people and want to spare them from me. Why should they have to shoulder or share my sadness when it's not about them? I want to sit in darkness and stay there alone, forever. There is no way anyone can talk me out of it. I need to let time elapse while my brain goes around its relentless cycle of turmoil. Being in this layer is like fighting a war—just me and my shield. Again, I can't eat or drink. I believe wholeheartedly that people are better off without me, and my brain doesn't stop. When I'm in this layer, I need medication to sleep in order to get away from the banter that plays so loudly in my head. Then, when I am truly exhausted, I become numb. I can barely talk. But I know if I make it past this point—if I can somehow push through the enemy lines with my last broken and mangled shield—I will survive. But holding my shield up alone and constantly fighting against the enemy makes me so tired, especially because I know another war is somewhere around the corner! I think to myself, I can win this war, but there's no celebration because my shield is more mangled and the enemy is always there.

So here is my last point. People with depression need an army of people behind them. They can't fight it alone, but they often feel they have no choice because of the powerful stigma. Their pride and fear of ridicule keep them suffering in silence. I can tell you from personal experience, the first step to healing is to have the willingness and courage to open up to a counsellor, to an AB, to anyone you trust.

But, for people who fought their hardest battle, their weapons destroyed or their shields too damaged to fight again; for people who didn't have an army, and sadly lost their internal war—please remember they didn't give up; the enemy simply won.

Thank you to everyone who has followed me on this journey so far. My army is getting stronger every day. And to anyone out there suffering in silence, please ask for help. Your broken shield can only last for so long, and if people don't know you're broken, they can't help you win your battle.

~ CHILD WELFARE

I feel my cellphone vibrate in Save-My-Life School, and I slip out of the room to take the call. I don't recognize the number. Immediately my mind goes to my eight-year-old son, Adam, who is at school. I hope he is OK.

Jon, Adam's dad, and I share custody of Adam. It is an amicable set-up where we have a one-week-on and one-week-off arrangement. Jon is also a paramedic, and we work hard to coordinate our schedules so we can each be there for our son.

"Hello. Nat here."

A matter-of-fact voice responds, "Natalie Harris?"

I start to worry a little. "Yes."

"I'm with the Children's Aid Society…" For a moment the world stops spinning. *Child Services?*

I hear her words, but I am not fully listening. I try to process why she is calling me. Then it hits me—I remember talking to a social worker at the hospital the last time I overdosed, and we called the agency together. I guess I just thought that was the end of it.

I am broken. I am devastated. I know I am sick, but I am *not* a bad mom. I don't need this added stress to my already-overflowing plate of bullshit and worry. My kids don't need this either.

As she continues to tell me I will be interviewed by the authorities, I wonder if she even has kids herself. Judging by her tone, my guess is no.

During break, my teacher approaches me in the hall to ask why I left class. I tell her about the phone call. I really expect her to be on my side and to agree this process is completely unnecessary. Why should I make a mistake and my whole family be punished for it?

I settle down a bit as my teacher talks with me. This is probably one of the most *real* wake-up calls I've ever experienced. I share with her what the social worker said to me on the phone, expecting comfort. Instead she says, "Well, is the worker not right? Is she not telling the truth? Did you not overdose—*twice*?"

This is a big, ugly reality check, and I feel as if I am being run over by a Mack Truck. It starts to sink in. I could have died, and my children could have found me. My teacher continues to give me the best advice she can—I should do what I am told.

As a paramedic, *I* was the one who called the Children's Aid Society about *other* people. Fuck. Who am I?

Now I am shaking uncontrollably. I am nauseous and feel as if I am in a dream—a nightmare, actually. Please don't take my kids away from me. *Please!*

~ MOVING

My heart is being ripped out of my body. Adam is moving in to live with his dad full-time today.

The Children's Aid Society interviewed all of us—AB; my daughter, Caroline; Leo; and me. In addition, they also separately interviewed Adam's dad, Jon. Jon is mad—not because he will have Adam full-time. Jon is a great dad and cherishes every moment he has with his son. No, Jon is angry because he doesn't agree with the agency's decision, and he has been very vocal about his opinion, too. Through it all, Jon still believes I am an awesome mother. But, I understand that the Children's Aid Society has a very important job to do. They are there to protect children, and prudence and thoroughness are part of that process.

The result of this now "open file" on me is Adam will live with his dad full-time. If I want to visit him, I can only do so supervised, in the presence of another responsible adult. My daughter Caroline is older, and with the help of friends and family she is able to carry on with her life without the interruption of having to move.

Every molecule of my body wants to fight this decision, but I keep remembering my teacher pointing out the bitter reality I don't want to accept—but must. I have to take responsibility for my actions. The events the social worker is concerned about really *did* happen. Sometimes acceptance is a difficult pill to swallow (pun intended).

~ PERFECTION PERSMECTION

I am running late for Save-My-Life School today, and I am nervous that I won't be on time when my friend sends me a text saying, "Go get a good grade. It doesn't have to be an A+ though. Lol. Be well, Nat. You are stronger than you give yourself credit for. Hold your head high."

I take a screen shot of it (like I have with many beautiful messages over the last week and a half) because it means more to me than she probably knows. I quickly reply, "OK, B+ it is!" and scurry into class at the last minute, that small text weighing massively on my mind.

Unfortunately, my perfectionist attitude does not always serve me well. I've enjoyed the accolades I've received over the years because they remind me of my hard work and dedication, but they were always somehow (at some point) never good enough. My college Board of Governors Award had to turn into first place at the Paramedic Competition, which then had to progress into a university Outstanding Achievement Award—you get the point.

Coincidentally, one of our topics in class today is "Perfection Versus Discovery," two dramatically contrasting attitudes in life. Our discussion brings me to the realization that many of my past hardships have led me to significant discovery—but also to inescapable perfectionism.

Allow me to explain. Having a daughter at eighteen years old filled my world with discovery. Being a new mom and falling in love with my child is something I can't describe with words. Discovering how to feed, dress, and care for her was a challenge, but I loved it. However, each night when I put her to sleep, I wasn't able to rest or be excited for a new day, because every second of downtime was used to formulate a future success plan—a plan I had no choice but to perfect. The quality of my daughter's life depended on it. When I was finally accepted into paramedic college, I didn't just scrape by. I needed to be the best in order to know without a doubt that I would be able to provide for my daughter. We weren't going to stay in the rundown apartment we lived in. She wasn't going to grow up in a bad neighbourhood—it just wasn't going to happen. I stayed up late every night to practise scenarios and study non-stop. Each test mark I received could have been better. *Are there bonus marks available on this test?* Because I would write out very long answers, the teacher would come over and take the test away from me mid-sentence.

"I'm not finished!" I would say.

"Yes, you are," the teacher would reply, eyebrow raised. The pressure I put on myself to succeed was slowly making me sick. I didn't get to truly enjoy school (like I usually did—don't judge) because the only mark that let me sleep at night was an A+.

Fast forward to today. I learn that I need to balance my perfectionism with discovery. I used to believe there were only winners and losers, but according to my handout there are winners and *learners*. Lame—but I guess it gets the point across. I also learn that I need to be less critical of my mistakes, and when someone compliments me, the only reply necessary is, "Thank you." On a positive note, I can say with certainty that the perfectionism I relied on years ago has subsided quite a bit—you should see the pile of laundry in my basement! But it still lingers and affects my response to challenges. I need to relax a little and discover new things that I may not be the best in. This morning my friend reminded me that in the school of life, you don't need to pull in A+'s, you just need to show up and keep trying—even if you're late.

Final line credit this evening goes to Miss AB—I love you.

~ WHAT DO YOU WANT TO BE WHEN YOU GROW UP?

Over the past two weeks, there have been a lot of powerful analogies put forth in class. Today is no exception. Our teacher in Addiction class asks us, "What do you want to be when you grow up?" Complete silence in the room. We know there is a catch. He continues on to say, "People recovering from mental illness and addiction exhibit many of the traits of adolescents." Oh goodie! I hated being a teenager. If anyone in class says high school was fun, I might punch them in the throat. OK, realistically, I can tell where he is going with this. Every one of us can relate to the following adolescent feelings—insecurity, not knowing where we belong in the world, pendulum-like mood swings, feelings of isolation, and a sense of being misunderstood. But on a good note, similar to an adolescent, we (once again) have the opportunity to decide who we want to become. Do we want to be an addict or not? Do we want to heal from our illnesses or not? What future do we see for ourselves? So, that's it? We just *decide*? Let's get real, we are all light years away from celebrating at sobriety prom.

The class starts to express their frustration in how easy the teacher makes this decision sound. The reality is that deciding who we want to be is often a minute-by-minute choice. Does the teacher know what that feels like? Similar to an adolescent, we all have constant internal battles. To carry on with the analogy, we have a high school bully living inside our heads, trying to convince us to numb the pain we feel from our mental illnesses with alcohol or drugs. It's what we all did in the past. It's how we coped—and how we almost died. And honestly, that bully is so convincing. He tells us: one drink will be OK; we're adults and can make our own decisions; no one needs to know about it; and everyone else is just overreacting. I want to hear the teacher say that the bully will eventually leave and that, with time and hard work, we can all have complete inner peace. But that is wishful thinking. Apparently, the bully will always be there, lurking in the back of our minds. However, we can control how much power we give him. Putting ourselves in situations where people are drinking—or *using* for many of my classmates—will make the bully stronger, more tempting, and easier to give in to. However, living a healthy, well-balanced lifestyle will kick the bully's ass significantly. But alas, it will take time.

Sadly, many of my classmates' bullies have been too powerful at one point or another in their lives. Some have relapsed after twenty-five years of sobriety (heartbreaking). It isn't going to be an easy road—it hasn't been so far. But at least for today we choose who we want to be—healthy human beings. That's why we are here. Together we already have our clique without any peer pressure—just acceptance and support. Now this is my kind of high school.

~ ANXIETY TO PANIC

In the interest of brutal truth, I want to take you back to the day of September 7, 2013—the very first time I overdosed.

~

I am under a lot of stress at work. My supervisor is excellent and tries everything to help me through this time, but there's only so much she can do. Day by day, work turns from a place I enjoy to a place I dread. I still love many aspects of the job, especially teaching, but when stress hovers over everything you do, there's only so much you can continue to love. I begin drinking quite a bit as soon as I get home. It is my only way to relax. I notice that on my days off, my anxiety slowly gets worse and worse. I never really feel like I unwind from work, and the stress is always on my mind. Noises start bothering me to the point of feeling nauseated. I can't sit in the room if the TV is on, and I plug my ears when anyone yells. There is a tractor that drives around our neighbourhood every day, every few minutes, all day, and I can't take it! I hope to see other neighbours run outside and stop the driver because they are going crazy too. But no, it affects me alone. What the heck is happening to me? I even ask AB, Leo, and my daughter to go outside and yell at the driver one day. They all look at me like I am crazier than a Saturday at Costco, but I am serious. I am about to chain my body to the backhoe. When that plan doesn't work, I have the brilliant idea to call the builder and lie, pretending that the tractor is waking up my small baby. What am I thinking? I hope that he starts to take a different route and think the desperate-new-mom image will pull at his heart strings. Well, it doesn't work. I'm such a bad liar—damn it.

As the tractor continues its tour of my neighbourhood, I start wearing earplugs. I can still feel the house shake when it passes, so it frustrates me even more. I download peaceful music and try to listen to that. It is futile. The only thing that gets me away from the noise is not being in the house at all. Why is something like this affecting me so much? Why can't I just come home from work and feel relaxed? To top it all off, being a shift worker means I need to sleep in the day. Well, when I come home from an already stress-filled night shift, my anxiety shoots to the moon when that tractor starts up. I have no peace. I can't sleep. I am living in stress 24/7—at work and at home! I feel myself growing angry and numb.

One night, while trying to listen to my peaceful music before work, something happens. I can't put my uniform on. There is no way I can do it. I cry uncontrollably and feel like a fool. I am angry, frustrated, and exhausted. Then finally my frustration spirals into a full-blown panic attack! For me, a panic attack feels like my brain is running a never-ending marathon that I can't keep up with—I breathe so fast, my muscles tense up, I feel paranoid, and it seems as if the world isn't real. I'm hyper-vigilant because I don't feel safe. Like with my deeper layers of depression, all logic disappears, and sadly it needs to run its course. After ten to fifteen minutes, I'm finally calm. I'm exhausted. I want to sleep for a million years, but after pumping so much adrenalin into my bloodstream, I can't sleep. It will take days until I feel back to my normal self—whatever that is.

Once I get through the panic attack, Leo drives me to the hospital as I continue to cry inconsolably. He can't bear to see me like this. I need something to calm me down. I am extremely embarrassed and very paranoid that I might run into any of my co-workers. It is bad enough I know most of the nurses—that can't be avoided. I want to be invisible. Leo scopes out the place before I leave the car. What an ordeal. Elaborate planning goes into hiding me during every hospital visit because I am embarrassed about my mental illness. It is exhausting—not only for me, but for anyone who goes with me. I think, "If only I had a broken leg, I wouldn't need to hide! People would never look at me differently, because a broken leg could happen to anyone." What naive thinking. I know what happens to me can happen to anyone else too, but I still think this panic attack makes me weak.

After completing our *Mission Impossible* task of getting me to the mental health unit undercover (we sneak through back halls with security to avoid being seen), the doctor assesses me and refers me to see another healthcare professional in a few days. I get a small anti-anxiety prescription, but when I try it, it doesn't help me at all. Of course! My only hope is that, in a few days, the appointment will reveal the answer I am looking for (to what question I don't know. I am a mess). He will fix me! That's his job, right?

The day of the appointment finally arrives; I am nervous but hopeful. After waiting over an hour to see the doctor, Leo and I sit down in his office and try to explain over the span of a few minutes what has transpired. My legs shake in the chair, and I stare out the window. I am on the brink of crying when I receive the "just think of positive things" speech! I immediately lose all confidence in this doctor, so Leo has to take over answering the questions. After what is maybe a fifteen-minute appointment, he writes me a prescription and tells me to come back in a few weeks. Are you kidding me? A healthcare professional just told me to "think of positive things!" I just *positively* want to punch him in the face. I am devastated, crushed, and deflated. I know there isn't a magic pill to fix what I am feeling. I need something more, but I don't know what.

That night I take my first dose of the new prescription drugs. It makes me feel is like a zombie! Leo keeps asking me if I am OK. I can barely reply. My lips can't make the sounds I need them to. I can't align my thoughts, let alone walk in a straight line to the bathroom. I don't like it at all.

"Maybe tomorrow you should just take half," Leo suggests. So the next day, I do just that. But half of each pill still makes me feel spaced out. The day turns into night, and I feel no better. When Leo asks how I am doing before he goes to work, I lie as I usually do and say I am fine. "Put your headphones on and try to get some sleep," he says. Thinking that I would be OK, I am left to my own devices, alone, and feeling like I am on another planet. I think that I just need to sleep it off. I take some more pills, listen to my music, and drift further into outer space. Because I am so far gone, I think it is a brilliant idea to shave the sides of my head! While rocking out to (I think) Miley Cyrus (don't judge), I take Leo's clippers and buzz both sides of my head. (I'm shaking my own head right now.) Time elapses, and I drift even further away. Apparently I take some selfies, proud of my new hairstyle, and send them to AB. She later shows me the texts and pictures. I am devastated. The rest of the night is gone. I don't remember it at all. I would later learn that I apparently made a sandwich and left it on the counter with one bite taken out of it. I'm surprised I even got that far.

When AB, Leo, and my brother get to the house, I am unconscious. I took almost an entire bottle of prescription medications, wrote in my journal, and left piles of hair in the sink. AB describes my room as "truly an awful scene." She says it is like the aftermath of a motor vehicle crash, except it is my house—hair in the sink, journal out with the pen dropped near it, crumpled tissue strewn around, and a dishevelled duvet.

I am taken to the hospital by ambulance. When I am finally conscious enough, I voluntarily admit myself to the psych ward, shamefully earning a minimum of three days in the mental health wing. Sad as this may sound, all the embarrassment aside, when I am able to put my thoughts together (and look at my horrible hair in the mirror), a part of me is happy to be here. It is quiet, and I can sleep. This is what I wanted all along—my mind to rest. How has the hospital become my safe haven? How did I get here? How do I move on? Well, I'm still learning those answers.

~ A GREY DAY

Fast forward to present-day Save-My-Life School. After a nice long weekend, I should be pretty good with heading back to school. However, generally speaking, I am more interested in gargling hornets.

After I find a seat in class, I ask my neighbour if the daily topics have changed this week. "No," she replies. "It's Tuesday. It's Anxiety Day today."

Gasp! I hate Tuesdays now. "Torturous Tuesdays"—that's what I will call them. I look for my doodle paper. The teacher enters stage left, "Here is your seven-page, double-sided handout everyone..."

OK, I'm aware that exposure therapy is a method of treating anxiety, but this repeat of last week is ridiculous.

"And we are going to skip Addiction class today and use its time to cover more of the anxiety module."

I'm on *Candid Camera*. I must be. Seeing that I promised to stay through every class unless the sky falls on me (and even then, I would probably muscle my way through it), I resign myself to the fact that it's going to be a long, anxious morning. Damn you, irony.

Deep breath. Big stretch. I'm ready. No, I'm not. Where the heck is my doodle paper?

The topic is "The Causes of Anxiety Disorders." It starts off by saying that anxiety disorders are brought about by a variety of causes operating on numerous levels. Pretty vague. I don't like vague. Some of these levels include (*deep breath*) heredity, conditioning, family background, biology, upbringing, recent stressors, your ability to express feelings, your self-talk, and your personal belief system— and so on. And so on? No, that isn't a long enough list—we should definitely add "and so on." That will clarify things (eye roll).

It feels like hours go by. We read about how our family background and certain types of upbringing can precipitate our likelihood of developing anxiety. As she continues to read, I hear a lot of the word "overly." Parents can be *overly* cautious and *overly* critical. I put up my hand, "What exactly is *overly*?"

I grasp the overall theory the module is trying to teach me, but while everyone else moves along with their heads buried in pages filled with highlighted sentences, I just feel frustrated. How do I know if I *overly* parent? How do I know when to encourage versus accept? Am I *overly* encouraging? Am I *overly* accepting? How do I know when to be cautious versus critical? Am I *overly* cautious? Am I *overly* critical? I hate not having answers when I'm learning something new. Up goes my hand again. The teacher calls my name without even looking this time. "Yes, Natalie."

I put forth my suggestion that maybe we should just make this handout our kids' first book. Then as they grow up they can point out what their parents are screwing up and save them a whole lot of anxiety—that would be helpful. (Insert sarcastic giggle by *only* me.) To me, the handout's lists, maybes, and different theories make it sound like every kid is just *overly* destined to end up in this class!

"Natalie, I can tell you don't like the grey areas." Well, I guess that's true. The grey areas of life suck and frustrate me, and every component of my mental illness seems grey. How I explain it, how I feel it, how I deal with it—and now how I educate myself on it—*all* grey. Now my anxiety is just making me irritable. The teacher doesn't deserve my attitude. I bite my tongue.

Sadly, I don't learn a life-changing piece of advice about anxiety today. I listen to a whole lot of causes that have no evidence and theories that will most likely change tomorrow. I am reminded that since I have mental illnesses, I need to work that much harder to continue to accept the grey. Good thing we skipped Addiction class because I sure could use a glass of wine.

~ HEARTBREAK

I wake up this morning feeling miserable. I drag myself out of bed only because our dog, Walter, lets me know he needs his morning pee. As he and I shuffle down the sidewalk through the foggy morning, my heart feels heavy. I can't shake the gross feeling in my stomach, and I totally know why. My heart is broken and I miss Leo. We dated for two years and still care for each other, but we need to break up in order for me to heal (it's complicated). You know that saying "If you love someone, let them go?" That's pretty much the story of our lives right now. I know Leo is not abandoning me. Don't hate him; this is a mutual decision. Trying to navigate my way through this mental health journey with a broken heart is not easy. It almost feels like a cruel joke. When I used to fall asleep, Leo would hold my hand. Now I hold Walter's paw instead. It's a very cute substitute, but it's obviously not the same.

When I finish Walter's walk, I talk to AB on the phone. I hope it will lift my spirits, but it doesn't. There is nothing that can make me feel better right now. She can normally make me laugh in a few seconds, but instead I choke back my tears as she speaks. I reply with a few mumbled words. If I start to cry right now, I will never make it to school. I take a quick shower and throw on some jogging pants. I know I will have a long day ahead of me.

The first topic of the day is "Situations, Moods, and Thoughts." You have to be kidding me. Throughout the booklet we learn how to develop a thought record. The purpose of the record is to see that once we work through some of the moods we have, we often realize that we are catastrophizing—or making things worse than they need to be. We don't actually possess any evidence to support the thought. I've been introduced to this concept before in counselling, and keeping it in the back of my mind did help me from time to time. But the mood I am in today is a very complicated example. I'm heartbroken. How do I talk myself out of that? Yay! Another grey area. As everyone works away on their thought records, I can barely hold back my tears. Why can't my mood be "discouraged" or "misunderstood?" I can bang those off no problem. Am I wrong to think that there is no such thing as a workbook that can teach anyone how to feel less heartbroken? Isn't that a normal emotion everyone has to ride out? I suppose that by my lack of questions and quietness, the teacher can tell something is wrong with me.

"Natalie, are you not feeling well?" *Oh, boy. Please don't ask. I've been holding it together so well.* What I want to say is, "You're right, I'm not feeling well. My heart hurts, and I feel alone. I worry every day about how I'm going to get through this. I hate how much work healing from this illness takes. I'm pissed off. I'm tired. I want a glass of wine, and the guy beside me has way too much cologne on!" But all I can muster is, "I'm just having a bad day."

I excuse myself during the "Enhancing Hope" section to bawl my eyes out in the bathroom.

At the end of the day, I am scheduled to meet with my teacher. She looks at me and says, "I know there's something wrong."

She sees right through me. I reply, "I feel very disconnected from everything that makes me feel comfortable. I desperately miss Leo—the transition isn't going well. And I even miss work." Oddly enough, I have never had an anxiety attack or depression at work—*ever*. This is probably because my mind is occupied, I feel confident, and I'm around people I love. But now I go home to a pretty lonely world. Writing is my saving grace. I hate feeling out of the loop, and I definitely hate feeling like my heart is out of my chest. She gives me a good "Keep practising your positive thinking" and "I'm here whenever you need to talk" speech, and I go home. (She is very kind; I actually like her. As you know, I'm in a super-judgey phase. But she's passed the test so far.)

I guess at the end of the day, it doesn't matter what diagnosis I am given or how difficult it is for me to separate a normal feeling from the feelings I'm used to in my overly dark world, heartbreak is an emotion we all feel. Not coming up with a miraculous solution after mapping it out with a thought record is to be expected. *Surprise, Natalie! You're still human.*

~ IT'S NOT HACKING IF I HAVE HER PASSWORD (AND PERMISSION)

Hi everyone. It's AB. I won't get into details as it's her story to tell, but I don't want everyone to worry. Very simply— Natalie overdosed yesterday morning and was taken to the hospital where she'll hopefully stay until she gets into a mental health facility very soon. Mental illness is a tough battle to fight, but she's trying. Sometimes the load is just too heavy to carry when you don't have the skills to manage.

Stay tuned. She'll be back. She's a fighter!
AB

~ THANK YOU

Hi everyone. I just got off the phone with Natalie, and she is in good spirits today. I read her every single message that has been sent. She loves them and is humbled and overwhelmed with gratitude. Your continued support means everything to her—and to Leo and me. So, thank you for the messages!

She wants you all to be updated. So, I will endeavour to keep you posted. Yesterday morning was a rough one for her emotionally. She called me in tears and couldn't believe she had landed herself back in the hospital. She felt like she let everyone down, but mostly herself. Nat talked about how proud she was of the progress she was making and how she felt sad that the anxiety and depression won again. She was moved from the mental health ward of the Emergency Department to the mental health wing yesterday. She said she has two amazing nurses on duty today who have been so kind and helpful, and she loves that! We had to talk about some behind-the-scenes stuff so we can keep her life running while she's in the hospital. Leo and I have divided tasks and each have our list of things to do. So many people have offered to help in any way they can. Again, the kindness and support is so overwhelming. As I type this, one of her co-workers is over at her house helping to close her pool—thank you. And that's only one example. We have been looking into a rehabilitation centre for Natalie. There's no news about an opening yet, but the push to get her there is in the works. Until then, she's safe and doing better.

AB

~ NIGHTMARE

My room in the mental health ICU is made up of four bare walls, a window with the blind permanently closed behind a pane of glass, a bed, a blanket, a pillow, and me. If I want to use the landline phone, I must do so under the watchful eye of a nurse and only during the allotted times. Dinner is served on Styrofoam plates with only a plastic spoon and fork to cut my meal with. Give that a try sometime! It's not a pretty sight. The powdered coffee is lukewarm—I'm guessing to make sure no one can burn themselves. I eat when I'm told it's time to because none of the rooms have a clock. I shower in an unlocked shower room with a handful of generic body wash, and I'm not allowed to wear street clothes or socks—only the scrubs and blue slippers they provide. The mirror in the unlocked washroom is a sheet of metal screwed to the wall and impossible to break. While I lie awake in my room, I hear patients being restrained down the hall. They are a threat to themselves I suppose, as I was. I plug my ears to block out the crying and yelling and feel relieved that I cooperated—or I would have been restrained as well. If I want a pencil and paper, I need to sign the pencil out. Then I am handed one sheet of paper. A camera is on me at all times, and for some odd reason I'm not allowed to sit on the floor. When I want my light turned off, I need to ask the nurse to do it for me because my room doesn't even contain the switch. It's lonely and sterile, but I'm here for my safety. It's been my home away from home—three times now.

How did I get here again? What was I thinking? How could I hurt the people I love so much? How could I have been so foolish? How did my brain not think of the consequences? These are all questions that swirl in my mind like a tornado. The level of guilt I feel after hurting my family, my friends, and myself is nauseating. I wish so much that it is all just a bad dream! I want so desperately to wake up from the nightmare and see that it didn't really happen. I feel suffocated by relentless distorted thinking—everyone is better off without me! They will never forgive me. They will never truly understand what the depths of my depression feel like. They won't understand that I'm not rational when I'm in that darkness and barely feel anything at all. It takes an army to convince me that my thinking is wrong, and days…weeks…months…to ever begin to forgive myself.

I want the cycle to end so badly. I can't hurt the people I love anymore. I can't hurt myself anymore.

Tomorrow is another day and a blessing. No catchy ending to this entry. This is all I have in me tonight.

~ IT'S ME, NAT

I've sat in front of my computer for over two hours, trying to find the right words. "Natalie, you're overthinking this again," AB tells me from the edge of my bed. It is so nice when she visits. I know she's right, but how do I express the spectrum of emotions I've felt over the last four days? Are there words in the English language that exist to accomplish such a feat? Well, I've decided that for tonight, in my still-foggy state, the best thing I can say is a simple and sweet thank you.

For all the love and support that you have given to me and my family—thank you.

For your compassion and understanding in my time of remorse—thank you.

For sharing your time and attention during your busy days—thank you.

For every single text, message, phone call, and prayer—thank you.

For believing in me—thank you.

I love you all! Every single one of you. XO

~ BELIEVING A COMPLIMENT

I am out of the hospital now and have moved in with AB. I am ready to attend Save-My-Life School again.

Thursday's class is pretty fun. Before Acupuncture and Relaxation class (which I totally love!), we all sit around the table and learn how to take a compliment. Sounds easy, right? Well, for people who have negative self-talk on a regular basis, it's not easy at all. Some of our mental illnesses cause our brains to convince us that we are not as valuable as we really are. The chatter that happens in our minds tells us that we aren't worth loving or that people are better off without us, etc. So, when someone tries to pay us a compliment, we think they are being sarcastic or that there is a secret message behind the positive words. In fact, they simply might be saying what they mean.

The teacher gives everyone a blank piece of paper and asks us to write our names at the top. Then he tells us to start passing the papers to our right, and everyone has to write a compliment about the person whose name is on the paper. This might be fun. Not everyone in the class has met before, so it is difficult to compliment personality traits, but no matter what, it isn't difficult to compliment something. Some of the compliments I receive include "I like the way you express yourself." That's very nice. I always thought I was horrible at telling stories, and me telling a joke is usually a disaster. "You have an amazing tattoo that suits your personality, so does your hair." Once again, a very nice compliment. I love my tattoo and hair as well, but I didn't know others liked them too. "Natalie is a strong person who is kind and caring towards others." I love this one. It makes me smile. "I enjoy your insight on addiction, and it's refreshing to know there are others who struggle with it like I do!" Wow, I think the same about everyone else in the room. We all have so much in common. They are like my new family members! The exercise is a success.

The compliments put a smile on everyone's face! It takes all of twenty minutes to complete, and we feel so great about ourselves afterwards. So why aren't we able to keep our heads held high and accept compliments every time they are given? We all deserve to be loved and respected, but sadly the mental illness stigma has taken away our ability to believe we are worth it. Our illnesses make us think that we look weak in other people's eyes and that compliments always have a catch. But they don't. We just need to learn how to accept them.

The class gets me thinking about receiving a compliment and also about accepting support and help. Before this journey began, I was the worst at asking for help. I felt I was putting other people out. Everyone has such busy lives. They don't really have time to help me. AB and Leo were two people who always told me to ask for help when I needed it. And it took them a very long time to convince me that doing so was OK. "Natalie, you just need to open your eyes. People want to help you," AB would say.

"Nut [my no-pun-intended nickname], you don't have to be every-thing for everyone. You can say no sometimes," Leo would remind me often. Well, I'm happy to announce that I am slowly starting to see that they are right. (I can picture AB and Leo high-fiving right now.) The love and support I've received over the past few weeks has been unbelievable! While I was in the hospital, a co-worker closed my pool and fixed the fence that needed to be kicked down to get into my house on the day I overdosed. No charge—just from his heart. People offered to make meals, help with the kids, and most recently help "watch" me until I go to the mental health facility. (AB and Leo have me abiding by some strict rules, but I agree it is for the best.) I am willing to accept the help I need. That's a big step for me. I feel like I'm finally on the right track. I have a long road ahead of me, but with all of you beside me, I don't feel so alone. I know you love me, and I can't thank you enough. Please accept my compliment.

~ APPROPRIATE GOALS

Well, you all know by now that I have experienced some huge highs and lows during my journey. But through talking to friends, class-mates, and my teachers, I've come to realize that that's just what recovery is all about. When I return to class after my recent over-dose, my classmates are happy to see me but not surprised I relapsed.

My teachers are so supportive, but they don't gasp when I tell them I overdosed again. They simply say it is part of many people's journey and they are happy I am back.

Their reaction makes me think about a point that is made in Codependency class: "Set higher standards for yourself and more appropriate goals." I feel it speaks to my perfectionist past and present. Let's not kid ourselves here; I am bummed when my tree pose at yoga looks more like a soggy noodle than a mighty oak. However, it reminds me that I'm allowed to have high expectations of myself, but they need to be reasonable. Relapsing and overdosing shatters my confidence and makes me feel like a failure—*again*. But I'm human. It isn't realistic to think that overnight healing is an appropriate goal. If relapse is part of recovery, I wish it took the form of me secretly skipping class instead of me almost taking my own life. But it happened—there is nothing I can do about it. I need to keep my recovery standards high, but appropriate.

~ CHURCH

I go to church today with a close friend. It is a mission I need to accomplish as per AB's loving direction. AB knows I am a spiritual person but not an avid churchgoer. She figures I will take something home from being in that spiritual setting again. I must admit, while growing up I found the weekly sermon often resonated with respect to some current contention in my life—and today is no exception.

"Love Your Neighbour as You Love Yourself" is the topic of the sermon. Interesting—and tricky! I promise I am the first neighbour to not love any neighbour who stands too close to me in a lineup. Anywhoo…the theme instantly reminds me of the few naysayers of my writing. To be fair, most of these devil's advocates' concerns (pun intended) revolve around the possibility of my writing distracting me from completely focusing on my own recovery. Interesting thought, neighbours, but allow me to share my own view on this topic. (Codependency class 101—have an opinion and don't be passive. I got this!) If I am to love you as I love myself, why wouldn't I share my journey in hopes of helping even one stigmatized mental illness sufferer? What an amazing thing to be able to do! Document my own turbulent journey, allowing me to heal as I write (which I love to do), and possibly help someone who is going through the same or similar experiences? I'm pretty much loving neighbours everywhere by loving myself. So I would like to thank the handful of people who have expressed their concern that my writing is taking up my healing time. I would like to remind them that writing allows me to breathe again instead of suffocating in darkness and stigma. If by chance some neighbours get to breathe along with me—well AMEN to that!

~ SMILING IN THE MIRROR

When I walk into class this morning, I notice that I'm not the little fish in the sea anymore. Five new timid, unassuming students have joined Save-My-Life School today. As they sit there, staring at the table or their hands, all I can think is, "I so know how they feel right now. They probably think that they don't belong here, that they won't like talking in a group, that there is nothing some silly class could do to help them, and that the stigma they use to shield their voice will never disappear." My heart goes out to them, but I know from experience that regardless of how uncomfortable they feel now, they will eventually see that they are precisely where they need to be.

Self-Esteem class is first on deck today. "Anyone want to tell me about something positive they did this weekend?" asks our teacher as her first at bat. Crickets. None of the new classmates are budging so I chirp, "I had a great night with some friends watching movies, eating junk food, and drinking cream soda!" (Big smile on my face.)

"Very nice," replies my teacher. Then she tries another swing. "Anyone want to tell me who you think determines your self-esteem?" Blank faces and uncomfortable coughs. I guess this one's up to me again. "We determine our own self-esteem," I answer confidently.

"Correct."

I'm such a prize student now. OK, last at bat: "Can anyone tell me a goal they have in their future?" Awkward stretches and coffee gulps. Don't worry, everyone, I got this. "I would like to have my master's degree completed by 2018."

Home run? Well, maybe not so much. My teacher smiles, but a new student a few seats over mumbles, "Wow, master's degree—my goal was to step outside my house today." *Aw crap. Maybe just getting on base would have been a better choice, Natalie.* All scores aside, the morning class is primarily made up of the teacher asking questions followed by me answering them to end the awkward silence. Nevertheless, I understand what the new students are probably feeling—like they don't even know who they are anymore. (And they definitely don't know who the punk with the short black hair and the tattoo is. P.S. It's me!)

The teacher then goes on. "We are who we see in the mirror. We determine and control our own self-image. If we want to change our life, we must change our vision of our life."

How true—and fitting for the day. Three weeks ago I saw a scared, anxious, guilt-filled mom and student in the mirror. I was the coffee-gulping, awkward-stretching student who had no idea how this class would affect me. My reflection in the mirror back then was probably what any one of the new students see in the mirror today. And that same reflection of myself probably would have rolled my eyes at anyone who mentioned that a master's degree was a realistic goal.

It's all perspective I suppose. I don't need to feel bad for saying that I want to complete my master's in four years, because that's who I see in the mirror today. (I may not have seen it three weeks ago—not crying each night was a good goal back then.) And the new student sees going outside and facing her anxiety as her goal in her mirror today. Both the new student and I give correct answers to the teacher's question about goals. And I think both goals with their equally evolving perspectives are home runs!

True side note: My fortune cookie tonight reads, "Vision is not seeing things as they are, but as they will be."

~ POSITIVE ANXIETY DAY—SAY WHAT?

On my Tuesday morning drive to Save-My-Life School, I notice I am experiencing an odd feeling for Anxiety Day—calmness. "How do you think today will be for you?" asks AB.

"I'm not sure," I reply. "But I think I've come to the realization that it's going to be what it's going to be." AB swings her head my way and gives me the serious "I don't believe you, Kissy" look.

"No, really!" I continue, "I can't change the way it's taught, and I always walk away from class with a poignant lesson. So, as long as the girl with the relentless phlegmy cough keeps her germs to herself, I will try to breathe my way through it." AB gives me the "mmhmm" look, but then she pauses and says, "I'm proud of you, Kissy."

After finding my seat (as far away as possible from Germ Girl), we are of course handed a multiple-page, double-sided booklet to read. *Breathe. Here we go.* But something odd happens again as the teacher starts reading. Drum roll please. I learn something in the first paragraph on Anxiety Day! My jaw drops as I hear the teacher say, "It's entirely normal to experience feelings more intensely when you begin to face situations you've been avoiding for a long time. If this is happening to you, you're on the right track."

Feeling extra anxious on Anxiety Day is what I should have been feeling all along? Eureka! Furthermore, "many people who are prone to anxiety tend to withhold their feelings, which only aggravates stress and anxiety more." So, let me get this straight, my rants about Anxiety Day are healing for me? Nice! Apparently feelings are not right or wrong—feelings simply exist. The perceptions or judgments we make that lead to the feelings, however, may be right or wrong. I also learn that over time the practice of continually suppressing my feelings can lead to increased difficulty in expressing or even identifying them.

Announcement to all those parents out there! When the process of suppression begins in childhood, we can grow up feeling completely out of touch with our feelings, leaving only a sense of emptiness. So, when your children are crying, they are sad. When they yell, they are mad—and those feelings are OK!

As we continue onto page 261 of Appendix B, Part 2 of the Second Edition (OK, I'm exaggerating for effect), something else in the reading rings true to me with regard to my EMS family and suppressing our feelings. "In some cases anxiety and panic itself may be a signal that suppressed feelings are trying to emerge." Interesting. I know that my anxiety doesn't occur at work. Maybe that is because it doesn't have time to set in until I am home. We, as first responders, are accustomed to suppressing our feelings at work largely because we don't have the time to deconstruct a call that potentially could be causing us anxiety or worry. In fact, we are often sent to the next call without even completing our paperwork. Our patients rely on our ability to be "on" and focused for that next call, so we have no choice but to suppress any lingering feelings from the previous call.

Likewise, according to our reading, every feeling carries a charge of energy. When we hold that energy in and do not give it expression, it may create a state of tension. I can definitely relate to this! After a long day of back-to-back calls, my shoulders are like rocks and my irritability is an eleven out of ten. Fellow paramedics, can I get an AMEN? But if I have enough downtime to eat my lunch, pee when required, and decompress after every call, I feel less tense when I get home—and I may not need to resort to that huge glass of wine to unwind. Wow, I may change today's name from Torturous Tuesday to Tell-Me-Like-It-Is Tuesday.

The last big point I can relate to today is that once we learn how to identify our feelings, the next step is learning how to express them. This usually involves being willing to share your feelings with others. *Check.* And we may choose to write out our feelings to express them. *Double check!*

"Kissy, was Anxiety Day actually good today?"

"Why yes it was, AB. Yes, it was."

~ TATTOO PROGRESS

Hey, everyone. I am super tired after sitting for another seven hours for my tattoo. I will write tomorrow.

Thank you again for everything!

~ MOM'S MAGIC SHOW

Today is a different sort of day at Save-My-Life School. Now that I'm almost finished Week 3, the revolving door of students starting and finishing the program has become very apparent to me. Earlier in the week, I was feeling great that I was no longer the new kid on the block, but today I feel uneasy and sad. I want to put an "Out of Order" sign on the revolving door and keep everyone with me. I am just getting to know fellow students and value their impact on my life. Now I feel as if I am witnessing a constant new-student inauguration, making my peer relationships noticeably less comforting. (It probably doesn't help that I am in Layer 1 of my depression today as well.)

Most of my life, relationships have been filled with uncertainty and confusion. It was only a matter of time until they would end. Growing up, my sister and I used to say, "Believe it when you see it, and enjoy it while it lasts." This is not a very comforting way to live. It's been hard to allow myself to be vulnerable enough to accept a loving relationship, except in one beautiful circumstance—being a mom to my kids. I would do anything for my kids. That love is certain.

But raising my kids while having a mental illness always feels like I am the magician in a multi-act magic show—lots of smoke and mirrors and extravagant illusions. David Copperfield has nothing on me! When I am depressed, I wave my magic wand and poof, I appear happy. When I am exhausted from my anxiety, I start the smoke machine and presto, I play the energetic mom role like a pro. But being such a wonderful magician is exhausting!

I never had a break because I didn't feel comfortable talking to my kids about my depression or anxiety for two reasons: First, I didn't fully understand what was going on with me, and second, I wanted to be everything I could be for my kids. To me that didn't include being sick—until recently. So, I've had many years of perfecting my act. Heck, I was so good at it, I even tricked myself sometimes. I'd often find myself saying, "I'm fine, totally fine. This feeling is normal." Then I would secretly go drink wine from my top hat. (Obviously I'm joking. I would never drink wine from my top hat.) I wanted to be the perfect mom, so the illusions I performed could have made me money in Vegas.

~

AB and I take my eighteen-year-old daughter, Caroline, out for dinner. It is the first time Caroline has been willing to talk to me since my last overdose. She is hurt and upset with what her mom did (again), and she needed time to process her emotions—which is absolutely OK. But her weeks of silence leave me to wonder what she thinks exactly happened. Are our views of the event different? Heaven knows I can barely wrap my head around it myself! I feel there is a disconnect somewhere. I know she has some tough questions for me, but now I need to answer them without my magic wand. No illusions, no smoke and mirrors—just authentic me.

"Mom, how were you upset enough to do this? You seemed fine the days before" is one of her first candid questions for me. My reply is the truth: "I was hiding my depression. I hadn't felt good for days."

"Why didn't you tell me?" she asks sadly. I truthfully reply, "I never wanted to worry you. I even tried to hide the feelings from myself."

"How could you do that to Adam? You made the choice to put those pills in your mouth! How could you hurt him like that?" She is quite angry, and I now see how my magic shows have negatively impacted everyone all these years. She doesn't understand my illness, and I instantly wish I had taught her rather than tricked her. I didn't have to scare her, but education of some sort might have erased her resentment towards me and healed her heart. She would understand that it was the illness that made me take the pills. She would understand that my depressed mind played cruel tricks on me, that nothing seemed more reasonable at the time, and that I felt like everyone would be better off without me. She would understand that when I am in those states, my rational mind is non-existent.

"Well, I can't trust you, and I need to make some boundaries until I feel better," she says sternly, and I am proud of her decision. Masking her true feelings like I have for most of my life would never work. She is wise enough to see that the truth is the only path to healing. If our relationship is going to grow rather than fall apart, packing up the magic show is the best performance of all.

~ THE DRY LAKE

I hate cold, rainy days. They cast a layer of sadness over everything and challenge my ability to put the new tools I've learned at Save-My-Life School into practice. Now that we are finished Week 3, there aren't as many new tools to learn about compared to previous weeks. I can see that I'm now at the stage where I need to remember and use my existing tools. I find myself reviewing my notes and making sure I haven't forgotten any of them. And now when I'm in a negative situation, I have to dig through my tool box, choose tools I think will work, and use them—trial and error at its best. For example, this morning I am painfully sad because I miss my family and my home so much. I feel lonely, frustrated, and confused—feelings that normally make me hibernate and avoid things I planned for the day, but shockingly I see it as a perfect opportunity to practise using my tools. Think, think, think. What should I do? Should I use my positive self-talk first to try and zap out this pain, or should I let this distressful feeling ride its course? One thing I know is that I definitely need to force myself to *not* hide in the bathroom and to continue going to class and participate. *Deep breath.* You can do this! So as I stand at the hall intersection, forcing myself to do the right thing, I make a left-hand turn down the corridor to my class rather than a right-hand turn to the bathroom.

Relationship Day. Perfect. Let's rehash how my family fell apart. One foot in front of the other, I walk over and sit with my classmates (on the brink of tears), and let the distressful feeling ride its course. Over the hour, I mix the ride with a bit of positive self-talk and even use my anxiety distraction tool (coping skills I have recently learned) to get the butterflies out of my stomach. And what do you know, as the class progresses I start to feel better! I make the right choice to push myself, and I use my tools better than Mike Holmes.

The day reminds me of an analogy my brother Mitch told me about a week ago. He came to visit and expressed honestly that he was still confused about how to help me. He said he knew I had so much support, but I needed to do the work myself. I couldn't agree more. The analogy went like this:

He pictured me alone and sitting on the bottom of a dry lake. I couldn't move without support, so the water (being my friends and family) rushed in to start to make me move. They were always there and always all around me, but I needed to swim on my own. More importantly, I needed to realize that I would eventually get tired and sink without building a boat to float on. So along came school, giving me the tools and wood I needed to build the boat, but no one could save me. Even though I had the support of my family and friends surrounding me and keeping me afloat, *I* was the only one who could actually build the boat. At first I would start out with enough pieces of wood to build a raft, but if I settled for that, the wind would get strong and blow the raft apart. I would need to keep gaining more tools and wood to build a ship strong enough to brave the harsh winds. Once I had built that ship over time, I would be able to confidently challenge any fierce storm, knowing that even if the wind blew some of the wood off the ship, it would remain strong enough to stay afloat. And I would still have all the tools to repair it.

It is the best analogy yet! And you all know how I *do* love a good analogy. (AB, your snow globe analogy gets an honourable mention.) I think I am on the raft today. The winds are pretty strong and try to sink me, but I keep building with the tools I have—and maybe add a compass to guide me through the small storm of loneliness. Heaven knows there will be more storms ahead, and I should probably prepare for a hurricane. But I can't sink anymore. I just can't! Not when everyone is still there, surrounding me and cheering me on.

~ WHY ASK "WHY?"

Do you ever find yourself asking "why" a lot? Why does a heartbreak happen? Why does a loved one die? Why do you have to withstand certain hardships? Why? We think that if we could just get the answer somehow, our grief would lift. We would know how not to repeat the past. We would just do everything better. Well, I ask this horrid question all the time—especially in my times of depression. But when I'm in my dark place, nothing about this question is simple. My "whys" about the world, the universe, our existence, and more are on a grandiose scale. It's not the type of calm, camping-under-the-stars-after-a-few-drinks "Why are we here?" question. When I'm in Layer 4 of my depression, nothing I see, touch, taste, feel, hear, or sense seems real, and "why" is an insatiable question.

I try to explain this feeling to AB and Leo because they have been so worried and confused while witnessing me cry on my bed, staring outside with my bleak outlook on life, and asking if there is any reason for us as humans to even be here. But it's so hard to describe. During these times, the world to me is just painted in pain. For example, the beautiful tree on my lawn that I admired the day before looks grim and scary and poses an overwhelming threat to the safety of the kids climbing on it outside—even when I cheered them on as they got to the second branch the day before. I feel impending doom all around me. Even if I logically know that everything is just the same as it was yesterday, the depression glasses I look through show the world in the form of a perpetual breaking-news highlight, reminding me of all the sadness on this planet. Nothing seems to be worth it, because eventually everyone will go through pain no matter what. Again, I could tell myself all day long that the struggles we have make us stronger and teach us amazing life lessons...blah blah blah. I could sing "Hakuna Matata" until Walt Disney rolled over in his grave, and I still couldn't see happiness when I'm so lost in my horrible darkness. It's such a dismal set of eyes to look through—all I see is sadness. (Depressing isn't it? *Exactly*.)

As you can tell, trying to describe this terrible feeling to someone who has never suffered from depression is profoundly difficult. With all respect, I liken it to how difficult it would be for me to try to describe what a rainbow looks like to a blind person. Words mean nothing. So, when some random person tells me that I should just change the way I'm thinking or look on the bright side, I want to scream! It's like saying to the blind man that he should just try harder to imagine the rainbow. *That* wouldn't be acceptable, so why is depression any different? Both of our worlds are only able to be understood through our eyes. I know most people mean well. I know they want so desperately to make us happy, but the only way to do that is through understanding and education.

My teacher says something very interesting. She says, "Why ask 'why' when the best answer we can possibly come up with is an assumption at best?" She then wisely suggests that maybe we should use that why-searching energy on learning how to accept the times when we just don't have an answer. I intend to take her advice.

~ VISITS WITH MY SON

Luckily for me, AB lives just a few short blocks away from Jon, which is where Adam is staying until I am allowed unsupervised visits with him. It's such a blessing to be able to simply put on a winter coat and walk a few minutes down the road to see Adam. Sometimes we watch a movie or just have dinner together. Jon is incredibly supportive— like always. He is a great dad! He's never made me feel bad for having a mental illness—and from what I hear, that is rare in relationships. My Save-My-Life School peers share horrible stories of unsupportive spouses and nightmare court battles. I feel as though the children always suffer the most in these cases. Jon has been sticking up for me when the social worker tells him that he should get a court order to get full custody. Jon is like a gentle giant, really. He is sort of shy, but when he is passionate about something, don't mess with him— especially when it comes to his family!

I am watching *Godzilla* with Jon and Adam tonight. We just snuggle on the couch, eating snacks. Adam is being his happy little self with both of us. I am grateful that Jon didn't go to court to take him away from me. I think it helps Adam a lot to know he can see me almost any time. And I am certain it helps me.

My brother Ross and sister-in-law Mandy also help to watch Adam and Caroline *a lot*. They make sure the kids get to and from school, and Caroline often sleeps there. I can never really thank them enough. I feel like a bad mom when I think of how much I depend on other people to help. My self-sabotaging mind tells me that they hate me all the time. I think, "How could they not?" It's the worst torture knowing that people are disappointed in me—and most of all that I am disappointed in myself! I *hate* mental illness! It feels like I am in a jail cell inside my own head and everyone is outside the bars waving their finger at me, telling me that I should know better. I want to scream out, "Should a person with cancer know better?" but that would make me feel like I'm being mean to people with cancer. But it's true! I didn't *choose* this! I didn't *want* to be locked up in my cell behind the bars of shame and guilt.

For now, all I can do is take some comfort in tonight, in this simple moment of warmth and family, watching *Godzilla* with Adam.

~ A PARAMEDIC'S COMFORT

My teacher tells us at Save-My-Life School that we need to get comfortable with uncomfortable. I know what she is referring to—we will be delving into deep, emotional topics that we normally would avoid. We will be experiencing distressing moods that we normally would numb. But immediately my brain also relates this complex phrase to something else—being a paramedic.

Over the last eleven years while being a full-time medic, I can definitely say I have become very comfortable with uncomfortable—and I am noticing how unhealthy this is. I've been acclimatized to live a life that includes horrific memories, relentless nightmares, and ingrained images of sadness and pain. That may sound barbaric to anyone not in the emergency services field, but it's literally part of our lives almost daily. Devil's advocates out there may be saying to themselves that we signed up for it, but we didn't. We signed up for an amazing career that allows us to help people on such an extraordinary level. No one signed up for mental turmoil. We signed up for the chance to save people's lives. No one signed up for memories of patients screaming in pain. We signed up for achieving educational goals. No one signed up for drowning our sorrows in vices. We thought we would be strong enough to avoid being uncomfortable, but no one is. Strength isn't measured by the number of deaths we pronounce. It's measured by the number of deaths we recognize we need to talk about in order to sleep at night. First responders are some kick-ass people! But signing up to be one doesn't mean we signed our hearts away.

It's not normal to have a person who is trapped in a car in agonizing pain from multiple fractures ask you to "just take their leg and arm off." It's not normal to try to resuscitate a man who just barricaded and hanged himself as soon as his son dialled 911, only for us to later discover our arrival pre-empted his plan to first kill his family. It's not normal to witness a young woman seven months pregnant rub her belly with the only limb she can move because she just had a stroke that would leave her forever disabled. It's not normal to see the cellphone on the road beside the obviously dead driver who was crushed between the pavement and the car because he was texting and driving. And it's not normal to know the three sisters in the other car are now two. It's not normal to tell a granddaughter that we did all we could after she begged for us to save her grandfather's life. It's not normal to experience and see the look of true evil when you learn how two innocent women were murdered. It's not normal to be handed a baby that's blue. It's not normal to watch a child have a seizure for thirty minutes because your drugs just wouldn't work. It's not normal to watch someone die right before your very eyes. It's not normal to hear a grandmother say that the baby in the highchair in front of you belongs to a twenty-seven-year-old who's dying from cancer. What we do *isn't* normal—so why do we think it's OK to be comfortable with that? Why is it any surprise to hear that first responders are dying every month because they can't take the memories any longer? I'm uncomfortable with how comfortable we've become.

P.S. I just got accepted into the University of British Columbia's master's in rehabilitation science program today.

~ GRATITUDE

Every day AB asks me enthusiastically what I will write about. She is always so excited to read my posts, and I love her for it. Some days Save-My-Life School gives me multiple topics to choose from; some days I'm a bit stuck. But it never ceases to amaze me how something will eventually come up to talk about. Today being the perfect example.

I am sitting in my room at AB's house, reading some of my messages when I notice that not everyone truly understands why AB is doing what she's doing—restricting my access to Facebook, Twitter, etc. This makes me sad, so I think I will let her know. But I am lazy, and I know her computer is on her lap in her room—so I send her an email. She thinks I resort to this communication method because I am farting in my room—she's so wrong. Anyway, here is a glimpse at what transpires:

Me: *I'm sad, AB.*

AB: *Why are you sad? P.S. You know I'm just down the hall, right? Do you want to meet in the living room in five?*

Me: *I'm sad that people have been lashing out at you. It doesn't make sense to me.*

AB: *Oh my heavens, don't be sad about that! Meatball, just so we're clear, you know you're emailing me from down the hall, and you could just come and talk to me. Here's what I think about the people who've been harsh or disrespectful towards me. Get comfy. People love you, and they are so worried about you. Lots of people don't know who I am and have no idea why there's this AB chick dictating that you can't go on FB or the Twit. Their defensiveness towards me is simply a reflection of love towards you, and I'm OK with that. Wait, why are you on your email?*

Me: *OK. That does make sense. I guess I'm so overwhelmed with the love and support people have been giving me, I wish it was always coming your way as well. I wish they knew how much I need what you are doing for me and my recovery. I would not be where I am if I wasn't forced to pay attention to me. P.S. I was emailing my dad. Remember you said that was OK. You're a dingle dork.*

AB: *Natalie Marie Harris, I hate "dingle dork" like I hate when people sneeze in their hands. LOL. People have been sending me love and support. It is beyond kind and overwhelms my heart—the depth of my gratitude has no measure. The people that have been a bit mean or have sent harsh messages—they simply don't know the whole story and the reasons why we have our rules. For me to focus on the few that have been disrespectful would dishonour all the people that have taken the time to write to me or talk to me when they see me. I'm grateful to everyone who has extended their kindness to me (and Caroline and Adam and Leo and, and, and). So please don't be sad. I went to the grocery store in my PJs today—NOT OK!*

Me: *True say! I will agree that you are right (I hate that!), but I won't agree that it's OK for people to be mean to you.*

AB: *Fair enough. Sidebar: I can hear you farting down the hall. OK, the mean people. I'm tough. I'm a dispatcher, remember? I can take it. But you can beat them up if it helps with your healing. Let's go down for dinner and we'll talk about all the wonderful things everyone else has done! Deal? P.S. Can you please make me some of those really big hamburgers we call "stomach burgers" for dinner? XO*

Me: *Lol. I just peed my pants a bit! OK. Yes, you are tough. But Sidebar No. 2: I just had a great writing idea! Stand by. P.S. We don't have stomach burger stuff, so you can have a bowl of "Luck Charms!"*

AB: *OK Redneck, I'll have some Luck Charms! I'm excited for tonight's idea. Are you going to tell me the topic?*

Me: *You're a loser! OK. Topic—gratitude. That's all I'm saying. I will meet you downstairs now. I'm done farting.*

So, that's a perfect glimpse into our ridiculous conversations! And I am so totally joking about the farting—I *wasn't* done.

Now that I've shared the evolution of today's post, it's time for me to share some more of my deepest gratitude (in no particular order).

To my beautiful kids: I love you with every inch of my soul! I'm so sorry for what I have put you through, but I promise I am on my way to getting healthy. Your hugs and smiles have made me feel better for years. I'm so proud of you and your strength. Words just aren't enough to show you how much I love you!

To Adam's father, Jon, and his family: Words won't be able to thank you all enough. Adam is the luckiest boy to have you as his dad, Jon! He has wonderful grandparents as well. I have always said that—and will forever. Thank you for everything you do. I mean it from the bottom of my heart!

To my family: Thank you for your help along my crazy journey. I know it's had so many mountains and valleys, but I hope you will always know how I hold you so close to my heart.

Thank you to Leo's family: You have all been so supportive and have shown me what unconditional love is. You are such a treasure. I will always keep my card and quotes close to me, and I will be reading them every day. They are so important to me. I am lucky to have you in my life!

Mama Bonnie: Thank you so much for the surprise flowers and card you left for me. It brightened up a very sad day. It was like you knew I needed it! I can't wait to dance with you again. Love you!

To Randi, all the paramedic faculty, and my paramedic students: Wow, what can I say?! Your card and gift brought me to tears (happy ones). Every heartfelt message meant the world to me. You are a pretty amazing bunch of people. I'm the lucky one! Thank you.

To AB and Leo (really, there aren't enough words for this): You have taken care of me for so long. I hope that one day I can show you how much better I am, and that I can somehow, someway thank you enough. It's probably not possible though! I would need to shout it from a mountain for the rest of my life if I was to even come close to thanking you enough. I love you both dearly. Thank you for saving my life.

To my co-workers and friends: Where can I possibly begin? When I sat down to write that first little piece as I was gearing up to step foot into Save-My-Life School for the first time, I had no idea how my words would create such overwhelming support! Paramedics, dispatchers, firefighters, police, counsellors—you have all made such a huge impact on my life! I love you guys more than you'll ever know!

To my dog, Walter (and your crazy eyebrows), and to AB's dog, Magyver (and your funny hellos): You guys pretty much rock! And always make me smile.

To strangers reaching out with support and love—to everyone who offered to help my family (AB and Leo included): Thanks for offering to bring food, close my pool, fix my fence, take care of my kids, etc.! You helped us all so very much. Thank you!

To my work: I am grateful for the time off to focus on healing. I miss the road very much and look forward to being back soon. I am so lucky to have such an amazing group of people supporting me.

To all the staff at the hospital (you all know who you are.): Thank you for taking care of me and holding my hand when I couldn't wake up. I received the utmost exceptional care, and I am so grateful to each and every one of you.

To all my classmates and teachers: I don't know where I would be without you! You have all impacted my life in such a positive way, and I will keep you in my heart forever. Thank you.

For double-cupped coffees in the morning and waking up to hope instead of despair: I am grateful.

And for David Beckham: I think he deserves a thank you just because...

And to all of you who read what I write: Thank you. I have been so fortunate to connect with strangers from around the world who are experiencing the same illnesses as I, or have loved ones who suffer. We can all get through this. I love you all. Thank you for your support and kindness!

Thank you to everyone!

XOXO

~ JUST ONE OF THOSE DAYS

I'm having one of those days! Everything about everyone is driving me nuts. I want to leave, sit by myself by the lake, and go for a walk. However, Save-My-Life School is a life prerequisite, so I can't. I'm telling myself that there is a lesson in this somewhere, but I don't quite see it yet. It's hard to find a lesson in loud coughers, over-the-teacher talkers, smelly-shoe wearers, slow readers, nose whistlers, door slammers, loud chair-pushers, over-exaggerating head-nodders, and unnecessary word-correctors. Just saying.

My anxiety goes to 7.8 on the Richter scale as I notice my leg-shaking and doodling get to an all-time high—and it's not even Torturous Tuesday! I even plug my ears (discretely) because the out-of-control noise in the class is making my ear drums bounce. *Sigh.* Lunch at a pub would trump the lake or a walk. Instead, here I sit on break in the hospital library. The lady behind me coughs all over the computer, and the person cleaning the floor emits intolerable noise pollution (slightly ironic). I think the hospital should employ "cough-watchers." If we are all so concerned about cross-contamination, the obvious coughers should get the boot. Heck, I would gladly be one! "Excuse me ma'am, we don't condone phlegm transmission in this healthcare facility, so I must ask you to leave and remind you to stay home if you have a disgusting cough. No one wants to listen to you. Have a great day." Easy peasy!

A lesson. Hmm, still not able to find it. I've always had multiple pet peeves that hover on the edge of phobias. Positive self-talk: "You are not as gross, inconsiderate, or as annoying as most of the human beings you have encountered today." There! Does that count? My question is, when is it OK to remove myself from areas with said people in order to decrease my anxiety? This is where the Save-My-Life School lines blur for me. I sit through the distress in the classroom like I'm taught to, but do I let it lead me to a panic attack? Will I be less of a good student if I go for a long walk to calm my nerves? Do I need to look at this as exposure therapy? If I give myself space, will I not learn the gold-star lesson of my life? I'm taking this too far I'm sure. I guess my lesson at this moment is that I don't know my lesson all the time. Tool—trial and error. Well, I feel like the tool box just keeps falling on my head today. Tomorrow will be better, I'm sure.

Oh goody. Coughing-Fit Lady just let the volunteer know that several weeks of antibiotics and puffers still haven't helped her. But I will rest assured that she's not contagious because *she* says so. Grrr, I'm out of here.

~ VULNERABILITY

"Walk in as vulnerable as you need to be." This is an extraordinary piece of advice I heard a student say on her last day of class to all of us freshmen four weeks ago. And I have reminded myself of it many times along my journey. I've encouraged vulnerability in both my student and everyday life; it helps me grow. It's uncomfortable at times of course, but it's imperative to Save-My-Life School success. Analogy time—I used to be like a nervous student, standing on stage, ready to speak. I would imagine that everyone in the audience was naked. Meanwhile, I was bundled in a hot, restrictive snowsuit to hide from what I thought would be unbearable negative judgment. But as this journey has progressed, I've been losing (or winning—depends on how you look at it, I guess) at stage-fright strip poker, and every day I have been the one getting naked. Vulnerability equals freedom! See you later snowsuit.

I, as a Save-My-Life School senior (la-*dee*-da), give the vulnerability speech to a new student today, and it reminds me of how far I've come. The new student is obviously frustrated with not having all the tools already and can't comprehend how she would ever be able to change. Rewind four weeks ago to my second-day post, "Patience, Natalie, Patience," and what do I find? I was feeling frustrated with not having all the tools and unable to comprehend how I would ever be able to change. Coincidence? I think not.

"Trust me," I say to the girl. "Just make sure you keep coming to class! I remember feeling exactly the same way during my first week. I had to allow myself to be a bit vulnerable and trust I would learn what I needed to learn. It's not easy, but it will be worth it." She agrees. I am so happy she finds the first drop of vulnerability she will need to succeed in all this. I don't tell her that eventually she will need an ocean of it to move forward through each week. Why try to drown her on Day 2?

I've had a few people tell me they love my writing, but they couldn't do the same—put it all out there into the webosphere. They would have a hard time letting people (including strangers) know about their mental health. And touché! Don't get me wrong; at first it wasn't easy for me as well. But layer by layer, I now find that the more I expose, the less weighed-down I feel. I sort of feel like a kid holding a hundred balloons that cause me to walk so lightly, I'm almost off the ground with every step. It's amazing what you can learn about yourself when you stop hiding from yourself. Some days the balloons pop because of my own negative thinking or someone else's negative influence. But I rest assured that when I least expect it, I will walk past a person who hands me fifty more balloons.

~ FILLING IN THE GAP

There's a figurative and literal gap in the timeline of my writing. My full recollection of October 19, the day of my third overdose, is very dim, and that fact haunts me. I knew I would eventually talk about that day, but I didn't know when—until today. Something awful happened, but I can't go into detail about it; it's not my story to tell. But I can say that it is an agonizing reminder that openness and honesty about this terrible disease is still so crucial.

You would think my balloon-lifting, light-footed feeling of freedom after opening up about my illnesses and experiences would make any writing easy. Wrong. The events that occurred on that day still embarrass me. They still make my body close in on itself with guilt. I've tried to (at the risk of sounding truly selfish) ignore a lot of the emotion I've had about that day because, generally speaking, I feel ashamed. It's bad enough for my mind to process the fact that I overdosed the first time. Wound so tightly with anxiety, trying to quiet the deafening noise of chaos in my head at the time, I made that first horrible choice. But then a year later a second overdose occurred—unacceptable! While I was saturated in wine, grief, and anger with the evil in this world, my actions were even too much for me to believe. I should have known better, right? But then, while still recovering from the "second time," thinking that the progress I was making would surely spare me and my family from the hell of another experience, it happened again. And this time was much different from all the other times. This time I had no vice like alcohol to blame. I didn't even feel it coming. It was a day like any other day until something snapped, and my world went dark faster than it ever had before. Talking about this is very hard for me. Here it goes:

~

I wake up and walk Walter like any other morning, then I drive Caroline to work. Easy enough. I had felt off the few days before, but today I still feel in control of my thoughts and actions. I just think I am in a bit of a rut. Normal enough. I get home and am alone, so I decide to go back to bed for a bit. Maybe that will take the edge off. Reasonable enough. I have my phone. So while lying in bed, I check Facebook and scroll to see some pictures. Innocent enough. But along come some pictures I am not expecting to see. There is Leo having fun with all my co-workers, drinking and laughing—*without me*. Suddenly my off feeling plummets to my Layer 4 depression. Just like that! No warning. No alcohol. No drugs. Just raw pain. I put my phone down and try to gather myself with reason. But nothing works. I feel like an alien on this planet, disgusted with myself, numb and cold. Who am I? How did I get to this shameful place in my life? How did I ruin everything? My distorted thinking soars off the charts. I can't drink or have fun. I can't hang out with my friends and laugh like them. Everything about my life has changed. I'm putting my kids through hell. What kind of a mother am I? And I've lost Leo. This disease has ripped away the person I have loved with all my heart, and I miss him so much every second of the day. My heart hurts so much! *Everything* hurts so much!

Suddenly I am just the girl with the mental illness history. Writing doesn't make me feel better in that moment—it makes me feel gross and uncomfortable. The rapid switch in my thinking erases every positive thing that has ever happened to me as a result of opening up. All I want to do is hide—from me and from everyone. I am suddenly reminded that my life and my brain are so far from normal. Nothing can change that. I am just a waste of oxygen.

Calm as anything I go downstairs. I let Walter outside to pee, get a dining room chair, and search deep in the back of my kitchen cupboard for the best sleeping pills I can find. But it isn't because I want a good nap. I, with a hundred percent certainty, want to go to sleep—*forever.*

With a bottle of sleeping pills in my hand, I call Walter inside. I'm not crying. I am not anxious. I am numb. Completely and utterly numb. I need to make sure Walter is safe, then I go upstairs and swallow about thirty pills. I curl up in my bed. I can't hear a sound in my head. I feel with all certainty from my calmness that this is the right thing to do. No more pain. No more roller coasters for my family. They will be better off. AB will take care of Caroline. Jon will take care of Adam. In that moment I'm almost positive I look through the window of hell, and I whole-heartedly believe that I *need* to die. I write a note to whomever will find me. "I'm sorry. You will be OK. I love you." Then swallow the rest of the pills.

The pills start to work as I begin to feel drowsy and a bit sick to my stomach. I walk into the bathroom and lie on the floor because I am so tired. I am positive it is just a matter of time—no more heart-wrenching pain, and I believe it is the best thing for everyone. In this state, I am certain I am doing the world a favour. My mind plays evils tricks on me; it's so scary to be so sure of something so wrong! (And it breaks my heart for anyone else who believed the same lies I did. That darkness shouldn't exist. I know that they are in heaven now, but no one should ever see hell.)

That's all I remember. But I feel the rest of the story is still important to tell, so AB will be picking up where I left off.

~ ANOTHER PERSPECTIVE

When Natalie asks me to write to fill in the blanks of her third overdose on October 19, I realize that she isn't asking me to do this because she doesn't want to have to relive it, but rather she very literally doesn't know what happened. I hold pieces of her story that she has no memory of. I find that absolutely chilling.

9:47 a.m.—that's when it all starts. The text says, "AB, I don't feel good." Five words on my phone, and I know it is happening again.

Natalie had some rough days before the nineteenth— none of us knew! The Queen of Facades fooled us again. Not intentionally of course. I'm guessing she thought she could manage the emotions on her own and didn't want to alarm us. I picture it to be like a juggling act. Natalie is an all-or-nothing girl, so let's use fire torches in this analogy. She's juggling three fire torches. The torches represent her stressors. She can manage three torches any day of the week. Bring it. Someone on the sidelines throws her a fourth—she loves a challenge. Look at her juggling away. Well, now her arms are getting a bit tired, but she's still giving it her all. Add a fifth and a sixth, and she's starting to get overwhelmed. By the time the seventh is thrown into the mix, she has no energy left. She misses a catch, and the entire act falls to pieces. On October 19, the proverbial seventh fire torch is a picture (on Facebook) of Leo beside two of his friends, beer in hand, after a long day at a hockey tournament. It is a completely innocent picture, but that's how you can tell when the anxiety takes hold—her rational thinking becomes distorted. That's the disease. It's not like her to get upset about something like that—the specific picture, or what it represents. And by the way, the fire torches might even top Mitchel's dry lake analogy! BAM! All right, it doesn't even come close, but you get what I'm saying.

Text after text flood my phone. It's one of the signs she's not OK and things are going sideways. She's not looking to have a chat, she's not looking for words of reassurance— she's scrambling to get thoughts out of her brain. I read them all, my heart aching, knowing what is happening. The text that finally sounds the alarms to move into action is, "AB, promise me you'll take care of Caroline. Just take care of her." My response, "I'm calling for an ambulance and police." That's the last I time she contacts me, so I try calling her. She picks up. OMG, SHE PICKS UP! The fact that she is still conscious and able to answer is a relief. There are no actual words though, just faint moans and pieces of words. I keep saying, "Natalie, talk to me...say something...stay awake Natalie...help is coming." The phone goes dead, and I am unable to hold back my tears. The idea that those may be my last words to her shatters my heart.

An ambulance is dispatched, and police are on the way as well—they'll be able to assist with any access issues. I call Leo and see if he can go over to the house with a key. Thankfully he answers. He is in his car and heads over immediately.

Police kick down Natalie's gate in hopes of gaining access to the house via the back door. However, Leo arrives just before the police bust down her door, and he is able to let everyone in. The paramedics run upstairs and find her on the bathroom floor. Leo sends me a text: "She has a pulse, but she is unconscious." I reply, "I'm on my way."

Yet again, Natalie has an amazing team of paramedics working on her—if there is any comfort in this horrible situation, it is knowing that she is getting exceptional care. I drive to the hospital. As I am parking, I see the emergency procession pulling in. It is as if time is frozen for just those few seconds. Standing there, I watch as the ambulance, supervisor unit, rapid response unit, and police car drive in one after the other, all there for one reason—Natalie. It is overwhelming. As the ambulance doors swing open, I get a glimpse of her. Lifeless. Vacant. I go to her side and tell her I am here—and that I love her. I briefly squeeze her hand and quickly let go.

That's all I can manage or I'll cry—and I don't want to cry. It isn't the time or the place to break down. This overdose is different. It feels different. It happened fast, and she wanted a specific outcome. I can't look at her. I'm not mad. I am overwhelmed with relief that she is alive, but the emotions are sitting right at the surface. How could this happen—again?

We stand in the triage area waiting for a room, Natalie lying on the stretcher, one of the paramedics holding her hand—such a simple but meaningful gesture. We finally get a trauma room, and all the amazing nurses immediately start to work on her. We try to help the nurses with their questions, but we don't know what or how much Natalie has taken (besides it being enough to render her unconscious).

OMG, I need to find out where the kids are. I send Jon a text and find out Adam is having a play date with his cousin. OK, he is safe. I assume Caroline is at work, but I want to be sure. I send a quick text. She replies right away that she is working until six. I tell her I'll be the one picking her up and leave it at that. I don't want this poor girl to be at work worried and terrified that this has happened—again. There is nothing she can do, so I'll just wait until six o'clock to tell her the news in a safe, quiet place. I'll be there to answer whatever questions she has or listen as she vents.

I stand beside Natalie's bed for hours. With bag after bag of IV fluids going into her, she still isn't coming to. Not a mumble, not a groan—nothing. She responds to painful stimuli. That's it. For hours. She looks awful. The nurses put a catheter in. Natalie doesn't even flinch. With Natalie's permission, I can tell you the girl almost peed on me. Yep, that's right. While holding one of her legs to help the nurse as she put the catheter in, my cold hands apparently gave Natalie a little jolt. Thanks a lot, Kissy! I know we're talking about a horrible overdose, but it's OK to laugh at that. Lord knows we do! I'm predicting we will have a conversation like this one day:

Nat: *Hey, AB, wanna go to the movies?*

AB: *No, I'd like to go for dinner though.*

Nat: *Come on, AB, I really want to see a movie.*

AB: *Remember that time you almost peed on me?*

Nat: *Rrright, dinner it is, love you.*

Hours go by. Nat starts to open her eyes and says a few garbled words. She reaches for my hand (which nearly breaks my heart). She tries to form words, but her lips stick together because her mouth and lips are so dry. I wet some tissue and wipe her mouth. I clean up her runny eye makeup and brush her hair.

I pick up Caroline and spend some time with her. I then return to the hospital. There is improvement. Nat is sitting up and drinking sips of water. She is putting words together, but she is still so confused. By eleven-thirty she is (medically) stable enough to move out of a trauma room and into a room in the mental health area of the Emergency Department. Leo and I get her settled, she eats a sandwich, we tuck her in, say good night, and leave. To say it's been a long day is a complete understatement.

The next morning the phone rings early; I recognize the hospital's number and my stomach drops. Is this a nurse calling to tell me something has happened? There is never any peace. You are always on guard. It is Natalie. Sobbing. Gut-wrenching, soul-cracking sobs. "AB, HOW COULD I DO THIS AGAIN? I WAS DOING SO GOOD. HOW DID THIS HAPPEN? I'M GOING TO LOSE EVERYTHING."

She asks if I am mad. I tell her I am not mad that she relapsed. I am heartbroken at the thought of almost losing her. I tell her the only time I'd be mad is if she stopped trying to get better, stopped wanting to learn, stopped treatment. I understand relapses happen, but man oh man, they're terrifying—and they hurt my heart. I'm grateful she's still here to tell her story. I'm grateful she's still trying!

AB

~ SNOWY FAIRY TALE DREAMING

It is an interesting Saturday, filled with different weather, different worlds, and different ways of thinking. In the morning, I wake up to the first snowfall of the year. Beautiful, soft, fluffy pieces of snow fall outside AB's window. And even though I'm not a fan of winter, the first snowfall is always something I look forward to. It's sort of… magical. Wanting to experience it all, Magyver and I bundle up and go for a "coffee-hunt walk" (AB doesn't drink hot beverages, so her house is coffee-less; I know, she's nuts) and find a surprisingly good cup at the Hasty Mart. Go figure. (Let's keep in mind I am also desperate, so I could have drank ground coffee beans and most likely would have thought it was delicious.)

AB and I are in love with the series *Once Upon a Time*. So after I return with my java, we snuggle up on the couch and start a fairly substantial marathon.

"When was the last time you had a day where you just relaxed and did nothing but stay comfy and watch TV?" she inquires.

"Hmm…I'm not sure. I guess I usually have errands or cleaning to get done every day. Why?" I answer.

"Really? No reason." She turns her attention back to the TV and lets out a tiny "hmm," and I see she is smiling from the side of her face. We then proceed to wrap ourselves in fairy tales like we wrap ourselves in our toasty blankets—and let the morning disappear as gently as the snow landing on the warm, outside pavement.

Sadly, my glorious morning bliss changes with the afternoon weather—dreary rain puts me in a dreary mood. I start to feel antsy inside the house, so I go for another walk with Magyver to get some blood circulating in my legs. But being alone gives me "busy head." I tend to overthink when I'm not distracting my brain. I appreciated the five episodes of *Once Upon a Time* distraction heaven, but quiet walks usually equal loud thoughts for me—so I am prepared.

As the busyness starts, I ask myself, "what am I feeling right now?" as my teachers have taught me to do in these situations. I need to be mindful and in the moment on this rainy walk, discovering what I'm feeling below the surface of the dripping shell of my rain coat. This question leads to an ache in my heart. I know the answer right away. I miss Leo. I still see him often because he checks up on me, drives me places, and visits, but it's a double-edged sword to the heart. (I could throw in a Prince Charming analogy here, which would totally fit, but I'll reel it in.) He's always taken care of me and didn't want to leave. However, my illness hurt us both, and we desperately need to heal. This new necessary distance between us rips my heart out. I love anticipating seeing him. It makes me happy every time—just as much as the first time we went on a date. I've never stopped loving him, and it makes me sad to still see that look in his eye when he smiles at me. It is so bittersweet. It's torturous that in order for me to heal, I need to be away from him. So even though the initial happiness I feel is still there every time I see him, I know the pain in my heart will always follow when he leaves. It's inevitable—just like how the first November snowfall always turns to rain.

Evening comes, and the rain is replaced with blustery, cold wind. I am plagued with a busy head again. Lovely. So, I go for *another* walk. The wind snaps at my ears and takes my breath away. I miss the soft winter wonderland of the morning, and I think, "It's funny how things that are wonderful and good can change so quickly into something that's painful and bad." But just as things can change from good to bad, so too can they change from bad to good—*eventually*. *Eventually* my heart won't ache as much. *Eventually* Leo and I will be happy again—just not together. *Eventually* things will settle and just be. So, as I walk in the dark, windy night, I remind myself to be patient with me. My heart needs time to heal like anyone's, and I need to not dwell on the past. So much easier said than done. I wish I had a magic wand like the fairy godmother in our show to fast forward the hands of time. But I bet even magic can't speed up the healing of a broken heart.

~ TEMPORARY HAPPINESS

I need to write. I'm frustrated as hell. I've been positive, positive, *positive* way too long. Today is balls! I feel so gross in my own skin. It's gloomy and dark outside, and that totally doesn't help. I'm exhausted working hard just to exist today. I think I haven't truly given myself permission to scream yet. I don't want anyone to worry, so I keep hopelessness inside—even hidden from me. Well, today sucks. It's one thing after another, and I feel like no matter how many steps ahead I take, a sledgehammer is waiting around the corner to whack me in the face—and then laugh at me.

Someone I know died by suicide two days ago. It's horrible and sad and tragic. My heart is being pulled in a million directions! I feel so devastated for the family—my heart breaks for the pain they are enduring. I think, "How can I be sad when so many family members are being ripped to shreds with grief?" But I still want to vomit with heartache. And then I think, "I could have put my family through that. How awful! Mental illnesses are ruining so many lives. I am extremely mad at this disease."

What is this world for anyway? Tell me. All I see right now is pain. All love seems to end in despair at some point, so what is the point? The clock of our hearts and souls are ticking only to stop at some cruel moment when we least expect it. We just all wait...for what?

Discomfort and sorrow? I can hear lots of you saying, "Wow, we've never really heard Nat like this before." Well, the exercise in writing is about honesty, and this is how I honestly feel.

I'm mad. I'm mad that I can't use any of my vices to release this pain. I'm mad that other people can drink and I can't. I'm mad that I can't drown this disgusting feeling! I'm heartbroken that while on the phone with my son, he asked if I had anything to drink tonight. I'm mad that I can't punch the walls and scream. I'm mad at the sadness in this world. All I can do is pace the hall, over and over. Or lie in bed with my leg shaking on the brink of an anxiety attack. I'm not depressed right now—*I'm pissed*! I am a hundred percent, legitimately pissed off with life. All I want is a sleeping pill and to go to bed. My arch nemesis today is time. *Time* heals everything. Let *time* do the work. Some *time* just needs to pass. I have heard it all! Hell, I've even given those awe-inspiring crappy pieces of advice myself. Well, *time* that heals just seems to lead into another *shitty time*—just saying.

OK, I'm going to lie in bed, stare at the ceiling, and hate my busy head. And hope with *time*, I'll fall asleep.

~ WHAT'S IN THAT TOOL BOX OF YOURS, NAT?

After four weeks of Save-My-Life School, I can definitively say I have a mental health trick or two in my tool belt, and I've used many of them along this complicated journey. I find some work better than others, but when I believe in their ability to help me—and actually practise them—they work. So I think tonight I'll share a summary of my favourite tools in case you'd like to try them too. Of course, I'm not trained in teaching these tools, and the best way to learn how to cope with these illnesses is through your doctor. But with that being said, I think a little extra experience-knowledge goes a long way.

The first tool may seem super simple, but to people who suffer from mental illnesses such as depression, it can be a tricky one to apply. When possible, in order to alleviate stress, do simple exercises such as deep breathing (I use this all the time to help me fall asleep), singing in the car, yoga, or walking a pet. Don't always think of exercise as an activity that takes all day to do or plan; that can be too daunting of a task for anyone with anxiety or depression. Instead, exercise your brain by doing simple things such as closing your eyes and breathing deeply for a few minutes. Be proud of yourself. Every small step leads to a healthier mind.

A tool I use for my anxiety (especially at the onset of my symptoms) is an easy distraction exercise to help me forget I feel anxious, thus often taking away the symptoms and preventing a panic attack. When I feel the butterflies or heaviness in my chest, and I know anxiety is looming, I focus on an object that is near me (this could be anything—the other day I used store names and licence plates), and I say any characteristic that comes to mind about the object out loud (if possible) for five minutes. This may sound funny, but humour me. For example: When I was anxious in AB's car the other day, I looked at the store names in front of me and said things like, "Zehrs. Z-E-H-R-S. The sign is green and orange. It's about fifteen feet long. It's above the Dollar Store sign. They are both rectangles, not squares. They have four points," etc. You can say anything at all, as long as you are taking your attention away from your anxiety. It sounds silly I know, but it honestly works for me if I commit to actually doing it properly. Then after five minutes of describing the objects, close your eyes and do deep breathing for two minutes. Repeat as many times as needed until you feel better. I usually need about ten minutes to get myself back to normal, but it's well worth the effort!

Positive self-talk is another tool I use. You would think this skill would be easy for everyone, but it's not. For people with mental illnesses, distorted thinking can block our ability to automatically implement positive self-talk during stressful situations, which leads us to believe that negative events (which are ultimately out of our control) occur just to ruin our day. So if you're sitting in traffic, livid that the highway is more of a parking lot than a freeway, squeezing the steering wheel so hard you could bend it, giving the finger to the guy who pulled in front of you, and tapping your foot to every headache-pound you feel—stop! Easier said than done? Well, not really. This one is pretty simple. Nothing you do, aside from getting a helicopter to land on your car roof to fly you to your Jays game in Toronto, will get you there any faster. Say to yourself, "Well, I may as well listen to some music and chill" because that's all you *can* do. Tell yourself that the guy who pulled in front of you won't be getting there any faster. We all know he will change lanes again, and you will crawl past him at the speed of a caterpillar in five to ten minutes. There's no need to get upset about it at all. The traffic wasn't made to make you late for your game, so stop telling yourself that it was. It's there just because it's there. I was horrible for increasing my stress with unnecessary road rage, which therefore increased the use of my negative, consequence-ridden coping skills. It wasn't worth it—especially when all I needed was some positive self-talk. I could have been singing with the windows down, knowing I would make it there eventually.

Watch for automatic negative thoughts caused by catastrophizing. People with mental illnesses tend to predict the worst-case scenarios (the catastrophe) of an event and worry about this for no justifiable reason. Which leads me to the next tool: look for evidence before worrying. This was a bit tricky for me to manage because as a paramedic I've been trained to imagine the worst-case scenario in order to prepare for anything I may walk into. Heck, "Worst-Case Scenario Harris" was the nickname my work partner gave me two years ago—and rightly so! But when I'm not in paramedic mode, this type of thinking is often pointless and stressful. So now, whenever I'm thinking the worst, I ask myself, "What proof do I have that this will occur?" And usually I don't find any proof at all. So why am I going to waste my energy on such frivolous thinking? Sadly, many people who suffer with mental illness have experienced past events which *did* turn out to be their worst-case scenarios. But these few past events still don't make it practical to think the worst about everything in their future.

Another good tool to help alleviate stress is to set healthy boundaries. Give yourself permission to practise trusting yourself and seek to understand your issues rather than let others shape how you think, feel, and act. Speak for yourself and stand behind your word. And remember, saying no to things you cannot do is normal and doesn't make you a bad person. We ultimately teach people how we want to be treated (good reminder, AB).

Here's a biggie that many of us overlook—learn from consequences. When you are about to numb or soothe yourself with destructive choices, say out loud what the consequences of that choice will be. For example, if I drink too much, I will not make rational decisions. I may take pills when I'm in that state, which will send me to the hospital again or kill me. My kids may get taken away from me, and I may lose my job. I will disappoint my family and friends. I know I don't make good choices when I'm intoxicated, so I will stay away from the liquor store and go to the gym instead. It would be magnificent to not have any vices with serious consequences, but if you do, you need to own it—or your consequences will be grave.

Healthy minds are able to think and act rationally. When an unpleasant event occurs, they allow intellect (rather than emotion) to dictate their reactions. Furthermore, healthy minds can manage the temporary feeling of distress and don't act impulsively to numb the feeling because they know the emotion will eventually pass. Which leads me to another tool: trust that distressful feelings will pass. You don't have to numb them or lash out because of them. For example, a healthy person may get pulled over for speeding and feel very nervous. But their healthy mind rationalizes this feeling using intellect, which allows them to get through their nervous emotions calmly. They know they will feel better once the officer leaves. Now take a person with borderline personality disorder who reacts to their emotion when they get pulled over. They leave no room for intellect until consequences are often being enforced. Intellect and emotion are in reverse order. This person may yell at the officer right away because they don't think to let themselves feel the nervous emotions. When they get a second ticket for lashing out, they then use intellect to realize that their actions were purely fuelled by emotion. So taking the time to breathe and know that the distressful feeling will pass may help people with mental illnesses avoid unnecessary consequences.

The most important tool of all is to remind yourself every day that you can only fix yourself and no one else. Stop managing others. They don't need you to tell them what is right or wrong (unless it's your place to do so). People have to take responsibility for their own mistakes, unhappiness, future, and personal growth. Pay no attention to ill remarks made about you. Remember, they don't cast doubt on *your* character; they cast doubt on theirs. I don't remember where I heard that line, but it is a good one.

The more you practise using these tools, the better you will become at using them. I am already noticing that I am doing them automatically, and it's only been four weeks—pretty good turn around if you ask me. In summary, remember to make recovery your first priority. Identify destructive behaviours, find alternative behaviours, and implement them—and practise, practise, practise.

~ OH THAT DEPLORABLE STIGMA

I am clearly the Save-My-Life School senior these days. New students are joining the class daily—we're almost overflowing with them. They even tell me I need to start weaning myself off the program because I'm getting close to the end. Yikes. It's bittersweet and a bit scary because the weekends can still be a battle for me to get through without class. So, three days off a week will take some getting used to (hence the word "weaning" I suppose). I digress. Today I want to write about the common themes I witness with every new student. One by one, each of them eventually declares they are still not able to (a) accept that they belong in the class and (b) admit to others that they have a mental illness for fear of being judged. They talk about complex webs they are weaving to cover up their actual whereabouts through the week because they are afraid co-workers and family will look down upon them if they are honest. Been there, done that—hated it!

Why these themes are reoccurring is simple—stigma. That loathsome, dark cloud of stigma hovering over every mental illness sufferer's head is unmistakable. It lies to us and says, "People won't understand the illness," "It's a sign of weakness," "People never heal fully" and on and on. This stigma kept me from joining Save-My-Life School a year ago and sent me to the mental health wing again. At the time, I thought I didn't fit the stereotypical mould—*I* was a professional and a kick-ass mom. Why would I need help with my mental illnesses? Only dysfunctional people in society needed that, right? Wrong. Even as a medical professional myself, I held the erroneous belief that only certain people joined Save-My-Life School. Even I was naive and let the stigma fool me.

Fast forward to today. I witness two students tell the class what they have already planned to say (or not say) so people won't know they are in the hospital program. *Sigh.* I zip my mouth. It's not my place to tell them what to do. They are adults. The deceit and pain the stigma causes infuriates me. Then my teacher points to me as if she's reading my mind! "Natalie, you had a rough-go with stigma not long ago..." I nod in agreement. Without hesitation, she signals for me to talk about it with a wave of her hand. I won't sound like a know-it-all, right? She gave me permission. Here it goes. "I lived with stigma every day before this program. When my boyfriend was at work, I would make sure he wasn't standing near anyone when I was crying on the phone for fear my co-workers would find out! I hid my illness from everyone. I played the Wonder Woman role to get by until I cracked after a bad call. Hiding them was exhausting. And now that

I talk openly about my illnesses, I'm not sure if I remember what hiding feels like anymore! Freedom from the stigma is like nothing I can accurately describe with words. In short, it feels amazing!" I see a big smile on my teacher's face, so I go on to tell the "new kids" about my writing, and that thousands of people from all over the world read it. There is no hiding for me anymore, and I won't change that for anything. A fellow student who already reads my posts even reminds me to let the class know that Clara Hughes, six-time Olympian, favoured a tweet about my writing (a fact that anyone would be proud of if they were in my mental health awareness and recovery shoes—she's kind of a big deal in that world).

I also go on to remind them that they are the furthest thing from weak. Hell, every person I've met in class is so strong! Strong enough to cry, strong enough to talk, and strong enough to keep showing up. They put one foot in front of the other through depression, anxiety, and more, willing to learn and heal, all the while knowing that it isn't going to be easy. Admitting you need help is not for the faint of heart—and making the choice to be a new student at Save-My-Life School takes a whole lot of guts! And I believe it's enough guts to one day soon wipe away their complex stigma webs.

~ I HATE THIS, I REALLY DO

Well, it's official everyone—I have writer's block tonight, and my brain hurts. I'm in Layer 1 (bordering on Layer 2) of my depression. It starts while grocery shopping. The "off" feeling settles in like the dark cloud it is, and everything seems weird to me. I just feel bored with this world.

Have you ever read the Berenstain Bears *Learn About Strangers* book? If you have, can you recall the page when sister bear sees everyone in her town as dark and mean looking? That's how I see people at the store today. Everyone just walks around like ants, monotonously searching up and down aisles, trying to calm their kids, complaining about prices, waiting in lineups, and worrying about what to make for dinner—*again*. Probably just like they did a few days ago as well. Ugh. Then I walk outside to the bitter cold; the wind pisses me off. Why? Honestly, I don't know why. And I hate it.

I walk past the wine store, and all I can think of is smelling a beautiful glass of red wine and taking that first sip—it would be heaven. (Figuratively, don't get the wrong idea.) All I do is look at the clock. I wait until I can go to bed—how exciting. I just don't get the point of it all. Depression is a horrible demon.

Sometimes it feels like a prison. I wish I could rip through the bars and smash through the walls and be free! I wish I could scream and strangle mental illness until it died. I feel like scratching my face off to show a small portion of the pain it causes me. But instead I get to sit and rot, alone in my cell of darkness. I hate that it sometimes makes me wish I could die—or even better—that I had never been born at all.

I want to stay in bed for days right now. I accept the fact that I will probably have a headache for the duration of this slump. There isn't too much to get excited about these days, so it's hard to smile. I barely have enough money to pay my bills now that I'm on disability insurance. I am unable to see my son whenever I want. My relationship with Leo is over. I feel so far away from my daughter. I have so much more exhausting mental health work to do. Important and amazing people are dying (two in one week). I can't look forward to having a drink at night. I don't have the energy to go to the gym or yoga class. I see so many people battle this disease at school every day. In addition to having nightmares every single night, I now have night terrors where I scream myself awake. I don't have my phone, and I can't be anywhere alone. I miss my dog, Walter, who isn't here at AB's with me tonight. And I don't know who I am anymore. It all pretty much sucks. That's all I have to say.

~ SORRY GUYS. NO POST TONIGHT

Hey. Sorry but it's been a long couple of days. I'm not really able to concentrate on writing. Don't worry. I am trying to work through this crappy time with my tools, etc. I will be OK. Just need a good night's sleep. I have amazing people with me. Night.

~ I WISH

I wish you'd see, but never feel,
This illness dark, to some not real.
I wish you'd know, it hurts to breathe,
My lungs collapse, when comfort leaves.
I wish you'd cast my scars away,
Repair the marks I formed each day.
I wish that answers existed near,
To rid my soul of unfound fear.
I wish each tear was never there,
They drown my courage left to care.
I wish I was brave enough to smile,
Sustain down heartache's endless mile.
I wish you'd camouflage each sting,
The blackness seems to always bring.
I wish I knew I'd be OK,
Believe tomorrow's a brighter day.
But I can wish with all my might,
It won't discount this ceaseless fight.
This wish will sail up to the sky,
With all the rest who've said goodbye.
I'll wish tomorrow, just for hope,
Or conjure up some way to cope.
Through darkness black, I'll make my way,
Exist again another day.
I wish...

~ CONFESSIONS OF CONFUSION

AB says I have to write tonight. Don't worry, she's not forcing me to do so, she just knows it will be good for me—and I need a push. In fact, she offers to give me all my responsibilities and freedom back (I think it is a test), but I decline. I'm not sure how I would handle being on my own all of a sudden. I like feeling safe with someone always with me. So, while I'm indeed weaning myself off Save-My-Life School next week, I'm not ready to be completely released into this mad world. It feels too weird. There are so many ups and downs.

~

I can't sleep at all. I toss and turn to no avail. The alarm rings at 7:15 a.m., and I realize that I got about two hours of sleep in total. *Sigh.* I have a headache from hell and feel like a zombie, which probably doesn't help my mental tug-of-war between the "you'd better go to school or you'll disappoint people" and the "but I feel horrible and not having a day to myself will make me feel worse" emotions. I'm not feeling depressed or anxious—I simply feel like crap! But now that I have a mental illness label across my forehead, I find it very difficult to explain to people that some of my choices are purely out of human necessity. Anyone would be frustrated with not sleeping at all. But alas, now that I have a collection of bad decisions longer than Santa's naughty list, I'm not easily trusted. Touché.

AB is already at work. I decide to stay home. Oh, God. I really hope everyone will understand my decision and not give me a hassle. I hope they believe I'm actually feeling physically sick. Well, I soon find out my loved ones are not impressed, and I feel horrible. And to top it all off, my confused brain thinks that "not impressed" means mad, but it doesn't. *Use your tools, Natalie. You have no proof of them being mad!* They simply always want the best for me. Over all, my emotions are very mixed about this outcome. One side of me is mad because I know in my heart I made the right choice for me, but I feel that no one (except one of my friends) believes me (again,

I have no proof). The other side of me doubts all my instincts and second-guesses my decision. I still have such a hard time not fully understanding where my distorted thoughts cross over into healthy thoughts—and it pisses me off.

Being a "normal girl" (whatever that is) feels as far away as the next galaxy to me. It frustrates me—my loved ones don't trust me because of my past actions. (Those damn consequences again). I feel I've disappointed so many people. This weighs heavily on my shoulders, and makes me second-guess my confidence in myself. I have no clue what normal is, but I used to feel like I had some idea. So, I try to do normal things this week, and it feels great. My friend and I pick Adam up from school on Friday then go to the Bulk Barn for treats (and a bone for Walter). Fun normal thing to do—*check*! I have a lovely girls' lunch with my daughter. Awesome normal girls' thing to do—*check*! We all hang out and play video games—well, *Adam* plays video games. Super fun, normal thing for Adam to do—*check*! And I make pasta for dinner. Yummy, normal dinner choice—*check*! I feel all sorts of normal, and it is amazing. I need it.

But time passes, and I want to hang onto that normal feeling for as long as I can. I love watching Adam play in the snow with his friends. I love just sitting and chatting with my friend. I love doing laundry (I can't believe I just said that), and I love learning with certainty that my broken heart will eventually heal. This normal girl is kicking ass with commonplace!

I also go and look at condos. I need to downsize eventually, and I'm really looking forward to it. I still have a lot of research to do, but it is nice to explore my options. Moving will also help me find another piece to the healing-heart puzzle I'm slowly putting together. I'm not running away from things (I have been known to do that from time to time), but rather I'm seeing that a fresh new start is what I need—*eventually.*

No sad poems or posts tonight, just rambling confessions of confusion—and I'm damn sure that's *normal*.

~ EXHAUSTING DREAMS

Dreams in general are exhausting for me—both the aspiration kind and the bedtime kind. This is likely because they are both so intangible to me—so out of my control. I notice that ever since the double-murder trial—and especially since my last overdose—my bedtime dreams are completely absurd! And night by night, the level of the absurdity is progressing. Allow me to explain. I know that most dreams don't make sense, but lately mine are off-the-charts outlandish. Screaming *Wizard of Oz* witches fly over my head while I try to jump off a Disney cruise ship because a gang of prisoners are chasing me. Seriously? Or I'm frantically selling mashed up paper in a mall as a meal replacement. What the hell is up with that?

Then when crazy witch-dreams aren't enough, I add a night terror or two to my nighttime regime—a new unwanted reoccurrence in my life. When I get a chance to go home on the weekend to stay with Caroline, I wake myself up screaming, covered in sweat, often scaring her when she is in the next room. A terrifying feeling for her, I'm sure. Even worse than that, the other day my daughter asked, "Mom, what were you doing downstairs at 3:30 a.m. for a half hour last night?" WHAT? I was never downstairs! All I can remember is that a night terror woke me up, and I thought I went right back to sleep. But no, I was sleepwalking—topless! I had no shirt or bra on that night because I took them off after finding them soaked in sweat after a night terror (gross but true). Thank goodness Caroline wasn't having friends over late that night! Could you imagine?! AB also remembers me walking around one night outside my room (luckily with a shirt on), and I don't recall a single second of it.

I've had reoccurring tornado dreams for as long as I can remember (probably a hundred times without exaggeration). In that dream I'm always yelling at my family to go in the basement, but everyone ignores me. I can see the tornado, huge and dark, right behind them. So I scream some more, but they still don't look my way. Then, just at the last minute, they slowly follow me to the basement where we can look out the window and see that it's about to hit our house. It feels incredibly real—even after the ninety-ninth time. The bricks in the wall start to shake while the wind howls. I try to cover everyone with stuff—or my body—as the roof rips off. I can see the swirling darkness coming our way. Even in my sleep, I feel sick to my stomach. Then just as the tornado is about to lift me away, I wake up—every time.

I researched what the tornado dreams mean, and according to the *Dream Dictionary*, "We have dreams of tornadoes when we are experiencing powerful emotions brewing [sounds familiar]. It may also suggest that perhaps there is a potentially destructive situation in your waking life, or maybe you are feeling overwhelmed or lack control [my life to a tee]. A tornado can represent a difficult period you are trying to get through [pretty much all the time]. They can also represent general stress and huge changes in your life." BINGO! My waking life has pretty much been a tornado, so it's fitting to add tornadoes to my sleeping life as well I suppose. (Screw you, Dorothy!)

Moving right along…I've now done a one-eighty, and for many nights now, I can't sleep at all (that is, without medication). Maybe it's because having horrible dreams is "exhausting sleep." (Ironic—possibly. Oxymoron—most likely.) So, the only dreams I have lately are my aspirations. I have a lot of these. I dream I will be healthy one day, and I can return to work as a kick-ass paramedic. I dream this nightmare (pun intended. OK, I must stop this) will end and be nothing but a tiny memory in the past for my family, friends, and me. I dream I will fall in love again one day. I dream mental illnesses will lose their stigma in my lifetime. I dream paramedics, dispatchers, and first responders of all kinds will never be afraid to talk about what's on their mind—good or bad. I dream I will one day fall asleep forever when my time comes, and not because of my actions. And most of all, I dream of peace and serenity. Sweet dreams.

~ THIS IS A GOOD DAY

This morning is like any other morning—I have no idea what the day has in store for me. At first it starts with AB and I shovelling her driveway. Then after the coziest post-shovelling nap ever, Leo calls me to let me know that the rehab centre called. Eeek! I call them back and learn my file has been approved, and it is just a waiting game as to when I will get a bed! Great news, but everything seems to be another "two to four weeks" lately, and I am feeling pretty antsy the last couple of days now that Save-My-Life School is weaning me from their program.

AB gets ready for the day and tells me she has a surprise for me. I *love* surprises! She asks me if I know the date today. I say yes and that it is November 19. She nods and turns her head to the side as if to say, "Yes, that's right, Meatball, but what else?"

I am stumped. "It has been one month since your last overdose, and we need to go out and celebrate your progress!" I am very excited! She continues on to say, "And we still haven't officially celebrated your acceptance into the master's program at University of British Columbia, so we need to do that too!" I am pumped!

After getting ready, we hop in the car and make our way to the mall. "I have seventy-five dollars set aside for you to use on *you*!" AB excitedly says. (It may sound silly to be excited about seventy-five bucks, but it's a big deal when you're on short-term disability insurance.)

Why does AB have my money? I've asked her to take care of my finances when I'm away at rehab because she is amazing with budgeting, and after my last overdose, she got an early start on it. Thank you, AB! "OK. Awesome!" I reply while clapping my hands like a kid in the candy store. "I don't know what to buy but will love looking around anyway." I haven't been to the mall in what feels like forever. And I do love a good trip to the mall.

The first course of business is to get a Starbucks coffee. *Nice!* Then I try on some awesome clothes at a store. But while I am trying on a beautiful jacket, my tattoo artist calls to tell me he has some time available if I want some work done on my sleeve. Perfect timing! He can fit me in at six o'clock. Why get a new jacket when you can get a sleeve instead? My seventy-five dollars has a new home.

Getting work done on my tattoo is still very emotional for me. Each piece represents a life-changing event I've experienced. Not only do I think the art of it is beautiful, but the whole tattoo perfectly reflects my journey so far—life, death, beauty, demons, and hope.

My daughter, Caroline, keeps me company while I get probably the most painful part of my tattoo done so far (under my arm), and she even shares her deep-fried pickles with me! Thanks, Loon.

All in all, it is a pretty kick-ass day! So, I'm off to bed. Wait, I think I'm forgetting something. What was it again? Hmm. Oh right. I got another phone call. I'M GOING TO THE REHAB CENTRE IN FOUR DAYS!

~ WHEN AM I "RECOVERED?"

You can make a plan, just don't plan the outcome.

A new student in Addiction class shares this awesome quote. With rehab on the horizon, I think everyone involved in my journey should deeply ponder it—especially me. I know that rehab will be the key that continues to unlock the hidden broken pieces of my mental health beyond Save-My-Life School, but where it will lead, no one knows. Everyone's treatment outcome is an honest mystery. Don't get me wrong; that's not to say that my future goals don't include being healthy for the rest of my life, or that I am anticipating relapsing again—hell no! It just means that putting a perfection stamp on my near future is the opposite of healthy. It's possibly a recipe for disaster.

I contemplate what would constitute me being able to say "I'm recovered" one day? Would it be after my hard work at rehab? Would it be a year later? Am I recovered now? I just don't know. As I've mentioned before, it's not like I have a broken leg that will recover in four to six weeks. Nope, every angle of mental illness recovery is much more complicated. There are no black and white answers, and what recovered means to one person is often up for debate by another.

Take being an addict for example. One day they may announce that they are a recovered addict, but that is not to say they don't fight the demon inside their head every day who tells them it's OK to use. Even a self-proclaimed recovered addict needs to continue going to support groups and/or ask for help when required. In short, they need to recover every day. Daunting. When I return from rehab, yes I will have many more tools in my tool box available to help me stay on the right track to health and well-being. But I won't be leaving with a certificate from my doctor saying "HALLELUJAH, YOU'RE HEALED" (which sucks, because I do love a good certificate). On the contrary, I will have a life-long—let's say *journey*—ahead of me.

This unclear reality can feel incredibly overwhelming to someone with mental illnesses such as me. Even after my stay at rehab, I need to face the reality that it won't be a matter of *if* my depression will strike again, but *when*. Of course I wish after doing all this work I could wake up every day to the comfort of peace and serenity. But alas, depression will eventually descend with the darkness I am all too familiar with. But when it does, it will be my job to battle it swiftly and capably.

The bottom line for me is I will never be fully recovered. *Sigh*. I will always be in recovery. (Get ready for Analogy-Nat.) For whatever reason, I've been dealt the hand of mental illnesses, complete with its clubs of stigma, hearts of sorrow, spades of confusion, and diamonds of pain, and I have to play it to the best of my ability. It's a shitty hand. No royal flush here! I was certainly used to bluffing my way through the game over the past thirty-something years, but now I'm folding in that option. My cards are on the table for everyone to see, and I will still need a cheat sheet to remember how to play from time to time. But even though my poker face is now washed away, I've been known to win the whole pot at times. I'm all in.

~ BIG CHANGES ARE HEADED MY WAY

I'm home tonight, and it's almost Rehab Centre Eve. Walter snuggles beside me, and the Christmas decorations are up.

Caroline, Adam, and I make ornaments while we laugh about nonsense. It is wonderful. I watch Adam play outside in the snow with the neighbours, and I chat with Caroline about her new boyfriend—a perfect day. But no matter what, the time I spend with them feels sad. I keep thinking about how I won't be here to enjoy the decorations, and we will all be separated over the holidays. I'm not even sure when or *if* I can come home. And I miss Leo.

I am extremely emotional. I cry at the slightest sad thing. Adam makes me a necklace—I bawl. Caroline hugs me—I sob like a baby. Walter lets me cuddle him like usual when I see him for the first time in days—nothing can make me hold back my tears. I pack up at AB's house and make the bed (really, I *do* make the bed)—tears. Lots of them. Jon tells me I'm a good mom—cry uncontrollably. It's all so bittersweet. I'm very grateful to be going to a treatment centre in two days, but I miss my life. Yes, this is me saying I miss my life—the same one who tried to die. But it's true, and the emotions I feel as of late are raw and agonizing.

AB asks me why I think I am so emotional. She is sure my "Yay, I got a bed at rehab" high will carry me until we leave. Secretly, I know it won't. The change will not be easy for me. I am settled in my routine, and I know that uprooting again will stir my dark world for sure. My answer to her question is, "I feel similar to the way I felt when I came home from the hospital and moved in with you a month ago—worried about my family and friends, filled with guilt that I couldn't take care of myself, and sad that my life was upside down." These feelings don't, in any way, discount my gratefulness. They are there for a reason. And I need to feel them and let them be in order to move forward with what Save-My-Life School has taught me. Distress will pass. *Have faith in that, Natalie.* Still not easy!

AB gives me my phone, my wallet, my passwords, and a bag of my medications that have been locked away for a month. *Gasp!* When they are in my hands, I stand there holding them, frozen in time, like a kid caught red-handed stealing a chocolate bar.

"What now?" I ask AB.

"You go and keep getting better! It's up to you."

I still can't move. Finally, I carry the bag of meds to my room on my finger like a bag of dirty diapers headed to the trash. This is just so weird. When I get to my room, I swing my "kryptonite" like a pendulum, turning around in a slow circle searching for a new home for my medications. I now have permission to have the substances that almost killed me in my possession. I am about to sleep fully trusted with them only feet away! I drop them on the floor and forget about them—the best I can.

Tomorrow will be my last day of Save-My-Life School. Now I'm crying again. I love every single person there! I feel this unexplainable connection because of our similar struggles and pain. They all taught me how to be vulnerable enough to heal yet strong enough to trust. Complete strangers became my extended family, and I couldn't have picked a better bunch if I tried. This includes my teachers, too! Crying is exhausting. Good night.

~ HAPPY REHAB EVE!

What a day this is! Here is the good, the bad, and the ugly:

The good: I say goodbye to all my Save-My-Life School teachers and friends. I respect them all so very much and will miss them—I already do. I made an "I Have Depression" shirt and wear it today. Remember I once said no one would ever wear a shirt like that? I guess I was wrong. It is a *big* hit! Not only do my classmates say that they want one, strangers in the hospital atrium start conversations with me about their mental health and medications. This is something I never imagined myself doing before. I've received multitudes of messages on Facebook and Twitter cheering me on and supporting my journey's new chapter. I make a clay necklace with Caroline like the one Adam made me, and I will wear them both every day and hold them when I'm sad.

A good friend at Save-My-Life School announces that she is finally ready to open up to her family about her mental illness. How wonderful. She trusts that talking about it will help her heal and lift the heavy weight of stigma off her shoulders. Everyone's bravery in my class never ceases to amaze me, but this friend's act of courage is icing on my last-day cake!

Back at home, I get to hug and reassure my kids that I will be OK when I'm away, and I remind them that they have an abundance of support here. I tell them that I will talk to them every day; they will never be alone.

The bad: I am extremely sad today—to be expected I suppose. So much more change is on the horizon for me, and there's no going back now—nor would I want to. A few days ago, I was so excited to finally get into rehab. But now that it's here, it's very nerve-racking. I keep asking myself questions like, "Will I be able to manage how open they will need me to be?" "Will everyone be nice?" "Will the group dynamic be as good as Save-My-Life School's dynamic?" "How many times will I cry?" and more. I guess we will just have to see.

The ugly: I will have to take weekly breaks from writing. I am not allowed to bring my laptop, and my phone will be locked away all week. So, sharing time will be limited to when—and *if*—I can access the few computers in the facility's library. Being without my computer makes me a bit nervous. This medium has allowed me to open my heart and mind fully to the benefits of speaking up about mental health, and I will never take that for granted. It also allows other people to see that they are not alone and that anyone can open up about their struggles. I always loved writing but didn't write much for many years. Now that I have been writing on a regular basis, my love for it has increased tenfold.

It's time for me to get some sleep—hopefully nightmare-free. I love all of you, and I thank you from the bottom of my heart for your endless support! I promise I will work my butt off at "Save-My-Life Boarding School," my new name for rehab. I also promise to continue to raise mental health awareness when I return.

~ DEAR AB

To my best friend: Get a tissue—this one's going to be a doozie! What a journey. Before all of this, I knew we were best friends. I knew we loved each other to the ends of the earth, and I knew we would do anything for each other, but the level of love and friendship you have shown me over the past few months is simply nothing short of amazing!

We have the kind of friendship that is completely grounded by trust. And for me and my huge trust issues, I've always needed it that way. Whether I like it or not, you tell me what you feel in your heart because you know I need to hear it. For example, when I asked, "AB, can I use some of my savings to get my tattoo done?" when the only real money I had was $1.20 in a paper napkin, you gave me the "Are you sure that's a good choice?" look, and I got over my disappointment quickly because you somehow always know what's best. Damn it. You see through me like glass. When I say, "Oh yes of course I washed the dishes with dish soap rather than hand soap," I know I'm not fooling you.

Thank you for sharing your home with me. I already miss so many things. *Sigh.* I miss yelling good night to each other multiple times down the hall. I noticed you always needed the last one; I was on to your games. I miss Magyver's face. I loved how he slept in his nest beside me. I miss how you never cared if I used a placemat, and you learned to deal with the water glass I always left beside the tap. I miss chatting for hours and watching *Once Upon a Time* together. I miss performing psychic readings and teaching you what a macaroon is. I miss borrowing your hair dryer every morning and showing you what the broiler in your oven does. I miss sitting at the table eating "Luck Charms" and laughing about boys until our stomachs hurt. I miss yelling at your neighbour—and your genuine concern as to whether or not I was constipated. I miss washing your dishes with hand soap (even though it drove you crazy) and driving with you to Save-My-Life School almost every morning. I miss having to move your cream soda out of the way to get the milk and learning that I fit into your bras. God, I was excited about that! I miss my bag of clothes on the spare room floor, and most of all I miss you yelling at me to put pants on! And that's just the tip of the iceberg.

You saved my life, AB. How is anyone supposed to put that amount of gratitude into words? You put my comfort ahead of yours—while I'm sure you were silently cursing my quirks when I lived with you. We have big plans, you and I—and you just wait, we will achieve them! One day we'll buy that beach house and name it Birchwood Bliss.

If I could scream "thank you" at the top of a mountain, I would! I love you from the bottom of my heart! And I would do anything for you too! I hope by the time we are eighty years old and arguing over whose petunias are better, I would have come close to showing you. And I especially hope by then that you will start using placemats. XO

Kissy

P.S. I will see you at six-thirty tomorrow morning!

PART II

~

Save-My-Life Boarding School

Never bend your head.
Hold it high. Look the world
straight in the eye.

–Helen Keller

Hi everyone. It's AB. Natalie asked me to let you all know about her first day at her in-patient program:

~

Our day starts early! I am working nights. Natalie and her daughter meet me at work at six o'clock in the morning so we can get on the road right away. We want to leave lots of time in case there is traffic, bad weather, or we get lost. I know, I know—a medic and a dispatcher getting lost is unacceptable. I'm embarrassed to admit it, but we do. On the way, we hit some traffic. Natalie and Caroline don't realize this. Because they are so exhausted from sleeping all night (insert sarcasm), they need to nap! We make it to Guelph in the hour of eight, which is perfect; it gives us time to stop for a quick bite to eat. Natalie is doing OK, but Caroline and I can tell she is nervous and antsy. She wants to sit and eat her breakfast, clean up and leave, talk and stay quiet with her thoughts—all at the same time. I am nervous, and this isn't even about me. I think it is just the unknown and the idea of this new chapter finally starting. We make it to the rehab centre around eight-thirty. We find parking, Natalie makes some last-minute phone calls, and we make our way to the admissions area.

It is surreal sitting in the waiting room—other patients and their families waiting to fill out their paperwork—no one really making eye contact. It is almost as if everyone wants to be respectful of each other's privacy and anxiousness. The staff work swiftly. You can tell this facility functions like a well-oiled machine. Natalie gets her hospital bracelet and asks if we can come and see her room. The lady happily announces, "Oh yes, we love to have family here." It is kind of funny; as we navigate our way through the hallways, the volunteer randomly declares to other staff "we have family here," "this is her family." Picture it in the voice of a train conductor yelling, "ALL ABOARD." I start to wonder if it is some sort of secret code because it is hilarious.

We finally make it to Natalie's floor, and we are instantly met by welcoming staff. They give the volunteer Natalie's room assignment and away we go. Nat is still quiet, and you can tell she is on overload. She looks timid and nervous. After the volunteer goes over the house rules, she leaves us alone to unpack and settle in. We put a few of Nat's things away, but she has more paperwork to fill out—and then she wants to lie down. While the nurses and staff pop in to do their own admission assessments, they want Caroline and I to meet with a social worker.

The social worker is very kind. She is very concerned about making sure the entire family has access to support and resources to help in their healing. She reassures Caroline that Natalie's illness is not her fault and that Caroline never did anything wrong to make Natalie do the things she did. The social worker explains to Caroline that treatment isn't about making a bad person good. It is about helping a sick person get healthy. I am so proud of Natalie's daughter. She speaks candidly and with such wisdom. She loves her mom so much and desperately wants her to get well. When our meeting is over, the social worker takes us back to Natalie's floor where we are told it is time to say our goodbyes. She has a big day ahead of her, and it is time to dive in. With a soft knock on Natalie's door, we find her sitting on her bed doing another intake assessment with a different nurse. We tell her it is time to say goodbye, and the sadness on her face is absolutely heartbreaking. After a few hugs and a few reassuring words, Caroline and I leave. It is time to let Save-My-Life Boarding

School do its thing, and it is time for Nat to start this part of her journey.

We drive back home, and I realize how incredibly tired I am as I walk into my house. After being awake for twenty-seven hours, and now having the peace of mind that Natalie is finally at the treatment centre, I can sleep—and sleep and sleep some more.

~ CAROLINE

Caroline here. Where do I begin? Today Mom leaves for the treatment centre. I have been worrying about this day for a whole week. In a way, I can't believe today is the day.

It's a five o'clock wake-up call. Mom and I pack the car. Neither of us is very chatty. I am sad as I watch her say goodbye to Walter—very sad. We get in the car and make our way to meet AB.

I am anxious and don't know what to expect. We arrive, and I assume we will say our goodbyes right here in the office; however, we are invited to Mom's room. I am surprised when AB and I get to talk to a social worker. It's nice, but my mind keeps wandering back to the fact that I will be saying goodbye. I can't help it. I am really, really nervous about it. It's almost making me feel sick to my stomach.

AB and I walk to Mom's room. As I hug my mom, tears come to my eyes. I hate crying. Part of me wants to curl into a ball and cry for hours, but instead I suck back my tears, of course. AB and I are welling up, so we make the goodbye quick.

It still seems surreal that she is actually here. All the talk about boarding school—and now the waiting is over. Thinking about Mom going to get in-patient help brought comfort and feelings of healing to me all last week. I thought this *place was Mom's saving grace, but now that I am here—she is actually here—I am not so sure. The next two months are make or break for my mom. That's scary. Can this place really "fix" my mom? I want to hope that when she comes home, she will have her life back—and my life will be back to normal too. I want her to be happy, and I can be happy as well. But, realistically, I think she will still have her struggles. I guess what I'm really hoping for is that she learns coping skills. Save-My-Life Boarding School seems like her last chance to save herself.*

~ HELLO! LET'S CATCH UP

Hi everyone. When AB, Caroline, and I first arrive here, I am a ball of nerves. I just keep telling myself that this is normal, but that doesn't help ease my anxiety. I am shown to my room and given a schedule filled with locations I have no clue how to find and classes rammed into all hours of the day. This is my first glimpse into how intense this program will be.

I feel like I'm in high school again. "Here is your agenda with all of your classes." "You'll feel lost at first, but you'll get the hang of it." This is going to be bumpy! *Think positively, Natalie.*

After getting through an initial orientation with the fire alarm ringing every few seconds—a total test for my anxiety (insert me wagging my finger at the sky), I say goodbye to AB and C. I have been dreading this part! We share tears through a sense of swiftness, as we all know lingering will inevitably increase our crying. And with a kiss and hug and a last look down the hall, I am left to my own devices, a freshman at Save-My-Life Boarding School—and all I want to do is go home already. I wish I had brought a lamp because the lights are super florescent. I sound like a spoiled brat—I hate that. I am grateful, really I am.

I feel very out of sorts not knowing anyone and soon learn the standard introduction line is, "Hey are you new? Don't worry, you will get used to it here. What's your drug of choice?" BAM—just like that! No smoke and mirrors here. You are encouraged to be who you are and talk about it. I announce in my first rounds with about twenty other people that I am an alcoholic and my dry date is September 23. Yikes! Talk about surreal—listening to those words come out of my mouth! I'm still struggling with accepting that this is the truth. People are actually hopeful and confident in the program, but my skepticism is cemented in my brain. I still can't fully see how leaving Save-My-Life Boarding School after fifty-seven days can lead to this dramatic healing and spiritual awakening everyone talks about. But rest assured, they are teaching me how to be present in the moment and not worry about the future or the past—and that my skeptical and angry stage is normal.

Generally speaking, I hate making small talk, but I learn that because everyone has so much in common, small talk isn't even required. Talking about our past experiences and struggles is usually the topic one minute into the cafeteria line. People just "get it" here. Everyone gets it. If I still can't get past my skepticism, at least I can take solace in the natural comfort everyone has around each other. Heck, I attended Horticulture class today filled with guys covered in tattoos. They placed delicate leaves into a pot with tweezers, and they all seemed so comfortable because they all just get it. I know they have never taken a class like this before (because they said so). And as I watched them create their own ecosystem with Zen music playing in the background, there was zero mocking or judgment being thrown their way. It is probably one of the best things I've ever experienced! It is such a pure example of vulnerability and acceptance—pretty amazing!

When I called home the first night, Caroline and Adam seemed very content and this makes me feel great. I know they are both cared for so wonderfully. This knowledge allows me to focus on my healing. In fact, on the topic of healing, one of the rules here is that we can't help anyone unless the person asks for help. It distracts us from our own recovery, and all the staff are big on focusing on yourself. So, I thank everyone at home again for taking care of my family while I'm here. You are allowing me the opportunity to truly heal! It's one of the best gifts I've ever been given.

~ 12 STEPS

Today I feel like I'm in Layer 1 of my depression as soon as I walk out of my bedroom door. The world looks so gloomy when you're surrounded by struggling people. Their pain is palpable. Their laughter seems partially forced. Their hope seems temporary. I want this to work so badly, but I'm only here for two months—and then what? Listening to everyone's story makes me want to drink so badly. I imagine myself smelling the red wine that could be right in front of my nose if I left and found a bar. I know I won't do that, but the cravings are so intense! I now understand why we are told that recovery is the hardest part of addiction. Screw withdrawal and the alcoholism itself. Relapse prevention is way shittier!

I go to my first 12-step meeting—*gasp*! Pun alert—it is *sobering. Groan.* A lecture hall filled with addicts from all walks of life provides my first introduction to the *Big Book* (some people out there will know what that means). I enjoy it and even get my first commemorative chip. I walk up in front of the crowd to accept this gift of welcoming sobriety into my life, and I feel like I am outside my body looking in. Great, the "How did I get here?" thoughts are back again. *Breathe!* Regardless of how nerve-racking it is, I am grateful to be here and part of an amazing group of such strong individuals.

P.S. We go to a meeting every single day!

By the second day, I learn I still have no clue how to love myself. I learn I'm still not completely honest with myself. And I learn staying this way is a welcome mat for my depression. Self-pity is such a huge demon in the early stages of recovery. "Why me? What's the point? Is it even worth it?" are phrases that I ruminate on in my head all day. I'm unravelling the biggest knot—being my life—and hopelessness keeps tying me up. My anxiety-ridden, pity-party mind causes me to bawl my eyes out in a hall filled with strangers. I crumble to pieces. I can barely breathe and nothing can stop the confused tears flowing out of my eyes! I have no idea which way to turn (partially because I am literally lost in the building), and all I want to do is cry, scream, and complain! My doctor and nurse just stand with me while my anxiety wants to scratch all the skin off my body; I remind myself that not knowing what to do is OK. They will guide me. I finally realize (a bit) that I just need to trust the process. I must believe the staff know what they are doing and my only responsibility is to try. Slowly but surely, it apparently gets better.

That's all for now. I have to go.

~ WOULD I HAVE BEEN LOCKED AWAY?

My third day here is incredibly long—almost as long as the walks we have to do to get around this place! The grounds (beautiful) and buildings (gorgeous architecture) are huge. Long hallways lead to some floors that are very sanatorium-like, making parts of the buildings also very creepy. The black and white pictures on the walls near the library show a time much different than now. Nurses in old nursing uniforms, often smile-less, pose in rooms that look familiar to me but appear more cold and hospital-like back then.

This reminds me that not so long ago, in the grand scheme of human time on this planet, people with mental illnesses were treated very differently. They were often just sedated and locked up. Recovery and rehabilitation weren't as much of a goal a hundred years ago, because the stigma surrounding mental illness was so powerful. Mental illness often came with the stereotype that patients who suffered from these illnesses were violent and capable of evil behaviours. It would take a long line of doctors, nurses, scientists, and other professionals to encourage the concepts of various rehabilitation methods beyond simply medication to change the way mental illness patients were viewed—and thus treated. It is a staggering thought. Would I have been locked away? This concept doesn't help my doomed-world mind. How did they survive? What a horrible existence. Was anyone locked in this very room a hundred years ago? Many of the floors have been renovated and have a cozy warm feeling now. Old fireplaces surround comfortable couches and leather chairs. But the old drafty windows with what appears to be a dozen layers of paint quickly remind me that I am in a building filled with so much history.

I miss my family a lot today. I'm grateful that I have the swirly, baked clay-necklace that Caroline, Adam, and I made. It honestly feels like a drug when I hold it. It makes me feel stronger and closer to them. It reminds me of the hope I need to keep for my kids and me.

I want this to work. OK, I'm off to another group.

~ RANT WARNING—INEVITABLE PAIN IS BALLS

I'm on the verge of pulling my hair out, and I'm going to go on a bit of a rant. I want to remind everyone that these are my thoughts alone and not intended to make Save-My-Life Boarding School look bad, because it's amazing. What's bad is my disease and what it causes me to think!

I am already feeling tense and frustrated today because I caught the cold that's going around here. But then my Connectedness class puts me over the edge! First of all, I'm not comfortable with a student addiction-counsellor—who is probably all of twenty-five years old— running our groups, and I *may* have inadvertently said so…to her… and the whole class…and the doctor…and the other counsellors. Yeah, yeah, yeah—I can hear some of you saying, "But Natalie, you are a teacher. How can you think that about a student?" An atrocity! And yes, I believe whole-heartedly that students need experience and the best way to learn is to do. However, I already feel incredibly vulnerable, and confessing details about my demon-filled world to someone who is basically young enough to be my daughter is very uncomfortable. To participate at all, I imagine she is an addict too, that she "gets it," and I am just being judgey old Nat. Not an easy task when my brain is already overflowing. Needless to say, I don't feel too connected.

I *may* have also told the whole group that I am bored and don't feel like I am getting anywhere…and I *may* have said that the class makes me look at the clock every two minutes and wish for a drink…and I *may* have said, in a super-pissed-off tone, that I think the 12-steps are balls! I *may* have done that. Yes, I *may* have.

I am pissed off at the program so far and what it's making me feel. I'm frustrated with being told to do one thing one second and another the next! "Make sure you take time to yourself to journal. It's so important." Then, "Make sure you don't isolate. Stick with the crowd." Huh? "Live in the moment and ground yourself." Then "Play the tape to the end and always think ahead about possible consequences." What? Frustrating as hell!

And you know what the most frustrating thing of all is? It's my disease talking. If my brain were healthy, I would be able to accept the support and understand the concepts. It's just so exhausting…

Fifty-seven days. I have fifty-seven days to understand all this and more, and some days are already gone, wrapped in bitterness and confusion. Please, dear God, I hope this starts to make sense soon. I hope I get to experience this spiritual awakening everyone is so confidently talking about.

The only reason I'm not in my room bawling my eyes out after my angry behaviour is because I know getting my anger out needs to happen. My doctor says it's good. So I'll roll with that.

Anticipating inevitable pain is exhausting, and I wish the travel mug sitting beside this computer was filled with a nice Argentinian Malbec. Don't worry—it's not!

~ TIME FOR AEROBICS

I wake up sad, anxious, and homesick. Every morning here at Save-My-Life Boarding School, we walk down the seemingly never-ending hallways to start the day with warm-up exercises in the gym. Just picture over a hundred adults (some who can still barely function because they are still detoxing) standing around the gym walls, stretching to the Spice Girls or some other upbeat group. Then we stand in a circle and do aerobics with the most bubbly counsellor *ever*. Smiling and totally rocking her dangly Christmas-wreath earrings, she tries to get the crowd pumped up like we are at a concert. I try my best to hide in a back row behind a huge muscly guy who appears to be a perfect candidate for the next NFL draft. No matter how hard I try to remain invisible, I get spotted by the cheerful counsellor. She kicks and jumps herself into a perfect position to see me hiding. She's *definitely* done this before. Other people appear to have fun with this, but it's really not my thing. Luckily when we go for a walk, a switch is flipped in my mood. The fresh air, the earthy autumn scent, and the spectacular beauty of the grounds make me want to stay outside forever.

Who needs aerobics when we have the outdoors?

~ LABYRINTH OF HOPE

It's a pretty nice Saturday at Save-My-Life Boarding School. The sun is shining, and after a week of being here, I am starting to feel a bit settled in. As it's only mandatory for freshmen such as me to stay at Save-My-Life Boarding School until at least next weekend, it's fairly quiet—hence I get a computer. So without all the normal hustle and bustle, I find the day perfect for working on my homework to find this all-important spiritual connection. Whatever that is. OK, where do I start?

The teachers here (I will call all the staff teachers for ease of writing) tell us how essential it is to realize that we are powerless against our disease of addiction. And in order to truly heal, we need to find a higher power who we can put our faith in. This isn't an easy task for many of us. You can probably imagine some of the comments people have made about this necessary component. "I don't believe in God," "I feel weird becoming a spiritual person all of a sudden" and on and on. And I get it! Even if you believe in God, it's not an easy task to remind yourself to be spiritual every day when you haven't most of your life. People who don't believe in God are equally encouraged to find some higher power in their life to surrender their disease to. Regardless of what we choose to believe in, spirituality is an integral part of our recovery so I attempt to figure this out.

All of us at the Save-My-Life Boarding School have experienced great atrocities. And our outlook on any positive or hopeful part of life on this earth is buried under the darkness we live with every day. We are accustomed to focusing on the heartache and misery that innocent people suffer—and we just keep asking, "Why?" Why would God or a higher power let these things happen? How do we get past looking at the anguish and see happiness in this messed-up world? Can you see our dilemma? Our minds have used the world's atrocities as our perfect excuse to numb the pain with addiction. It's all we know. And because everyone of us here has been blessed (insert sarcasm) with the genetic addiction-switch in our brain's limbic system (where the evil lies), which is responsible for our disease, we can't allow the rational part of our brain (the frontal cortex) to tell the limbic system to shut the hell up! We think and talk about our tormented past like others think and talk about the weather.

With my spiritual homework in mind, I go for a walk on the beautiful grounds. As I have mentioned before, they are truly spectacular. Not long into my walk, I come upon a huge labyrinth made of stones near the gardens. In a roundabout way, the nearby sign explains that it exists to help us clear our minds. It represents the path we are going down to a new, healthier life. When we get to the middle, there is a large stone we can sit on and concentrate on whatever we would like to. All right. Let's give this a whirl!

I start to walk and get a bit dizzy. While I weave my way through the twisting pathway, I realize I am letting go of all my negative thoughts. I concentrate so intensely on getting to the centre and staying on the path, my mind clears and I feel peaceful. I feel calm and relaxed without wine. It is really awesome. That's my spiritual word for the day—*awesome*!

When I arrive at the middle about ten minutes later, I sit on the thinking rock and notice how peaceful it is. OK, this is a good time to practise my meditation I suppose. I close my eyes and notice all the small noises around me—the wind blowing through the trees, the squirrel running over the damp leaves (Walter would be all over that. *Focus, Natalie!*), and the birds chirping in the air. I also feel the cold wind rush over my face from left to right, making my nose run. Too much information? Well, I never said this spiritual time would be without its flaws. When I open my eyes, I see the sun shining straight ahead as it sets for its rest for the night. It is incredibly peaceful. It is the quiet my mind always craves. These moments allow me to feel some sort of happiness in this mad world—and it is awesome.

I think I do a pretty good job with my spirituality homework. My nurture-your-spirit teacher from Save-My-Life School would be proud of me. I feel a sense of accomplishment today, and I may even do it again tomorrow.

~ANOTHER NEAR-DEATH EXPERIENCE?

You meet a lot of people here and get to know them quickly. The commonalities we share are strong, making facades less necessary. I wish the world were like this—one big happy Save-My-Life Boarding School.

So, when at some point someone announces they are making a trip to Walmart, it is nothing for me to ask to tag along. Suddenly it's completely normal to jump into a truck with four strangers and trust we are going where the driver says—without batting an eye. Of course it's my luck that the driver is a crazy driver, causing me and the two other strangers in the back seat to clasp hands as if we've known each other since birth. The simple Walmart adventure ends up being a near-death experience that we may all have to share about in group tomorrow (I'm being facetious). However, the peanut butter cups I obtained on the mission make me forget it even happened as soon as I take a bite.

~ I HAVE BROKEN MY SILENCE

One week and a bit into Save-My-Life Boarding School, I wake up feeling refreshed. I just had the first really good sleep since being here—without sleeping pills. However, the shower I step into is icy cold. I dry myself off, get dressed, and have my blood work done. I'm getting used to the random urine tests, but I'm not getting used to keeping the bathroom door open while I go.

I speak up at rounds about the topic of resentment. I say that I resent having to feel all these emotions in order to heal. I also resent that everyone else has to experience them too. I suppose I understand the saying "misery loves company" now. It doesn't mean that you want other people to be miserable; it's just nice to know that you're not alone. So now that I've broken my silence and spoken up, watch out Save-My-Life Boarding School, Nat has something to say!

~ TRIGGERS AND GROUNDING

Until now, I have participated in *just* the addiction program. I start the PTSD phase of my program today. According to my peers, it's exhausting and very emotional; I am trying my best to mentally prepare for it. Today's topic is "Triggers." Even before this class, I was aware I have some very serious triggers when it comes to my PTSD, but I have no idea how to effectively manage them. I always feel like I walk around with a big tangled mess of stress that ultimately leads to an even bigger mess of triggers, that in turn grows into the biggest mess of shitty coping skills. And not knowing when or how most of my triggers will arise puts this messed-up perfectionist's brain over the edge!

I learn in class that I will never be able to eliminate all my triggers. Some exist in daily life, and short of locking myself in a dark room, I will inevitably crash into one eventually. The old coping skills I used to use when my triggers appeared made me freeze on the spot and curl up in a ball of anxiety. All I wanted to do in those moments was lash out, run away, and numb the feelings they gave me.

That usually meant I ended up drinking, oversleeping, using pills, or literally running away. Poor Leo. I used to run away on a regular basis. I once got frustrated for some reason and decided to drive four hours away to a town by the water, get a hotel, and drink myself into oblivion. I barely texted to say that I was OK—how selfish of me! Back then, I could barely see how manipulative I was—and overall, I didn't care. Life was hard for me. No one understood me. ME, ME, ME...UGH! So selfish, so sick, and so scared. I remember during that particular trip, I was so drunk I almost slept in a cave in the rocks by the water—and at that time it made complete sense to do so. I remember walking along the piers and docks, drunk. I am surprised I didn't fall in. Looking back now, I think my selfish, sick brain wanted to make Leo worry. We were breaking up, and I desperately wanted him to love me again. In my deluded mind, if he was filled with worry, I thought he would show me how much he loved me—like he used to do when we were first together. With my sickness progressing, I became a different person—one who I despised but somehow couldn't change. I became jealous and didn't trust him anymore—I used to make fun of girls who were like that. My confidence vanished and turned to paranoia. These feelings just made me drink even more. I lived in such an endless cycle of fear and anxiety I no longer want to experience. I need to learn how to stop the cycle.

In class, I learn that intentionally exposing myself to known triggers this early in my recovery is unhealthy and sometimes dangerous.

During this early phase at Save-My-Life Boarding School, I am still re-wiring my brain. Therefore, it's unable to cope effectively with repeated exposure to trauma. But then the question arises: What happens if I do come across a trigger? Well, that's where grounding comes into play.

I still have quite a lot to learn about this skill, but what I do know is grounding moves me to the present, reminding me the trigger doesn't bring me back to the *actual* trauma. Some grounding techniques are similar to my anxiety tools. I can recognize the trigger is there, then focus my attention on an object that is with me now, in that moment. My choice is to hold onto the necklace Caroline, Adam, and I made and squeeze it tightly. It will hopefully remind me that I am not in danger and distract me from the trauma my memory wants to reenact. In essence, grounding reminds me that I'm safe!

Grounding also allows me to *live* my life rather than run from my life. The old Natalie would bolt from the scene of a trigger, possibly messing up my plans and definitely ruining my day. But I am told that if I become skilled at grounding, when I realize a trigger has struck again, focusing on the now may allow me to regain trust in the safety of the present. Why couldn't I have learned this a long time ago? Of course, tools are not always guaranteed to work, but it's sure worth the effort of trying.

Going along with the lesson that I shouldn't purposefully expose myself to triggers so early in my recovery brings up the point that these triggers can be people too. If I find I'm with a trigger person, I need to ask myself, "Where has this person gotten me? Am I truly happy when I'm around them?" That's not to say that the person has any fault, necessarily. It just means that, for whatever reason, I am not able to communicate effectively with them or cope with our interaction—so I have to remove myself from such personal triggers. The necessity to remove myself from these trigger people doesn't have to be forever (unless I want it to be), I just need to do what's healthy for me right now.

There you have it, my one-hour lesson transformed into a few paragraphs. I hope it helps anyone out there battling with daily triggers. If I need to practise my grounding today, I will—but I'm still choosing to stay away from tractors, anyone being bullied, articles about the murders, or any disruption to my family relationships— piece of cake. *I wish!*

~ ROOMMATE AND LAUNDRY WOES

I still don't know where I'm sleeping tonight. I need a new roommate. Hopefully I will find out soon who that will be. I feel bad for the amount of suffering my current roommate is going through, but I can't take on her problems. She talks non-stop about her marriage difficulties when all I want to do is sit and read in my bed. She's making me want to drink, and I need to stay away from what the doctors call "slippery people." I feel I have been doing pretty well with that. *One point for Natalie!*

I feel good tonight. I'm cheerful and not anxious. I want to fully enjoy this emotion, but I often wonder when it will end. I shouldn't do that. I need to be present with this feeling and this moment.

I'm waiting for my laundry to finish in the washing machine and am wondering what the laundry room etiquette is. Can I put the mystery person's clothes on top of the dryer so I can use it in six minutes? I will probably take them out. In the meantime, I am just going to sit here on the counter, living in the moment, kicking my feet, smelling the laundry soap aroma, and sweating my balls off. Four minutes. The mystery person better get their laundry out soon. Two minutes—no mystery person. Time's up! Your laundry will be safe on top of the dryer for you when you arrive. I need some fresh air!

~ ROOMMATE UPDATE

I'm exhausted again, but I finally have a new roommate. She is lovely. We just finished removing any mice-attracting food because, apparently, she caught one last week! EEK!

Sidebar: I'm not a fan of handshakes. Anywhoo...

~ KNITTING

News flash: Everyone at Save-My-Life Boarding School has an annoying cough. 'Tis the season. But there's an even bigger epidemic spreading through the halls of the building as of late. People seem to have caught a serious case of—*knitting!* You heard me correctly. At any given time, in any given room, you can find people hovered over a ball of yarn, creating toasty-warm masterpieces. This is what our addiction-free lives have come to. You see, once you take away the one thing that occupied most of the hours of our day (i.e. drinking or using drugs), we end up having a lot of free time on our hands. So we, in turn, play a lot of dominoes, volleyball, badminton—and we knit! I'm not going to lie, watching a tattoo-clad, hard-exterior guy learn how to purl one, knit two is quite endearing.

~ WEEKEND PASS

After two long weeks, I'm home for the weekend and comfy all tucked into bed. Bliss, I tell you. The night is filled with great talks, fun walks, and clean socks. In short, it's wonderful! Hugging Caroline and Adam fills me with so much love I could burst. And playing with Walter calms me tremendously; I know his wee spirit is connected to mine. These are the feelings in life I want to have. Clearly Save-My-Life Boarding School is doing a pretty good job so far.

It's remarkable what this treatment centre has done for me. AB says she can see transformations in me already. Actually, her exact words are, "Your hair looks great, your eyes don't look sunken in, you don't look like a waif, and you may have gained one whole pound."

Love you, AB! But on a serious note, it's true. I feel great not only physically, but mentally and emotionally too. I'm on the right track and it feels...refreshing. I'm very used to the routine now, which helps calm my brain. It's funny, I used to hate getting woken up at six-thirty in the morning to do stretches in the gym sans caffeine and go for a winter walk. Like who goes for winter walks? But now I love it! My day doesn't feel right if I don't make a fool of myself, dancing in the gym and huffing my ass back to the building in last place. I have little legs—they can only go so fast!

Well, that's it for tonight. I'm ready to have a great sleep in my own bed with Adam snoring beside me.

Good night, everyone. Sleep tight.

~ NAVIGATING LIFE AS AN ALCOHOLIC

My weekend pass includes some adulting, and I trade in my car today. I don't need an Acura, nor does my bank account, which is easy to deplete when living on short-term disability insurance. I love this car, but at the end of the day, there is so much stuff I don't need. What I need is my health. In a sense, I'm doing a deep clean of my entire life—materialistic things included.

As I wait at the dealership while my tires get changed, I look over the reading material I brought along. But instead of bringing the latest fiction-romance book, I brought a much more relevant piece of literature—my 12-step-program book. When I placed it in my purse, I wondered how many looks I would get in the waiting area while I read it. Now, as I pull it from my purse, I think, "Wow, how did I even get into this alcoholic predicament? Where exactly did I lose my way and spiral so deeply into such a serious addiction?" The illness is a gradual process I know, but how did I not see it coming?

I come from an alcoholic family, and as most of society knows, this piece of my heredity is nothing less than an inescapable beacon, warning that I may suffer from the disease one day. But heredity isn't the only factor at play. In very simple terms, according to

Save-My-Life Boarding School, people with the alcoholism gene also need a traumatic event—or events (I may have gotten this information wrong before and said that they didn't)—to turn the genetic addiction-switch on. *Check. Check. Double check.* The old me would stew and blame, blame, blame, wondering what the exact event was. But I now see there's no need for me to search my inner soul to try to isolate which event turned the switch on—it's futile. I will never know. And in my eyes, it really doesn't matter anymore. I need to focus my energy on getting better.

It's amazing how we can fool ourselves! If I'm being completely honest, I didn't believe I had this disease until a few days after arriving at Save-My-Life Boarding School. I used to think I merely abused alcohol from time to time. Rude awakening! Any stress or event in my life was a good enough excuse for me to drink. If I had a long day—I needed a glass of wine. If I had a short day—I needed a glass of wine. If I had a busy day—I needed a glass of wine. If I had a slow day—I needed a glass of wine. If I was cooking—I needed a glass of wine. If I was doing laundry—I needed a glass of wine. If I was eating, breathing, tired, sad, happy, celebrating, fill in the blank—I needed a glass of wine. If it was winter, spring, summer, fall, the harvest moon—I needed a glass of wine. And let's be honest, my glass of wine always had an endless bottom. More realistically I should have written—I needed a *bottle* of wine.

My drinking didn't start to get out of control until maybe five years ago. Relationship breakups, school, kids, post-breakup financial stress, and life in general increased my cravings, and I truly loved how alcohol numbed my pain. When I went back to school to become an advanced care paramedic, I started replacing bottles with boxes of wine. I couldn't fall asleep without being drunk, and at the time I thought it was totally fine. At school we all joked about how much we drank because of the stress. But what I didn't joke about was that the amount I drank each night would leave me hungover on a regular basis—*really* hungover. One friend would call or text me almost every morning to make sure I was awake, and I dreaded being asked questions until the afternoon because my head was pounding and foggy. Looking back now, I'm not sure how I wrote my tests sometimes, let alone made the Dean's List.

More time went by, and my drinking got heavier. What did the trick before didn't cut it anymore. I went to the liquor store every day. I experienced some scary blackout moments—one being when Leo found me passed out in the hot tub with the water over my mouth. But still, I didn't think I was out of control. I told myself, "Lots of my friends party and drink. We all have such stressful jobs and see horrible things. I drink a lot because of that." But waking up with the shakes on a regular basis that could only be relieved by time or another drink started to scare me. I was the Queen of Manipulation when it came to convincing my friends that my drinks with lunch or that second bottle of wine was totally fine because, "I had a big meal," or "I had been drinking slowly all day so it's metabolized." *Right, Natalie—lies.* But when I was saying these things, even *my* brain believed them. The voice of this disease is a powerful thing!

Finally I got tired of convincing my family that my drinking was under control. I hid bottles of wine in the laundry and chugged from another bottle any time I was alone in the kitchen. I filled wine bottles with water to make it look like I hadn't had too much and returned empties as often as I could. At one point, I had an orange liqueur bottle hidden under the sink in case I needed more alcohol before I went to bed. My day revolved around my cravings. Sometimes I even lied to my kids, saying Scouts or swimming was cancelled. How could I have done that? And when I did take the kids places (out of horrible guilt), getting home was all my mind could fixate on. I never truly allowed myself to enjoy where I was if I was sober. And if there was an opportunity to have a glass of wine, I would. My mind would race "I'm almost home! I'm almost home!" a thousand times in the car, and I would curse every yellow light and slow driver. I couldn't wait to have that sip! And when I was in the throes of these thoughts, I was the Queen of Irritability. (I still feel so much remorse for that.) When I eventually got home and poured a glass of wine, smelled it, and took that first, beautiful gulp—all the world was good again. I was happy, cheerful, and physically feeling better. What kind of life had I created?

My life was completely out of control with alcohol. And Save-My-Life Boarding School is showing me how serious my disease has become. I now realize that I am sick, and I know I made it to rehab just in time. I still have a long road ahead of me, but I have completed the first of the 12 steps with flying colours. Here is the first step: "We have admitted we are powerless over alcohol—that our lives had become unmanageable." *Check. Check. Double check!*

I'm sorry to anyone I have ever hurt due to my drinking—I know there are many. When the time is right, I will be making official amends. I love you all. Thank you for still loving me.

~ MY ALIEN WORLD

I learn something amazing in PTSD class today. I solve a mystery that's been bewildering me since I was a child. You may remember me talking about how I feel disconnected from the physical world during my times of depression. The best way I can explain this sensation is that I feel like an alien and that everything around me doesn't seem real. I feel like I am outside my body.

I told very few people about this feeling while growing up because I was embarrassed by it, and my attempts at trying to describe it usually resulted in one of two responses: "I'm really not sure what you mean," or "You worry too much, Natalie." *Sigh.* For as long as I can remember, I kept my mouth shut when my depression demon descended. I frequently dragged myself through life in my alien bubble, lost and utterly alone, because I just didn't know what was going on with me. It was such an isolating feeling. When it happened, I hated it and couldn't wait for the feeling to go away. I wanted to finally feel human again. If I only knew what caused me to feel that way.

Fast forward to today. Have you ever heard of "alexithymia?" Well, I just heard of it for the first time a few hours ago. It means to have "no words for a feeling." I relate to this odd definition instantly. So do many of my peers. My teacher goes on to tell us that it's used to describe the sensation from a condition called dissociation, a.k.a. my alien feeling. "What is dissociation?" you may ask. Well, sometimes when people experience major trauma(s), they teach their bodies to numb, or they remove themselves from an uncomfortable feeling as a protective response. Dissociating can make us feel like we are outside our bodies looking in, but there are no exact words to describe the feeling. Eureka! Does this mean I haven't been crazy all these years? Other people experience this phenomenon too!

Dissociation is a highly effective coping mechanism—but not necessarily healthy. It allows us to create a different world that is void of any emotion, hence saving us from the pain that a traumatic event causes. But after months, years, decades of dissociating when a trigger reminds us of the trauma, this alien state can emerge without us even recognizing the trigger. It becomes our normal coping mechanism when we least expect it. My alien world is now starting to make sense to me.

The traumas I've experienced over my life caused massive depression (and most likely a dissociative state) in order for me to hide from my painful emotions (Layer 1—weird feeling). Coupled with the fact that I was never encouraged to express my emotions growing up, dissociation would have been the perfect escape route for me.

Now, in my adult life, when my depression starts to rear its ugly head, my dissociative feelings bubble up, with or without trauma, because they've been so closely linked to my depressive world all these years. Yes, I have only just learned about dissociation today. My eagerness to link my alien moments to it may be premature, but it sure makes a lot of sense to me.

If you think you may have experienced moments of alexithymia too, remember, you're not alone—and you're not an alien.

~ THEY JUST GET IT

I survive several weeks of laughs, tears, confusion and awakenings at Save-My-Life Boarding School—it goes by so quickly! And I do it alongside some pretty amazing individuals. I want to take a moment and recap some of the experiences I have with my peers.

I am an expert mover now. I hate moving. But with patients cycling through the doors of the treatment centre on a regular basis, it's not out of the ordinary to have to move rooms from time to time. But I have moved five times in two weeks. It's not a complicated procedure, but it certainly affects my level of comfort here—being that I haven't quite found it fully. It's not the staff's fault. Sadly, I collide with some severe rule-breaking occurrences, making my habitat not available for some time. So seeing my sorry self wheel my few belongings down the halls of boarding school is now a comical event. They say, "There she goes again!" There are those who want to take pictures of my sad little hobo state, but alas, pictures are not allowed.

Did I mention that the people here are amazing? It's one big family. Cliché? Yes, but it's true! We all form an intricate web of support, kindness, and understanding. I know I have said it before, but we all just "get it." One guy in my group rightfully describes the atmosphere here as "disgustingly happy." We welcome newcomers like they are our baby birds. We reassure them that their wings will heal if they trust the process. We understand perfectly what each other is feeling because all of us have crash-landed here too. When we walk through the doors for the first time, lost and scared, we have that special person pick us up and fix our wings, so it's only natural we return the favour. Everyone smiles and says hello and there are no cliques. When it's time to eat, we don't need to search for our table like in high school. Thank God! You literally walk to an empty seat and sit down—just like that! Everyone starts talking to you instantly. It's probably the least judgmental place on earth. We all feel safe— and we say it often.

We divulge some unbelievably painful personal information in group, which not surprisingly solidifies peer connections even more. While learning about each other's blood-curdling pain, we cry until our eyes burn. We know these tears will heal us. We encourage per- severance when we can tell someone can barely go any further. We know we're not alone; our secrets are safe.

On a happier note, we have some super-intense hockey rivalries going on here. People from across Canada wear their team's jerseys up and down the halls, showing undying dedication to their home- town city (even Toronto—I love the Leafs! Please don't send me hate mail). It's an amazingly diverse community here at Save-My-Life Boarding School. Oh, and if you want some candy to munch on dur- ing the game, you're in luck. We deal chocolate bars and sour keys out of duffel bags and side-drawers like...well...you know.

Yes, students at Save-My-Life Boarding School are still knitting and playing dominoes. If you want to learn any of these skills, you're in luck. At this facility, somebody nearby would love to teach you! Who needs drugs and alcohol when you can have a heart-pounding game of checkers? Am I right? OK, so I may not be knitting socks yet, but on a serious note, these things are actually pretty fun with the people here. Who knew? Not in a million years did I think I would be sitting in a greenhouse planting cacti with a bunch of addicts—or showing my neighbour how to use a glue gun on his Christmas orna- ment at two o'clock in the afternoon—*sober.*

All in all it's good to be here. And I can even say that, through burning eyes as I had a pretty excruciating session today, if I have to be away from my family and friends, I will take being with this gang any day!

~ STEPS TO FREEDOM

Before being a member of Save-My-Life Boarding School, my exposure to 12-step programs had been confined to movies. I would see characters stand and announce their name and their disease, followed by a room of people replying, "Hi So-and-So" in unison. But that is all I knew. I had no idea how lifesaving these fellowships are, or how spiritually connected everyone in the room is, regardless of who or what their higher power is. I suppose I had a stereotype in mind that the people in these meetings just came to complain about their vices, and when they finished, they would all go out for a beer. How bad is that? Well, my preconceptions are superbly wrong!

Now that I'm in the addiction program at Save-My-Life Boarding School as well as the PTSD program, it's mandatory that I go to a 12-step meeting every day. Yes, you are hearing me correctly—*every day.* Furthermore, we are encouraged to try different types of meetings that focus on different addictions such as alcohol, cocaine, or narcotics. They all use the same 12 steps for recovery. In the end, an addiction is an addiction, so any meeting is suitable. Each fellowship has their own style of meeting, and my peers and I are told to choose whatever ones fit us best. This recovery world is really alien to me, so it's nice to have some options. Many meetings have speakers, while some forgo the speaker and partake in discussions about pertinent topics instead. But no matter which meeting I attend, I hear one thing that undoubtedly resonates through all of them—you can gain true freedom if you follow the steps.

The people I meet while attending these meetings have shattered the stereotype I had of them forever. Gone is the image I used to have of addicts sitting around relentlessly venting about their misery. It's not like that at all! Yes, there is some talk about past addiction experiences—but most discussions are very solution-based.

Generally speaking, no one wants to listen to anyone bitch and complain. Everyone wants to hear how sobriety can change their lives for the better and how others have come to achieve it. People of all ages and from all walks of life attend meetings—the other day I sat between a police officer and a doctor. It's plain to see that addiction doesn't discriminate.

In 12-step programs, it is reiterated over and over again that everyone is encouraged to trust in their higher power whether it's God, nature, the power of the group, or anything you choose. Recovery on your own terms is too much to bear. You can always go to a meeting just for the unconditional support. Twelve-step meetings are simply rooms filled with hope, strength, and determination—as well as reassurance that you don't have to fight the demon in your head alone.

The people at meetings are fighters. Their stories depict years of internal war with addiction and relentless battles with compulsion. I admire every person I meet within the walls of a meeting. Their honesty and vulnerability gives me hope that I can heal. Their stories resonate in my mind days after a meeting and reassure me that I'm not alone. How wonderful to not be alone. I can see myself making lifelong friends with these fighters because their unconditional support was instantaneous. I feel blessed to be introduced to this world and look forward to the freedom it promises.

~ WHO WOULD YOU SAVE?

There are a lot of healthcare professionals walking the halls of Save-My-Life Boarding School. If you name a profession, it's probably here. Strangely, this helps me feel fair-minded, as it reminds me that educated people have this disease too. I know, how ignorant of me, but it's truly how I felt. Speaking on the topic of education, whether I have a high school diploma or a PhD, no amount of education can stop the predisposing factors of addiction I inherit throughout my life—nor can it shelter me from PTSD. In the textbook of life, there are no answers to some important questions no matter how hard I study. For example, my ever-curious brain wonders, "Does my education and passion for my career help or hinder my recovery?" "Why do I crave being back on the road when it hurt me so much?" and "Will I ever be able to return to the road and not risk relapse?" My doctor informs me that, right now, these questions don't have an answer at all. Allow me to elaborate...

The question as to whether or not my healthcare education helps or hinders my recovery rages war in my mind with its double-edged sword. Deceivingly, it fools me into thinking that I have more control over my disease than an uneducated person would. Knowing what I know must surely curb my addiction and automatically heal my PTSD to some extent, right? Wrong! But on a positive note, my education grants me temporary serenity when I feel embarrassed about being sick because I understand the disease process behind my addiction. I know that, on a pathological level, weakness isn't a causative factor. But with all that being said, like society, I still have so much to learn about my disease and illnesses.

Being so passionately enmeshed with my career and education transfixes my mind on a particular question—one that I hear many other healthcare professionals here ask as well, "When can I go back to work?" But why are we so eager to rush back into our uniforms? What is it that makes us confuse our careers for our lives? You may be reading this and saying to yourself, "My career isn't that important to me," but I challenge that statement. Whether it's for financial or self-pride reasons, I would wager a bet that any of you would feel lost if I said your job was gone tomorrow. Think about it—careers become so much of who we are. No wonder I dream about going back to the road as a paramedic—even when relapse may dangle over my head like lethal Christmas mistletoe. I don't know what the future holds for me just like I didn't know what my next call would be. So for now, I need to just focus my attention on my recovery in the present.

During an interesting discussion today, our doctor tries to encourage us to explore who we truly are minus our profession. What the heck would that look like? One by one we start to follow his direction, but then, one by one, our minds always wander back to the same career-based thoughts and concerns. "If I don't go back to work, will I be able to afford my lifestyle? Will I be viewed in the same light now that people know I am sick?" and on and on. I watch the doctor sit and grin as we slowly make the conversation about work again. We can't remove our career psyche. At one point a comment is made that someone doesn't want to have a minimum-wage job. An atrocity! "How could we possibly live without our salaries?" they ask. The doctor's response is crystal clear—security and money didn't stop us from getting here.

The doctor repeatedly asks "what's the rush?" when we talk about going back to work. Why do we not want to use this time to learn how to live? Why can't we see that our careers aren't the centre of our lives? Then we do an activity. He tells us to look around the room and choose the person we would save in a disaster. Everyone scans the room and starts naming names. Then the doctor suddenly stops us. He lets the room go quiet and speaks in a serious tone. "I knew you would all be ready to save each other's lives. Now it's time to save your own." Touché, doctor. Touché.

~ I HATE TODAY

I hate today. Group rips our hearts out. Someone's aching soul spills onto the floor. It hurts. It enrages me with the disgust of life. It makes me disbelieve that things can ever be good. Good people go through so much pain only to have the people that hurt them walk away unscathed. Evil. Darkness. Torturous pain. There is no fairness. I can't see why this needs to be. I hate today's lessons. Pain has a colour, and I see it. It is blacker than the vastest hole in the darkest midnight sky. Pain has a feeling, and I experience it. It seizes my soul and massacres my heart while my breath becomes hopeless cries. I feel it so strongly—crushed and numb in the palm of strong and calloused hands. Left alone. Empty. I hate today.

~ SUICIDAL IDEATION

Suicidal ideation feels like I pull hell from beneath me and inject its toxic thoughts and delusions into my veins. When my heart beats, it screams to be stopped. When I breathe, it physically makes me want to vomit because it reminds me over and over again that I am still on this earth.

There are times when my mind relentlessly replays ways of killing myself—such as crashing or drowning. I analyze every possible way to die because I want to be sure it does the trick. The last thing I want is to choose a way to die that doesn't work, which is what happened when I tried to kill myself with the last overdose. Can you even imagine what this is like? How it feels to *never* have a peaceful moment in your mind?

I haven't crashed my car or drowned in the pool after my last overdose because I have kids. I used to get drunk all the time to become even more delusional and to convince myself that dying by suicide wouldn't be that hard on my kids—that they would get over it and move on, that they would understand. Then I would wake up hungover and back to some partial reality that reminded me I was still in hell. I would see a bush as I walked my dog and think of waiting until it's cold enough outside for me to crawl under it and freeze to death, out of sight from anyone. I would pull my own hair so hard to try to feel a different kind of pain from my internal pain. I would scratch at my legs and dig my nails into my skin.

At times I hate my body and being trapped in it. I want to bleed so that some of the hell in my veins will escape and hopefully bring me relief. I don't fear death at all. I don't understand when people say they need to eat well or exercise so they can live longer. There are times I can't conceive how anyone *wants* to be alive.

I would "get it" when I went to a suicide call at work. I could understand how the person couldn't take the hell they lived in anymore—and how people around them didn't understand and expected them to just smile or look on the bright side of things, making their inner turmoil feel even more hopeless and misunderstood. My heart would break when I attended patients with scars on their arms and a void look in their eyes. They were so lost on this earth, bombarded with media that told them life was supposed to be good and happy. I get that all they saw was the pain in the world. I get that they didn't *want* to feel that way. I get that they weren't afraid of any physical pain suicide may have brought them, because *no* physical pain can compare to the pain they feel while hell is pulsing through their veins.

~ THE ESCAPE

I miss my old life so much today! I can't bear the pain. I try to talk to nurses and counsellors, but nothing eases the broken heart I have and the worry that consumes me about the future. I have been on my bed crying so much that I can't breathe. Hugging the photos of my kids and dog is reminding me of how much I have hurt them, and the shame I feel is unbearable. When the nurses leave my room after trying to calm me down, I take my robe belt and tie it around my neck. I look into the mirror and start to pull it tight. I hate my reflection, and I can't take another moment in this building. I don't keep the belt on long enough to die. I'm weak and need some type of release, so I decide to leave Save-My-Life Boarding School at night without anyone knowing and start to search for a bar.

It's the weekend, so I have my phone. I text AB and tell her I am leaving, and I don't text her again. I walk down the street in the freezing cold night, back in my self-centred, self-pity phase, and I am spiralling fast. I ask a stranger on the street where I can find a restaurant, and he directs me. As I walk, I imagine what it would be like to even order a glass of red wine. I dream about how amazing the smell would be! I would just go for *one*—it wouldn't be that bad. But as I walk I can't stop thinking about how much AB must be worrying about me. I decide to text her and tell her I am OK. But when I try to, I realize my phone battery is dead. I had plenty of battery when I left, and now it is randomly dead. I stop in my tracks. I have to go back. It isn't fair to do that to AB! She doesn't deserve to be worrying about selfish me again. I can continue walking in the direction the stranger showed me, but instead I turn and jog back to Save-My-Life Boarding School (well, as much as I can with the cold air freezing my lungs so badly). I get past the nursing station without a soul even knowing I left.

I pray for my phone to hurry up and charge. I text AB and let her know I am OK.

~

I believe my phone died for a reason that night. Before discovering the dead battery, I wasn't thinking about the consequences my heat-of-the-moment decision would have had on my entire life. I was just falling into my selfish behaviours and previous negative coping methods.

In retrospect, the consequences would have been enormous. Not only would I have been kicked out of Save-My-Life Boarding School, I would have disappointed everyone—myself included. Most importantly, I would not be jumping up and down right now because of the fantastic news I just received from the Children's Aid Society! They are officially closing my file. This means that when I go back home, I can see my son unsupervised—whenever I want.

If I hadn't turned around, I could have lost all of that. Or worse, I could have died. But I believe, because of the grace of God, I realized what I was doing was catastrophic and changed my course. Thank you God for allowing my phone battery to die instead of me.

~ CRUMBLING WALLS

I'm exhausted from crying. Today is another tough day. I knew it would happen; I have to talk about the double-murder call and trial. With reluctance crushing my heart with every beat, I recount the horror of those life-changing days—the days I unquestionably saw evil in a man's eyes and felt spirits in the room where those poor women were brutally murdered. My walls are no match for the emotions that flood my soul. Today I am forced to remember hell.

As I recall the event in group, I bawl—like I knew I would. And when I am right in the middle of recalling the horror, my mind dissociates again. Thankfully, this time I can name the once indescribable sensation—I don't have to feel so alien when my mind pulls me away from the reality of the room and the people around me feel like characters in a play. I also know how to ground myself, but that skill is going to take some practice. I'm not used to controlling the dissociation while I'm in it, as loss of control is the cause of it in the first place. Fortunately, I have more support from my peers than I could have ever imagined. While reliving two of the worst days of my life— the day of the murder call and the day I had to testify—I gratefully feel blanketed in safety and trust.

My peers can connect with many of my immense feelings. Outrage spills from me in the form of words and is an emotion everyone can feel. I explain how infuriated I am that evil always seems to inevitably triumph over happiness. To me, it's only a matter of time before any contentment in my life will be overshadowed by deep sadness. Remember the saying my sister and I had when we were little? "Believe it when you see it, and enjoy it while it lasts." This truly is my adage in life. How depressing is that?

What appears good at one moment in my life seems to disappear so quickly, leaving me guarded by walls and wary of any future happiness. Sometimes I think people who say "there's a lesson in all this pain" deserve a punch in the neck! I don't like painful lessons. They suck and happen all the time. I also don't like when people say, "It's better to have loved and lost than to have never loved at all." These dorks deserve a kick in the nuts. My heart is still broken, and it hurts with every passing moment. To me, love wasn't better at all.

The stress of the day gets my addict and PTSD brain going a mile a minute, which I am told is quite normal. Craving wine and sleeping pills all night, I can't force myself to come out of my room. My depression lands on me like a heavy wet blanket, and I am unable to crawl out from underneath it. It is the first time at Save-My-Life Boarding School that my depression is *this* bad. While lost in self-pity, I doubt my true intentions for being here. Am I here for me? Or everyone else? My distorted thinking is cunning and plays sly tricks on me. The only thing I know clearly is I need to stay and trust the staff.

This time I ask for help when the darkness hits me. I am proud because I never would have before. Since arriving, I have learned how important it is to talk when I'm lost. (I needed to feel like this in order to heal.) It's another painful lesson. It's horrible! Apparently I have to see that I am allowed to crumble to pieces, and when I do, the whole world doesn't fall apart without me. I am so used to being the strong person because for so many years shit needed to get done or people wouldn't survive—or so I thought. There was never any time for falling apart. I had a daughter, a little brother, and a mom to take care of. Feelings just messed everything up. In fact, having a glimmer of sadness made me feel selfish and weak.

After taking a closer look at every aspect of myself, I realize the only thing that is weak now are the walls I built to save me from my feelings. When I first got here, I thought, "Good luck tearing them down." But with a lot of tears, a few bricks crumbled today. I tried to catch them, but they were already falling. They are old, decayed, and of no use to me anymore. I let them fall, then noticed the smallest glimpse of light shining through in their place. Now the trick will be preventing myself from rebuilding this wall.

I could really use a sunny day!

~ THE POISON OF RESENTMENT

I'm home on a weekend pass. The poison of resentment is not a very cheerful Saturday topic, I know. But nonetheless, it's a very important one. How much do we really enjoy anything, let alone Saturdays, when filled with this powerful emotion? I heard a saying that resentment is a poison you drink, expecting it to kill another person. It casts us onto an island of loneliness and anger with the only ship to rescue us called forgiveness. Lonely and angry, we let that ship pass by, over and over again, because being rescued by forgiveness isn't easy. I know, because I've been a castaway for a long time.

Resentment is one of the topics at the 12-step meeting I go to, and the discussion immediately reminds me of so many things stemming from the double-murder call. It dawns on me that I have probably been stuck on resentment island for a long time. I harbour deep anger, which leads to resentment with regard to this call—especially towards my patient, the murderer. This covert emotion is hurting me. I know this because no matter how much I delved into my feelings this past week, I still feel burdened by something. I naively think that sadness and anger are the only emotions that are making me sick. But after opening up these wounds, there's still an odd heaviness in my heart.

I resent everything about that call. I resent the things I saw, the voices I heard, and the spirits I felt. I resent the lack of support afterwards. I resent the nights I've been woken up by nightmares. I resent the anguish it would have caused every first responder at the scene. I resent having to prepare to testify, only for the trial to be cancelled, then back on a year later. I resent the misery those women went through. I resent the tears I cried alone for days after the call. I resent that the murderer was my patient. I resent what I heard him say. I resent that I had to see him again at the trial. And most of all, I resent the evil this appalling human being showed me, causing my gross lack of faith in humanity to this day.

I resent May 2, 2012, and the moral injury it caused.

I want to get better. I don't want to drink that poison anymore. But if forgiveness is the only means of rescue, how do I go about doing that? How do I go about forgiving everything in my life that I hold resentment for? So many bad things have happened that seem unforgivable. I'm going to pray on this one. I don't have the answers tonight.

~ LOCKED AND LOADED

According to a doctor at Save-My-Life Boarding School, living as an addict in recovery is like living with a loaded gun to your head— figuratively speaking of course. What he means is that the danger of relapse is a real life-or-death situation. One more drink or drug could be our last. It's that simple. And sadly, many people who graduate from this program will lose their lives within the next year. It exhausts me just thinking about how on guard I have to be for the rest of my life! I wish I could just remove the bullets. But alas, rehab can't teach us how to do that because the bullets are our genetics.

We as students learn that ten to fifteen percent of people are born with the addict gene. Simply put, if we have a reason to justify why we numb our minds through addiction, we use it. Our addict brain craves being numb. It doesn't care who, what, where, when, why, or how it happens. That damn limbic system and its impulsiveness wants to win every time.

I am frustrated with the amount of mental energy it takes to stay sober. It's on my mind 24/7. I have nightmares about relapsing and losing everything I hold dear to me. I wake up in a sweat, grateful that it is just a dream, but with a sickening feeling in my gut that lasts for hours. Just when I think I've got Steps 1, 2, and 3 of the 12 steps conquered, my addict mind confuses me and makes me doubt all the work I've done. And it's a vicious cycle! The cycle goes: I doubt my strength; I stress; I want to drink; I gain some hope; I doubt my strength; I stress; I want to drink—and on and on.

The 12-step meetings are just monotonous now. Sure, I learn things every time, but I tire of listening to the same preamble and stories. How do people do this for forty years? I'm confused about my future, and at this point I am exhausted from trying to figure it out. Yeah, yeah, I know, one day at a time. But that isn't the way my brain works. I want to be successful, but when does my mind get to rest a little bit? It's a rhetorical question. I know the answer is never. Rest only comes when the figurative trigger is pulled.

I have a few weeks to find some clarity, but right now all I feel is confused. One thing I cling to is the doctor says he is happy when we are confused—it means we aren't complacent and are striving for a lifelong recovery. Short and sweet, confusion equals effort. OK great, I get an A for effort on my Save-My-Life Boarding School report card. But my positivity still needs improvement.

~ MERRY CHRISTMAS

Save-My-Life Boarding School is decorated with Christmas trees and dangly paper-snowflakes; I love it. The grounds are a winter wonderland and make for some slippery morning walks. My trips to Starbucks with my friends are a production because of the amount of snow we need to remove from their cars. I hate the cold, but I love Christmas—especially because I will be going home to see my kids and my dog, Walter!

Not everyone is as excited as I am though. Some people live across the country and can't afford the flight there and back, so they will be spending their Christmas in what I am anticipating will be a pretty quiet and lonely place. Even sadder are the people who *do* live nearby, but won't be going home because they don't have one. Many of the Save-My-Life Boarding School students are "between homes" for one reason or another. Some have been kicked out by loved ones who needed their own space to heal. Some have lost their homes due to financial stresses that their addictions placed upon them. And some simply chose to live on the street. Christmas mass will be held in the chapel, and Christmas dinner will be served in the cafeteria. However, I can't help but feel the unmistakable loneliness that no amount of praying or feasting can remove. And I know that many will be wishing that they could drink or "use" their worries away.

After I spend the day making a Christmas bulb ornament in Horticulture class, I pack up my bags and get ready for the ride home. One last Merry Christmas urine test, and I'm off to see my family!

The drive home is an overly chatty and snowy one (God bless the friend who drives me home, but he's chattier than a grandma at a quilting bee!), but I don't mind. After weeks of Save-My-Life Boarding School, I am ready to hug my kids so tightly that their heads may pop off! And Walter—he's going to get a long, snowy walk. There won't be many presents under the tree, but recovery life has taught me about what is truly important—and it's never found in a box with a bow. True gifts are found in our hearts, in hugs, and in cherished moments because we are blessed enough to have them. Merry Christmas.

~ FUCK CHRISTMAS

I have such an idyllic vision of arriving home on Christmas Eve. All the way back during the chatty drive, I imagine the warm glow of a lit tree, the smell of home-cooked food, and the warmth of family. This vision shatters almost instantly when I walk through the front door. I am enveloped in a heavy, suffocating energy, and it makes me feel sick to my stomach. The tension is palpable.

It's not anyone's fault; I'm just not strong or well enough—yet. A miracle is needed this Christmas. When I see the faces of my beautiful children, I experience complete and utter despair and guilt.

I tell myself to stop dreaming that this Christmas will be happy like the previous ones were. All I am able to do is remember the pain I have caused my family. This cloud won't vanish just because I want it to.

Walter is happy to see me, and yes my kids are happy to see me too, but they are hurting so much because of my absence—and rightly so. Their faces are so lost and confused. I want to die when I see and feel their innocent eyes almost look right through me. The truth of what they are going through is hard to take.

The pain and incredible guilt—the utter gut-wrenching, heart-ripping, run-me-over-with-a-thousand-freight-trucks-please pain—is so hard to smile through. How could I have done this to them? I wish I had never been born. They wouldn't have to sit here, experiencing this immense confusion and uncertainty. The best I can do is try to find a Christmas special on TV so we can pretend to be a normal, happy family.

I wake up the next morning, but my mood isn't any better. Christmas morning…happens. That's about it. I hold back tears every second of the present-opening and stocking-emptying festivities so my pain won't ruin my family's only opportunity to be happy on Christmas. The presents are minimal, and I want desperately to stand on my roof, crack my house open, and release the sadness trapped inside! I want to witness some kind of peace radiating off my precious little souls. I would do *anything* to see them smile for real, but it doesn't ever happen.

Jon comes over to pick up Adam after the presents are opened. I try so hard to accept that I won't be seeing my son for several weeks again. Caroline eventually leaves to hang out with her boyfriend, so I sit alone on my couch, snuggling Walter, wanting to see Leo or someone who can take away my pain. I want to drink. How selfish and sick is that? I just witnessed the looks of despair in my children's eyes because I was away in rehab, yet I still have the urge to drink!

Fuck you, addiction! Fuck you and every moment you have ruined in my life! Fuck you for choosing me to infect! Fuck you for hurting my kids and my relationship! Fuck you for leaving me alone on Christmas day!

I can stay home until tomorrow, but I am not ready to handle this. I make the choice to return to Save-My-Life Boarding School. I know if I stay here, I will make a horrible decision of some kind. I call my daughter and ask her and her boyfriend to make the three-hour drive back to Save-My-Life Boarding School *right now.* I feel ashamed that I'm not yet capable of being home alone.

The drive back feels long and uncomfortable. My throat is tight, and I want to scratch my skin off. Right now I hate myself. Actually, hate isn't a strong enough word. I *despise* myself. I feel like I am a waste of other people's oxygen.

Fuck you, Christmas, and fuck this existence!

~ HAPPY NEW YEAR

Now that Christmas has passed (thank God), all of us addicts and alcoholics at Save-My-Life Boarding School get to white-knuckle our way through New Year's Eve. Yay! NOT! We have been invited to some celebrations at the local church basement by our 12-step group friends, but our curfew is eleven o'clock. I'm not sure what could possibly be more depressing than walking in the bitter cold to a church basement decorated with tacky decorations, only to stand around and drink punch without a shred of hope it is spiked (and we would be foolish to drink it if it was, as I'm sure we will have a ring-in-the-New-Year urine test extravaganza tomorrow morning), awkwardly chat with strangers about—I really have no idea what—and then leave by ten-thirty to be sure that we don't miss curfew, which is an hour *before* the ball drops. Shoot. Me. Now.

My best Save-My-Life Boarding School friend and I decide to go to the variety store and buy chips and pop. We sit on the floor of her room and watch the clock torturously tick until we go to bed at eleven, only to have visions of champagne and drunken kisses dance in our heads.

I'm a total bitch at the 12-step meeting tonight. When it is time for me to share, I have nothing constructive to say. With my arms folded and tears welling up in my eyes, I say, "This New Year's Eve sucks! How can *anyone* be happy right now? Sitting sober and alone on the night that is by far the biggest alcohol- and drug-filled party night in the WORLD! Remembering the fun times we had at those parties and trying to accept that those times will *never* happen again. Thank you for listening, I pass." Jaws are on the floor. I've clearly put a damper on things. Oh well, I really don't care. Unless the doctors and nurses barge in through the door with streamers, New Year's Eve hats, and shooters, nothing is going to make me happy tonight.

~ BEING SIX FEET UNDER IS COLDER

Recovery is a life-or-death situation! There's no cutting off the crust to make it taste better. It's hard to swallow, but it needs to happen! So much so, that if you don't have supportive family and friends, get new ones. Yes, I just said that, and I mean it. We are learning that it is very important to avoid certain people, especially in recovery. This includes family and friends that continue to drink, use, or trigger PTSD symptoms. Boundaries need to be set. This is not my expertise by any means. As you know, I am a people pleaser and a perfectionist. I have no idea how to say no when it comes to setting boundaries that suit my needs.

We are learning that we need to seriously accept that ending relationships is essential to our recovery if those relationships cause us to feel shame, guilt, or less than others. We finally need to step up to the plate, stand tall, and do exactly what is good for us. Long explanations are not required. If people don't understand how dire our future decisions are to our ability to live, they are not people we want in our life. It may sound cold, but being six feet under is colder!

Interesting lesson I learn in class today: We cannot simultaneously set a boundary and take care of another person's feelings. We will be tested when we set our boundaries. We will probably feel ashamed and afraid to do so. When we decide that we need to set a limit with someone, we need to do it clearly, without anger and use as few words as possible. Anger, complaining, and whining are clues that boundaries need to be set. Be prepared to follow through!

~ OUR DISEASE, THE LIAR

It's a bigger revolving door here at Save-My-Life Boarding School than I thought it would be. There's no dicking around, and I totally get it. They are in the life-or-death business here! And if you're not ready to follow the process that the doctors and nurses have clearly outlined, they have no qualms with sending you packing. That may seem harsh, but there is a long line of dying addicts waiting for their chance to get better, so Save-My-Life Boarding School is tough-love central.

Almost every day the who-got-the-boot gossip gets around. "Did you hear that So-and-So got kicked out?" Followed by, "No way!" is a normal conversation here. I'm usually so shocked because I still find it difficult to see people beyond their faces, to see them as sick human beings. Some people are more physically sick than others. The reality of how powerful the disease of addiction is comes shining through when those who look so sweet and kind lash out at the doctors. Misguided by their disease, addicts think *they* know what is best for their recovery. It's a grim reminder of how close everyone here is to death. Their disease fools them into thinking they aren't *that* bad and that they "don't need this place anyway." And it's even more of a reality check when I see that type of person on a regular basis looking back at me from the mirror.

The physical transformations here are dramatic! People who are so frail, hunched over, and detoxing are brought in by wheelchair on a regular basis, and week by week (if they trust the process) they begin to gain some weight (the food is pretty good), get some energy, and start to smile, and eventually walk. I feel incredibly blessed to be a part of their recovery support system! We truly are a family here. But we are warned not to get too close to one another as we need to focus on *our* recovery.

Addicts and alcoholics have a disease that lies to us. It tells us to manipulate and take advantage of people, and we do it even without realizing it. Our addict brains can stay very much in dire need of our drug at any expense for a very long time. In fact, on my second day here I got moved to a new room because my roommate was caught using heroin. Our room got searched, and I am surprised that she didn't hide stuff in my belongings, because that happens here. Our addict minds are ruthless and selfish. Until we fully surrender to recovery, our future is unknown but guaranteed to be painful.

~ A GOOD DAY

Going to church today is really nice—minus the coughing girl who coughs (loudly) the whole time! I can see myself occasionally replacing a 12-step meeting with a church service. I feel comfortable and I like my connection with God here. My goal today is to really focus on increasing my spiritual connection, and I want to do this on a daily basis. I'm at least feeling less bitter today—maybe because I had a great sleep. I think I will go for a nice walk on the grounds.

~ QUIET

I know where I can find God now...in quiet. When my brain is peaceful I know He's there. In that quiet I can really see the evil that clouds my mind and blocks Him out. My mind is always too busy. When I slow it down, alone, in silence and concentrate, He's there. I remember the few times recently where I felt my soul was at peace: at the lake, at the labyrinth, and at yoga. I was peaceful and calm. Maybe that's why I overdosed the third time—to quiet the madness and noise in my head. Ironically, it almost brought me right to God— too soon. He wants me here still. I trust Him. And when I need to find Him, all I need is silence. This is an important discovery.

~ LEAVING

I am leaving Save-My-Life Boarding School prematurely. I will graduate a week early, and apparently this is quite unheard of —something only superheroes do. (Insert me laughing hysterically.) In light of this recent development, one of my very good friends has now nicknamed me the Dark Knight.

You may be wondering why I am leaving early. Normally people leave the treatment centre early because they get the boot. Miraculously, I didn't get kicked out—thank God! The reason I am leaving early is that, according to my team of care providers, I am actually starting to regress in my recovery.

I was making huge leaps and bounds in my first weeks of the PTSD phase of the program, but something changed. In the beginning, sharing my stories in group helped me tremendously. But as the days went on, I heard more and more of my new friends' tragedies, and I began to dissociate. I tried hard to shake the gross feelings off me after the group each day, but they never fully went away. I grew very angry at life again and almost relapsed.

I am scared, but I am ready to go home. I have fully and completely given my will over to the 12-step program and to the big guy upstairs. I need to do exactly what I am told to do when I get home. If I do, I will be OK. Now it's time for real life.

PART III

~

Save-My-Life Grad School

*Some changes look negative
on the surface but you will soon realize
that space is being created in your life
for something new to emerge.*

– Eckhart Tolle

I am now out of the Save-My-Life Boarding School bubble. I have new hurdles to jump over, and there have been changes in life itself. As I fumble towards a new rhythm, AB and I find ourselves no longer hanging out on a day-to-day basis. Life consists of seasons. It is a mutual and amicable shift; there will never be a day that I am not eternally grateful for everything AB has done to literally save my life.

Being back home is nice. Sidebar: I have to confess a story showing how delusional and self-centred I was before I went away. I was hoping that people would have a welcome home party for me when I got home! What the hell? When I tell this story to my 12-step friends, it causes them to almost pee their pants laughing. Now, I'm ashamed to even acknowledge I thought that way. What I am blessed to have is a small welcome home cake from my family, but there was no rented hall or streamers waiting for my arrival (insert embarrassed face). Just more proof that an addict mind truly thinks of itself first.

Being home does involve me thinking about myself—but in a healthy way. Recovery is a moment-by-moment mission! And if I don't consistently use my tools, relapse can rear its ugly head. My days are pretty consistent and peaceful. I go to hot yoga every morning, hang out with my kids, eat healthy, walk Walter, read books, pray, meditate, and go to meetings—lots of meetings. I start another out-patient program that is twice a week and develop a great network of recovering-addict friends. I also join a 12-step group, and I'm responsible for bringing cream and sugar to every meeting—it's a big deal. I'm still on the hunt for a sponsor, but I want them to be right for me, so I'm not rushing into that. But don't worry, I won't leave it for long—it is a pivotal component to successful recovery.

I'm very grateful for how much Save-My-Life Boarding School focused on the addiction part of my PTSD recovery. As you can probably remember, at first I was very resistant to the idea that I was an addict and that a 12-step program could actually help me. I used to think, "Why would I want to go to these meetings all the time?" Ugh. I was convinced I had it all figured out. And in turn I made the initial weeks at Save-My-Life Boarding School very difficult for myself. Once again, self-righteous Natalie thought that a program that helped *millions* of people around the world live happy, clean, and prosperous lives couldn't possibly help her! When I finally decided to surrender and follow the simple steps provided to anyone willing to recover, my mind started to become calm. I now tell myself to stop complicating things. Just…follow…the…steps! And you know what, they do work—if you work them.

My PTSD symptoms have been at bay for a few weeks since I've been home. And for this, I am very grateful. But I am not so naive to think that they are gone forever. I haven't had a bout of depression or anxiety since I've been home and am genuinely living one day at a time so much more peacefully than before. I finally got the help I had been craving for years (pun intended)! And it will be a work-in-progress for the rest of my life.

~ TAKING TIME ON THE PATHWAY TO RECOVERY

I have nicknamed this phase in my recovery "Save-My-Life Grad School," which consists of classes at the hospital—and I am doing some independent study too, learning from life itself. I am attending an out-patient hospital program, and it is being held at the same location as my initial Save-My-Life School program.

The number of life lessons I am still learning to survive in this confusing, messed-up world are amazing! I am back in the original rooms at the hospital where I attended classes every day at Save-My-Life School, and I can't help feeling happy to be in the loving atmosphere again. While in these rooms, I learned how to breathe. Now I revel in the opportunity to be with my teachers again and show them how much I have grown.

Today's topic in class is "The Pathways of Recovery." Its lesson revolves around the feeling of hopelessness, which is incredibly common in people with mental illnesses. You may have told yourself, "Why try? Everything goes wrong anyway." Or maybe you have thought, "Things that are going well today won't last." Well, I sure have! These phrases used to fuel my pessimistic outlook on the world, and if still used, will force me to have trouble believing recovery will make a real difference in my life. These self-defeating beliefs are not OK to live with.

Now you may be thinking, "But, Natalie, so many bad things have happened to me! It seems like just when I get my head above water, something pulls me down again." And you know what, sometimes this is true. But all kinds of things can and do happen in people's lives—some good, some bad. Hard times don't discriminate. We all experience terrible losses that hurt us to the core. We all face sadness that we thought was never even possible. Some people are diagnosed with cancer, go bankrupt, or get divorced—and some have even experienced the loss of a child. Sometimes life just sucks! But what I am learning is that choosing to cope with these terrible circumstances in a healthy way, rather than going numb and hiding from our emotions, *is* possible. Yes, that is correct; the way we cope with the atrocities of life is a choice. I never thought those words would come out of my mouth.

Before learning any coping skills over the past four months, when something bad happened to me, I would numb it right away, usually with alcohol. I would also hide from situations in my life that may have caused conflict, which in the end really only caused me more pain. This avoidance of pain is an unhealthy way to behave and often slowly led me into a horrible depression. Rather than tackling a problem head on and getting it sorted out right away, I would ignore, ignore, ignore! I thought it would disappear! What was I thinking? It only grew into a bigger problem every day.

The bottom line is I didn't like to feel. But if I want to stay on the recovery path, I need to trust in my ability to get through hard times, no matter how gross they make me feel. I can't just run to a bottle of wine or down a jar of pills at the first glimpse of sadness. Clearly those choices make everything worse. Adopting the ability to choose to accept the normal pain life brings us is going to be tough at first. Thinking with a rational mind when all I'm used to thinking with is an emotional mind will take time and practice.

What I learn in school is that we must give ourselves time and permission to process a painful event. We need to allow ourselves to experience all the normal human emotions that may come with the situation; that's when things get scary for me. Then we need time to develop and implement a game plan. Healthy people do these things instinctively. Buggers. But with practice, this can be second nature for anyone with mental illnesses too. I usually want the pain and discomfort to go away fast! But oddly enough, the sooner I accept that it will take time to get through a loss, the sooner I will heal from it.

Recently, I experienced this ability to get through pain by allowing time to pass, and it's quite empowering. My heartbreak with Leo hurts me *a lot*. And at first I definitely didn't cope with it in a healthy way. I wanted to rip my heart out of my chest rather than feel the pain of losing someone I love. But as time goes on, it's getting better. I tolerate the distress adequately and allow time to go by. I still have bad days and need to talk it out with a friend, but overall, I am able to tell myself that what I'm feeling is normal and that it won't last forever. Even though it is a big heartbreak in my life, I still haven't picked up a drink because of it—to me that's cause for some pride.

Shit happens. At times life sucks. The fight to get through tragedy can also be a fight for a mental illness sufferer's own life. I am by far no expert in this give-yourself-time-to-heal world—I'm a freshman at best! I am starting to see that, through effort and determination to stay on the pathway of recovery, we can gain life stability and improve life outcomes.

~ OFF WITH THEIR HEADS

Over the past five months, I have grown and changed. I now automatically recognize many negative emotions when they pop up and use mindfulness and patience to navigate through them rather than push them away. I am taking things one day at a time rather than ruminating about the unknown future. I have learned so much about my addiction, how it controlled my life, and how recovery life can be a life I never imagined—a happy one. I have crisis plans and a network of friends who have been where I have been and who I contact every day. But, there's still (and probably always will be) huge hit-me-in-the-gut, make-me-want-to-vomit, what-was-I-thinking? lessons almost daily. Today is no exception.

Today, the topic at Save-My-Life Grad School is "Challenging Extreme Judgments," and we discuss the difference between our emotional mind and our rational mind. *Oh Lord, Natalie. This chapter is going to sting.* It speaks of how many of us often use a hundred percent emotional mind when in an argument and don't realize how much exaggeration is occurring on our part when we do so. When we feel hurt or upset, we tell people that they *never* do anything nice for us or that they are *always* being selfish. In truth that is merely our emotional mind's perception in the moment. We feel like no one cares about us because they aren't instantly remedying our insecurities or making us feel loved. But if we turn on our rational mind, we would see that the "never" and "always" statements we throw out like daggers aren't true and the people we are upset with feel very criticized.

And class also teaches me that when we label people in extreme ways, they become defensive because our statements are unrealistic and one-sided. They then get upset that all the positive things they've ever done for us are discounted and ignored. When we lash out with extreme judgments, our loved ones don't want to make us feel secure and loved. They are hurt and sometimes end up pushing us away. When we accuse people of things they don't do, it slams the door shut on negotiation, causing hurt and misunderstanding for both parties involved.

This chapter hurts my heart to the core because I was the Queen of Extreme Judgments, and I hurt a lot of people in my life with my harsh opinions. I feel embarrassed that I wasn't able to see how my behaviours were destructive and painful. I always felt terribly sorry after horrible arguments and eventually realized that I was definitely overreacting. But I had no idea why I couldn't control my emotional thoughts before it was too late. My inability to turn on my rational mind until much later in the day slowly sabotaged the relationships I wanted to desperately keep. By the time I had said sorry, it was too late; the people who I loved so dearly were tired of hearing it.

By having false extreme judgments about others and myself, I created a self-fulfilling prophecy that destroyed the relationships I wanted to keep. Allow me to explain. Whenever I disappointed myself by hurting someone I loved, I felt unworthy. I told myself over and over that I was crazy and no one could ever love me forever. I was stuck in self-defeating ways. The negative labels I put on myself had long-lasting effects on my self-esteem. This clouded perception slowly crumbled the foundation of any loving relationship I was in. People would eventually become tired of trying to convince me that I was worthy of love. Eventually, they would need to walk away for their own well-being. And if they didn't, I would push them away. I thought that relationships would never work out, because they hadn't before. But what I didn't realize was that my extreme thoughts sabotaged my relationships from the very start. I had no idea that words and thoughts driven by a self-defeating emotional mind should never be trusted. I thought I knew what was right, but I was very wrong.

Save-My-Life Grad School teaches me to take a stand and rationally challenge extreme judgments right when they occur! I'm learning to defend myself from these judgments, which will in turn protect future relationships from them as well. Like all lifework, changes don't happen overnight. Sadly, I've been called the Queen of Hearts before because my all-or-nothing emotional judgments were equal to me yelling "off with their heads" if anyone threatened my heart in any way. How I couldn't see that this caused undue grief when I tried to sew their heads back on once I rationally woke up, I don't know.

I'm not a stupid person. I've just been living with a dysregulated, out-of-control mind. My mind (whether or not influenced by mental illness, addiction, or past experiences) did and said mindless and impulsive things because I only acted on my emotional mind—especially when I was in a desperate state. My all-or-nothing outlook on life and love wasn't rational, and it made me believe that death was the only way to be free of the turmoil and darkness that consumed me. My suicide attempt is the ultimate example of an extreme decision I wouldn't be able to apologize for when my rational mind kicked in. Thank God I have the opportunity to be a different Queen of Hearts now—the queen of my own.

~ MINDFULNESS AND VALENTINE'S DAY

Valentine's Day. Blah! A day I've never been too fond of anyway now involves me finishing *Confessions of a Shopaholic* at home in my pyjamas with my Valentine (dog) Walter (he totally forgot to get me flowers, but whatever, he would have eaten them anyway), drinking copious amounts of coffee, and taking Cold-FX to hopefully ward off my sore throat. How romantic. But as this silly day of love goes by, I am very conscious not to let my emotional mind start to take over for fear of heartbreak rearing its ugly head tenfold.

Last week in Save-My-Life Grad School, we discussed the topic of mindfulness quite a lot. Simply put, mindfulness is awareness in the moment, in the here and now. It involves being aware of what we're doing and what we're thinking about doing. This is a skill many people implement instinctively when they are in an upsetting situation, but not me. One of my biggest problems in the past was doing before thinking, especially while I was in an upsetting situation. In fact, in the past when I was upset, my emotional mind would tell me that the only way to feel better and calm the demons in my head was to drink, a lot. I used to never play the tape to the end and be mindful of the consequences of my actions. Back then, all that mattered at that moment was getting rid of the awful feeling in the pit of my stomach. With today being Valentine's Day and my heart still only partially healed, the old Natalie would have used this day's sadness as the perfect opportunity to numb! But on February 14, 2015, I am proud to say that the only numbness I experience is when my nose is about to fall off while walking Walter outside in what feels like a Yukon winter.

A common theme I notice with mental health therapies is balance. A healthy life involves taking a little from Column A and mixing it with Column B. For example, while in recovery it's very important not to isolate, but it's equally as important to take time to meditate on your own. Confession time: We Save-My-Life Boarding School students quickly learned the secret to being able to take a nap is to say that we are "meditating." Another secret is if you want chocolate milk, you better be early for lunch because it is gone faster than a parking spot on Christmas Eve...but I digress. Another example of this balance is when we are told to practise mindfulness yet also told to keep ourselves occupied every day to discourage our minds from being too busy. Can you see how the Save-Your-Life School lessons can be a bit confusing at times? No wonder I study every day. My point is that on days like today, a little mixture of mind*ful*ness and mind*less*ness may be the perfect balance for this girl. I'm mindful that I need to keep my emotions in check, but I'm mindless enough to forget to put deodorant on. Too much information? Oh well, I'm way past the worrying-about-what-I-say point anyway.

I am mindful that I am quite sad at times today and a bit lonely. I can't help but think about the good times Leo and I had and how nice it was when we first started dating. It's difficult on Cupid's Day to not think about the flowers he would bring me home or the first time he told me he loved me, but I don't beat myself up for thinking about it. I remind myself that the feelings I have today are normal and that I am human. In the past, these thoughts would turn into emotions that would kick-start the perfect negative, self-defeating cycle of self-pity. I was a pro at it. If I was heartbroken a year ago pre-Save-My-Life School, I would have been a blubbering mess. I don't even want to think about the drunk texts I would have sent. But overall, I'm super proud of myself. I am managing all of my emotions in a positive way today, and I remind myself that they are only temporary—and that I *will* feel better. I say my prayers like I'm supposed to and ask God to keep me on my recovery path. I trust that He still has good plans for my heart. And even though I honestly am not up for a meeting tonight, I am mindful that not going is a typical relapse behaviour, and I get my butt out that door!

So, if mindfulness is Column A, in order to keep mental health in balance today, I also add a little of Column B—mindlessness. Way more fun! I'm equally as proud to say that I mindlessly eat what feels like four hundred and fifty-seven of Caroline's Valentine's Day chocolates; take two naps; eat cinnamon buns for breakfast, lunch and dinner; snuggle Walter when needed; and sing in the car louder than usual on the way to my 12-step meeting. How's that for balance?!

As my Valentine's Day draws to an end, I remind myself that the love I have in my life is immense. There's no need to numb or be sad.

And even though Leo and I are apart, his love taught me more than words can say. And above all, I now have love for life every day, not just on February 14.

~ EASY DOES IT

I'm sick. It's just a chest and head cold, but I'm cooped up in bed. I don't like the feeling of diverting from my daily routine by staying home as my new-found education teaches me that isolating is relapse behaviour. But am I truly isolating? Or quarantining myself for the good of the public? I find myself juggling whether or not to rest my physical self or try and battle the elements (and pray I won't cough until I vomit when the cold hits my lungs). Should I focus on my mental self? I constantly go back and forth between thinking, "Well, I personally wouldn't want anyone hacking up a lung in the yoga studio," to "Well, maybe if I just push myself half as hard I will be OK," and then, "But yoga etiquette says I'm not supposed to leave the studio until the class is finished and coughing for ninety minutes is horribly rude," right back to "Well, going means I'm definitely still on my recovery pathway because I'm out of the house." Ugh. That back and forth is how my mind works. But when I give myself a break and really think about it, even being mindful of making sure I stay on my recovery pathway is more than I ever did before.

Being that I'm a mindfulness rookie, differentiating between what is being mindful and simply being too judgmental of myself is tough. In Save-My-Life Grad School, I learn to avoid extreme judgments because I often base them on only an observation or two rather than a bigger picture. Furthermore, if I'm in too emotional of a mindset when I am making these judgments, my perceptions often get distorted. Making incorrect judgments is part of being human; I get that. But when mentally sick and physically sick get rolled into one (like today), making the right judgment and recovery choices can be a matter of life or death. For me, making decisions regarding my health in general are a little overwhelming.

At the end of the day, I do think I'm balancing things quite well. I'm keeping my germs away from the public (you're welcome!), but I'm very mindful to make sure that sitting in my room for most of the day doesn't put me into a downward spiral. I need to give myself a little slack sometimes and remember "easy does it." I suppose I am taking this as a learning opportunity, which is good. And over time, the decisions that seem so big to me now (go to yoga or not go to yoga) will become easier, more natural, and rather automatic. I learn that it takes a lot of dedication and practice to change our old habits, but the end result is well worth the effort.

~ LOVE IS ESSENTIAL, BUT SADLY NOT THE CURE

Seeing someone you love suffer from a mental illness, including addiction is heartbreaking. Let me know if any of these phrases sound familiar to you: You would do anything to take their pain away. You would trade places with them if you could. You eat, sleep, and breathe the feeling of helplessness, not knowing what to say next. You never know what tomorrow will bring. You walk on eggshells day in and day out. You get mad at the universe and wonder why there is nothing you can do to fix them. You agonizingly watch them get deeper and deeper into a world of despair, into a darkness you don't understand. You wish you could grab them and shake them back to health. You pray, beg, counsel, reason, threaten—but nothing seems to work. Years go by while you think they've finally reached bottom—only to see them get even worse.

The following advice is for anyone who can relate to that first paragraph. It's for the caregivers who suffer alongside their sick loved one, baffled by the disease of addiction. It's for the people who wonder time and time again why they can't fix their sick mother, father, spouse, sister, brother, friend—whoever it may be. For those pillars of strength who have researched enough on a particular illness that they can rival any specialist's lecture on the topic. For those of you who travel miles to treatment centres, psychologists, cognitive behavioural therapists, naturopathic doctors, and drug trials, praying that this time your loved one's illness will be cured. For those of you who try everything, but nothing seems to work.

I'm not here to tell you to stop trying or loving—not at all! Your love and effort is invaluable to anyone who is sick. But I am here to tell you that you need to breathe and ultimately realize that you can't *make* any treatment work. Some people, sick with mental illness, lose their homes, jobs, freedom, and even children, but if they aren't truly ready to get better (or they can't), they won't. It's probably one of the hardest things for a healthy family member to accept or comprehend. Even if doctors warn the sick person of possible death, it may mean nothing to their diseased brain. Sadly, to many who suffer from mental illness, dying is often the only cure they can see.

When I was at Save-My-Life Boarding School, I heard story after story about how people had been in and out of treatment centres and hospitals for years, only to find themselves still sick. Family members probably shook their heads in disbelief when relapses occurred, saying to themselves, "But I put them in the best care facility! I made sure they stayed until the program was completed!" Sadly these relapses occur with this mental illness because the person who is sick couldn't give themselves completely over to the treatment program they were being offered. They may have wanted to, but something about their illness kept stopping them. Something about their illness kept lying to them. Something about their illness kept winning. It wasn't anyone's fault! It wasn't due to lack of help. Mental illness a cunning and baffling disease.

I don't have all the answers, but I'm here to try to ease your restless minds. There are times when no amount of therapy or love guarantees that a sick person will truly comprehend the gravity of their illness and accept help. You may be mad to hear that all your love still can't (or couldn't) fix your loved one. Please take my word for it; it's not that the love you gave wasn't amazing. It's not that the sick person didn't see, feel, and appreciate that love. Love is a huge part of recovery for anyone! It's just that sadly all the love in the world sometimes can't cure a illness that keeps them from loving themselves.

Why does one person finally accept or ask for the help they need and another person doesn't? I don't know. Every individual is different. Just know that if your loved one didn't, it's not because you said one prayer too few. You didn't love them too little or ask too few questions. You didn't choose the wrong doctor, treatment centre, or therapist. You didn't fix them—because you couldn't.

My heart breaks every day for the people who have lost a loved one to a mental illness. And my deepest condolences go out to the family of my thirteen-year-old niece's friend who is living with the loss right now.

Love one another—that medicine *never* hurts. But remember that even love can't cure everything.

~ WISDOM IN THE RING

Some of you may know that I have a love for MMA (mixed martial arts). I've been to every UFC (Ultimate Fighting Championship) fight ever held in Toronto. This passion comes from years of watching boxing growing up with my brother Ross (Oscar De La Hoya is our all-time fave). Most guys are surprised when I am able to have an extensive conversation about fighters from the past and present— and hopefuls for the future. The series *Ultimate Fighter* is pretty much this girl's *Days of Our Lives*. And I'm so OK with that.

One of the main reasons I love this sport is because I admire the skill it takes for fighters to wisely take control of their physical and emotional selves in order to perform effectively in an out-of-control atmosphere. If they are not in control of their emotions, they can suffocate any attempt at a mindful and effective fight. Yes, emotions are a definite part of any fight (getting punched in the face is surely going to piss you off and fire you up), but being in control of these emotions takes practice—a lot of practice, and I respect that.

This fighter analogy brings me to this week's Save-My-Life Grad School topic, "How to Use Our Wise Mind." This mind turns on when we blend our emotional and rational minds together. While I learn about these minds, I imagine a wise-minded fighter in the ring who remembers to play by the rules and make calculated choices versus an emotional-minded fighter who doesn't analyze their opponent, breaks the rules, and fights strictly with impulsive reactions. Sure, fighters who use only their emotional mind may get lucky and win a fight from time to time with a rage-filled punch, but their career longevity is limited—their luck will eventually run out when fighting with a hundred percent emotional mind. Thankfully, during my biggest struggles, *my* luck didn't run out.

Before Save-My-Life School and Save-My-Life Boarding School, I was completely an emotional fighter through and through! When I would feel an uncomfortable emotion, I reacted immediately. I would throw that figurative rage-filled punch over and over without even noticing that I was barely winning the fight. And more often than not, I would throw in the towel before even putting on the gloves. I thought that "being strong" (a.k.a. stubborn and bitter with life) was the only characteristic I needed on my UFC resumé. I thought my passion in the ring made any fighting strategies irrelevant, and when I was exhausted I selfishly thought that retreating to the corner would simply make my opponent have compassion for me, forget how much I hurt them, and love me again. Only when I was finally down and out for the count would my wise-minded fighter awaken. But by then it was too late—I was already a bloody mess, and no one was in the crowd anymore. When I finally pulled myself to my knees, all I would do was rehash the emotional fight over and over in my head or beat myself up for retreating. The only way I ever knew how to fight in this world was through unnecessary exhaustion and pain.

I'm now learning that taking the time to practise using my wise mind before throwing that emotional rage-filled punch is a key to having peace and stability in my life. I can still be strong but show my strength through patience and mindfulness. I don't need to knock everyone out to protect my heart. And I now know that I will have to feel a punch or two in life, rather than numb myself, in order to grow. Furthermore, I am learning how to mindfully decide if a battle is even worth the fight at all! Sidebar: Jerseying a girl in Walmart when I was twenty-one because she got all up in my grill about me flashing my high beams at her after she took my parking spot—not worth the fight. But man, it's an awesome story! Moving on…

When I look at all the impulsive things I've done through a totally emotional mind, I feel foolish and embarrassed. I don't think that shame will go away for a long time. But now if I am ever in crisis, mindfully moving through emotional mind, rational mind, and then on to wise mind, allows me to see that I have way too much to lose by acting impulsively. The consequences of me jumping into the ring of pure emotions and swinging are too damaging. After all those years watching boxing and UFC, never did I think I would be called into the ring for the fight of my life, literally. But I'm no longer the underdog. I've been practising this fight for my entire life, and I'm finally winning.

~ A LOTUS'S JEWEL

Life lessons seem to hit me in the gut left, right, and centre lately. Just when I think I'm due for a lesson lull—BAM, I get hit with a doozie! Do I have a sign on my back that says, "Please rattle my view of the world and humanity"? It's totally possible. OK, let's see how I can describe how I'm feeling in words: "Overwhelmed" doesn't seem right. I feel that word sort of has a negative connotation, and what I'm feeling is anything but negative. "Mesmerized?" Partially. "Gob-smacked?" I don't really know what that means, but it sort of sounds appropriate. "In awe?" Yes, but it's still not right. "Awakened!" Yes, that's it! Last night's lesson awakens my knowledge of a subject I admit has baffled me for years—love.

I have this awakening when I join my sister-in-law for an hour and a half at a Buddhist centre. Upon arriving, all I know is the topic of discussion and teaching is "Love." *Gulp*. Meditation is involved, but I don't know what else to expect. I am thrilled to be invited, as I have been practising meditation at night to help me fall asleep sans prescriptions drugs—and I love it. But the meditation I participated in at the Buddhist centre is much more challenging than the count David Beckhams—I mean sheep—technique I am used to. More challenging as in it takes what feels like a small eternity to complete. (I'm used to only reaching sheep thirty-two-ish). However, tonight I sit patiently through the duration of the meditation because the topic speaks volumes to me.

The teacher tells us to close our eyes and envision a lotus seed in the murky, muddy water. This seed represents our potential to find the purest of love. We then envision the lotus growing out of the dark water and blooming into its breathtaking colour. With a little more patience, the beautiful flower reveals its jewel inside. This jewel represents a love that would have been hidden for eternity if the seed had not been brave enough to make its journey through the darkness. It isn't always easy for the lotus to grow in its dark conditions, but nonetheless it does—and is beautiful.

After the meditation, we are told that the ideal meaning of love is found in the phrase "May you be happy, may you be well." Love simply wishes someone happiness and wellness—that's it, that's all—no hidden clauses or fine print, no expiry dates or restrictions applied. Love is pure and simple. Love doesn't say, "May you make me happy and well"—love is selfless, giving, and comes from a special home in our heart.

As a society, we are so used to thinking that someone's love for us completes us, but it doesn't—only we can complete ourselves. We think that love from another person is what is necessary to make us happy. We also unknowingly attach ourselves to someone who we feel happy around. We don't want to lose that feeling for fear of being not-whole again, and the attachment this fear causes puts a lot of strain on a relationship. Furthermore, we often idealize the way a person treats us at first through that glorious honeymoon phase and make no room in our head or heart for the natural evolution of the relationship. Sadly, we believe that any change in the relationship means a change in the love we have for one another.

No one completes us or is the key to our happiness. Pure happiness comes from accepting ourselves with all our faults and blunders, and in the ability to give love to another human without hidden resentment, ill feelings, or expectations. Love simply says "May you be happy, may you be well."

~ TORNADO WARNING IN EFFECT

I have had tornado dreams all my life, and they always feel so real. And I never used to understand why they were so frequent. Enter today's Save-My-Life Grad School topic: "The Importance of Distress Tolerance." Research brought me to the conclusion that my tornado dreams mean there is some type of chaos in my life, and they occur so frequently because chaos seems to *be* my life. Growing up, I didn't know how to process and heal from sad experiences through natural grief, which is probably true for a lot of kids. I didn't realize that emotional pain would be temporary and was necessary to experience in order to thoroughly heal. I ignored any chaotic pain and tried to hide from it because, well, pain is painful. This poor coping skill stayed with me throughout my life, and over time the burden of any loss built up and caused even more pain and suffering. Throughout my life the tornado just grew and grew—and in exponential proportions. What used to be an F1 as a child became an F5 by the time I was in my twenties.

When I was twenty, I took care of my mom after her aneurysm. I also was responsible for my one-year-old daughter and my five-year-old brother. I couldn't make time to grieve the loss of the mom I knew before her brain injury. When I was sent away pregnant, I was unable to take the time necessary to grieve the important relationships that were lost. I couldn't make time because things needed to get done, mouths needed to be fed, medical appointments needed to be made, homework needed to be completed, kids needed to be bathed, and bills needed to be paid—all while trying to take care of my mom who was battling side effects from her serious brain injury that included horrible paranoia. My life was a tornado, and I did not have any clue how to stop it—nor did I think I had time to.

I cried when I went to sleep at night (a lot). That was the extent of my emotional healing—and I never truly felt happy. I was stuck in a life I didn't necessarily want to be in, and I was only twenty years old. I responded to the life I was given the best I thought I could and tried to look away from the tornado. If I only knew what a mess it was leaving behind.

Eighteen more years of tornadoes inevitably brought me almost to my death. I did everything I could to ignore any distress in my life, including the distress certain calls at work caused me. I filled up many years with certificates, diplomas, and degrees, but never graduated from distress-tolerance kindergarten. I tried to avoid pain at all costs. I didn't know how to accept that pain is a natural part of life and that I could heal if I stopped avoiding it. Bitterness silently made me more mad year after year, loss after loss. Pain from original situations that were supposed to be temporary turned into long-term pain and suffering, and that became harder and harder to ignore. No wonder my tornado dreams were more frequent as I got older—my psyche was trying to tell me to open my eyes to the chaos in my heart and mind. "But who has time to deal with tornadoes anyway?" was my response less than a year ago. But now, after all the emotional work I've done, I feel like an emotional weather radar tracking system, tracking the smallest of storms—preparing for them, managing them as they come, and more importantly, staying away from tornado alley.

After my last overdose, with a lot of support and encouragement, I slowly came to ask myself, "When is enough, enough?" Yes, it hasn't always been a smooth transition from being a tornado chaser to a common citizen who carries around an umbrella just in case it rains.

Recovery doesn't come easily when the amount of destruction left behind seems impossible to repair, but I am slowly learning to be patient and wait for positive changes I've made to take root—like the seedlings planted after a storm. (The old impatient Natalie would go to Lowe's and purchase an expensive full-grown tree.) I haven't had a tornado dream since being home from Save-My-Life Boarding School. Maybe I've finally moved from Kansas.

~ GRATEFUL, SAFE SADNESS

It is six whole months since my last drink and six whole months since I was transported to the hospital almost dead (again). Six whole months since I saw no light in this world. Six whole months since I thought my family and friends would have been better off without me. It's been six whole months…that I have been healing.

Six months may seem like such a short period of time to you, but for me and my sobriety and health, it feels like an amazing lifetime. Going to Save-My-Life Boarding School was a blessing beyond my wildest dreams. Not only because it helped me with my PTSD, but because it exposed my alcoholism. Through 12-step programs and fellowship, I grew into a happy and healthier mom, woman, sister, daughter, and member of society. After balking at a program that I thought couldn't possibly be for me, I finally surrendered. Not only did I grow to heal my alcohol addiction, but I also made leaps and bounds in improving my mental health. Life is good—words that are becoming less foreign to me now. But this good life still takes hard work to maintain. I pray and meditate every day that I won't take advantage of any blessings a new day may bring. And I shake my head in awe as I type this, because six months ago the only thing I prayed for was for God to take me away.

~

My daughter and I go for an eight-hour drive for a university open house. We wake up early to make the long trek, chatting and singing songs as we drive. Miracles seem to be happening to me a lot (and maybe they were before, but I was just too sick to see them). As we drive into massive amounts of construction, a huge miracle happens right there in the car. Caroline looks at me and says, "Mom, you know that a year ago you couldn't have driven this far without your anxiety being so bad you would want to stop for wine." My heart skips a beat as I remember the exact day last year when I told her I couldn't take her to this exact university open house she had been looking forward to. My anxiety was too severe and my depression wouldn't even allow me to muster up the energy to brush my teeth, let alone drive for eight hours—only to stand in a crowd of noisy, pushy teenagers and parents. A year ago I remember sitting in my basement in the dark, feeling like the worst mother in the world because I couldn't take her. Looking at Caroline, I smile and say, "You're right."

I am suddenly mindful of the calmness I possess for the trip. I am aware of the absence of any craving to hurry up and find a restaurant with wine—or to hurry up and get home so I can drink my anxiety away for the night. I am simply at peace! The old Natalie would be cursing the construction and how sore my tailbone was from sitting so long. The old Natalie would have been so irritable and would have taken away all the excitement Caroline should have for the day. But the miracle doesn't stop there—Caroline tells me how she no longer wakes up and walks on eggshells until she can decipher my mood. She tells me I am just happy now—and patient. What a true moment of bliss. Hearing these words from my daughter's mouth makes my heart pour out joy! We are enjoying a day I never could have enjoyed before, and words simply cannot express the gratitude I feel at this moment.

Not all the miracles I experience involve smiles and happiness (which you would think all miracles would). After six months in recovery, I also experience what I call "grateful, safe sadness." What I mean by this is that I am trying to not be afraid of my emotions even if they are sad. Feeling *any* emotion is slowly starting to become second nature.

I'm working on Step 4 of my 12 steps, which involves a "searching and fearless moral inventory" of myself. As I move through my moral inventory and analyze my resentments, old and new, as well as my shortcomings and selfishness, reminders of memories of the old days flip my stomach over and make me very sad. My sponsor warns me that this type of emotional response is to be expected, so I allow myself to feel all the emotions the inventory brings forth.

When I get to reviewing recent relationship losses I've experienced, I cry and cry. I sob loud, sorrowful cries, which make me feel out of control and uncomfortable—feelings I would have most definitely numbed in the past. But now I choose not to numb them. In fact, I don't even think of it. I simply allow myself to feel, and when I finish crying (half a roll of toilet paper later), I feel fine. The tears don't make me feel depressed or anxious. I discover this sadness is a safe sadness. It's what healthy people feel. Sadness is a normal emotion, and feeling it doesn't hurt me. It actually helps me. After I finish crying, I jump in the shower and get ready for my 12-step meeting. Nothing in me wants to stay in my room and wallow in self-pity. Nothing in me wants to dissociate and hide for the rest of the night. I am OK, and I love it!

And if learning about grateful, safe sadness isn't enough of a blessing, while I am crying another miracle occurs. Caroline hears my sobs (as most of the city probably does), so she comes in to hug me. But after she gives me a good solid hug, she leaves the room and goes about her day. When I tell her I am just "normal sad" and not depressed, she believes me right away. She trusts me. She doesn't need to worry about finding me unconscious on the floor in an hour.

She is just a healthy girl, seeing her healthy mom have a good cry. Pretty amazing, if you ask me.

Now don't worry that I might be in over my head with this enormous quantity of positive change. While I write and reflect about what has changed for the better in my life over the past six months, humility still races through my veins. I know that one bad choice can still lead me back to the darkness. I know that my recovery will always be a work in progress. But once in a while, it's nice to share the good experiences—to show there is always hope. My 12-step book tells me, "I was in a hopeless state of mind and body," but I'm happy to say that all the work I am putting into my recovery is actually paying off. Remember when I said that I always wondered how someone I saw walking down the street even on a beautiful day could be happy? Well, I don't think that anymore. Now I think, "How could they be sad?"

~ CULTIVATING POSITIVITY HABITS

As weird as this may sound, it's not always easy for me to talk about happiness. When I do, I feel as if I am a fraud. After all, who am I to share about happiness when I've only *just* started to experience it? But I know it's only my mind telling me that it's not a topic I have enough knowledge of to be able to share. I suppose it's realistic to think that there may be a lingering demon in my mind whispering, "How dare you suggest how anyone else can become happy?" But I sure am willing to kick the demon's ass (again) and remind myself that I'm a pretty awesome testament to how it's possible for anyone to achieve genuine happiness—and why wouldn't I want to share that? While my collection of writings are primarily filled with documents describing my darkness and pain, now that I don't experience that dark world quite as often, I can't help but share how this rookie happiness-experiencer experiences happiness.

I have become quite educated in the science of addiction. I have been taught that my drinking became a habit and that (a) I perceived value in it, (b) I criticized myself for doing it, and (c) I was persistent regardless of the outcomes. My addiction was so strong that I had to be hospitalized and go to a treatment centre to basically reprogram my mind. Over the course of my entire lifetime, my mind was made up of negative habits so ingrained, I could not see a way of changing them on my own. I constantly wondered how I, of all people, could ever be truly happy when even all the love in the world from my family and friends couldn't change me. I always thought that if I ever did learn how to experience happiness, I would never let it go! I would do just as much work to keep my smile as it took to find it.

I had little belief that anyone could change my negative habits. I was deeply convinced that I knew best and that there was no way to teach me how to be happy! Luckily, I eventually saw how much of a stranger I was to myself. I learned to surrender and chose to accept the lessons that taught me how to be aware of my actions. And when I did that, hopelessness turned into joy, and fear turned into love.

Old habits are hard to break, but here's the exciting news: through my recovery studies I have learned that I can quite possibly now practise positive habits and have a positive addiction—an addiction to love and happiness. Yes, you may be saying, "Whoa, Natalie, you should stay away from all addictions." Hear me out.

I can make happiness a habit if (a) I perceive value in it, (b) I don't criticize myself for it, and (c) I can be proud of myself regardless of the outcome.

My alcoholism produced negative habits, which inadvertently tested me and taught me many lessons. There is no need to learn from pain, though! We often end up hiding from our painful lessons anyhow, making them a blur at best. So why not implement positivity habits into our lives and see what lessons we can learn from them? When we learn from joyous experiences, those lessons often remain clear in our mind, making recollection of them not such a tedious task.

When circumstances become unbearable, we are motivated to change, but why wait until that moment? From experience, I think that many people sleepwalk through life. We are rarely mindful of the occasions when we could choose positivity over anger or fear. If we wake up, we could make positivity the best habit we ever had! Practising this doesn't have to be difficult, but recognizing the opportunities can be easily lost in our dream-filled day. In order to find opportunities to practise, we must be mindful of our day. An example would be to notice when we feel frustrated or annoyed and try to see the lesson that the particular emotion is teaching us, then let it float away. Don't hold onto it, even if you think it's just a minor negative emotion. I once read that annoyance is a veil drawn over fury—and I agree. We tend to lessen or ignore negative emotions as they come our way (because they suck) rather than mindfully recognizing them and moving through them with positive thoughts and actions. If you're like me, you will have many opportunities to practise being aware of negative emotions every day. And I'm happy to say that even through my rookie experience, using positivity habits has become, well, quite a habit already—making my negative emotions now few and far between. (Even in a Costco parking lot!)

Practising positivity habits increases our positive energy in general. And the more we feel good, the more we crave that feeling and inadvertently share it with the world.

We were all born to add value to the world—every single one of us. And positivity habits can be one of the best values we can share. Cultivating happiness doesn't happen overnight. Just like a seed in the garden, it takes time to grow. But that seed knows to grow by habit. Try nurturing that seed today, and I promise it will positively grow into something beautiful!

~ CONTENT AND COMFY

Currently I find myself at a fork in the road, with a "very important decision" being the destination. I have just over a month to accept my master's offer from the University of British Columbia, and I don't know if I'm ready to undertake this commitment yet. As many of you may know, this is usually not a difficult decision for me. Normally if I hear "education opportunity" I say, "Sign me up!" before I can blink. But this time around feels different. Now that I am enjoying my life and health, I am wary about adding anything extra to my plate. I am now able to see that while I do love education, many of my expensive pieces of paper were obtained as a form of numbing myself from the real world. It was easy for me to get lost in a research paper rather than address my crumbling mental health and family life. So here I sit, with a "yes or no" email defining a significant part of what the next four years of my life will look like, and I'm personally shocked at which road I'm leaning towards going down.

My sponsor recently told me a story that struck such a huge chord with me. She told me how, before her recovery, she was always a person who needed to make it to every sale advertised. She felt that if she missed that one opportunity to get that awesome "thing" (let's use shoes for this analogy), she would miss out on having them forever. But as she grew and explored this personality trait, she came to learn that there will always be another sale.

I find this profound—and true! I immediately associate this idea with my fear of not accepting the master's program now. What would that make me if I missed this "sale"? What version of Natalie would I be without buying (a.k.a. accepting the offer) the fancy shoes (that I can't afford) tomorrow? Sure, the shoes would look great, but would they give me blisters and make me hate every step I take? Or would they be super comfy and put a spring in my step? Yes, I know I can't have an answer unless I buy them and try them on. But do I absolutely need new shoes right now? The ones I'm wearing are the best ones I've ever had! I'm not so sure I'm ready to trade them in.

Just like there will always be a sale, there will always be time for me to complete a master's degree. And for now, I'm more comfortable continuing the "life education" I am already enrolled in.

~ HAPPINESS AND POSSIBILITY

Happiness to many is a very simple emotion to grasp. You want it. It feels good. You get it, right? Well, it's not that way for everyone. Crazy as this may sound, happiness can also be a very scary emotion for some people. But why? Why is it easier for many of us to stay content with emotions that block happiness? Why are we often more comfortable having emotions like anger sewn into the fabric of our personalities? It certainly doesn't feel good to be angry. But at the end of the day, when it's all we've ever worn, it feels... comfortable.

I think many people are afraid of things that feel different—even if that "thing" is supposed to feel good. I bring up this topic because at times I notice when I am not mindful, happiness seems to hide in a corner. After all the healing I've done, I sometimes find myself subconsciously content with an undertone of anger in my gut. It's like an old friend who shows up unexpectedly, convincing me that I should let them in. I'm comfortable with that friend—we've known each other for a very long time. So, I sit all cuddled-up with my friend "anger," and let it slowly convince me that my dreams are impossible to fulfill or that I don't deserve to be happy. It can convince me that happiness just isn't my forte. In fact, lots of negative emotions convince me that answered prayers or granted wishes only lead to responsibility, and who wants that?

Equally scary to some people is the concept of possibility. Many of us don't like not knowing where possibilities may lead. In fact, we often lock possibility's proverbial open door before we even take a look outside. We shy away from a road that may lead to fulfilled dreams because the road is so unfamiliar. When the saying "the possibilities are endless!" falls upon the ears of a happy person it's like, well...music. But when those four words land on angry ears, the promise of anything endless can be far too intimidating.

If your dreams were scheduled to come true tomorrow, would you say you're ready for that? Or when the time came to act upon your dreams, would you rather retract them for fear of the unknown? Finish this sentence; I'm afraid that if I start dreaming...What is your answer? And if you do have this fear, how can you overcome it? I personally think that a lot of fear of happiness and possibilities comes from the fact that in order to truly appreciate them, you have to allow yourself to be vulnerable. Take the happiness of love, for example. It takes courage to learn how to love. The emotional stakes are high when the possibilities of the heart are exposed. When we are in love, it's like our hearts are beating behind a cellophane wall—so easy to see and so easy to break. Therefore, rather than possibly experiencing the magical happiness that only love can provide, we hide behind our armour of anger, which in turn protects our hearts from damage.

Will I always have a difficult time not welcoming my old friend, anger, in? I hope not, but if there is one thing I do know, it's that this girl is ready for her happiness. I'm good with making vulnerability my new friend and seeing where the possibilities of this journey continue to take me.

~ SELFISH OR SELF-CARE?

Selfish—it's a word that has evoked so many emotions in my life; emotions such as anger, sadness, guilt, shame, and most often confusion. I was told I was selfish a lot as a kid. Depending on the day and the mood of the house, I was told I was selfish when I wanted to show my achievements in school such as my report card. I was told I was selfish when I needed a break from all the responsibilities in my life. I was often told I was selfish whenever I wanted to better myself—and I didn't understand why. This confusing emotion kept me questioning my own personal-growth motives for years. If I was told I was selfish for so long, I must be, right?

While moving through the 12 steps, I have come to realize how much my misconception of the word selfish has affected me. Deep down I knew that the word should be linked to a negative action and *not* to taking care of myself. But because my feelings surrounding this word were so volatile and confusing, I moved through life on my tippytoes, careful not to be selfish in anyone's eyes ever again. I learned through trial and error who I could share my accomplishments with and who would be proud of me. For example, I learned months after I "lost" my college report card that my brother Ross had it in his wallet all along; he had been showing it to his friends because he was so proud of me. I learned that my colleagues were genuinely happy with my career advancements and didn't see me as selfish at all. I learned that my kids were proud of me when I walked across the stage and accepted my advanced care paramedic diploma and when they both helped me press "enter" to send the last research paper I had written to the university in order to obtain my BHSc degree. But all these examples of happiness in my achievements still couldn't erase my misconception of the word selfish. In fact, any personal accomplishment left me feeling that "selfish" just masqueraded as pride.

The shame-based messages I received growing up also affected my ability to set healthy boundaries. I would often go with the flow and not voice my personal opinion for fear it would appear selfish or hurt someone's feelings. In a crowd, I never rocked the boat. I wanted to be honest and direct with people, but outside of work the line between selfishness and self-care was as clear as a puddle of mud. I had confidence in my skills at work and knew my role and responsibilities well, so I rarely had a problem saying what I needed there.

But in my personal life, if someone seemed to be helping me, regardless of whether I wanted that help or not, I went with it because I was too afraid that they would leave or that I would appear selfish if I questioned any of their motives.

Through this amazing journey, I have come to learn the importance of self-care and its vast difference from selfishness. Doing what is best for me, regardless of anyone else's opinion is what I should do! Who knew?! I don't need to justify my choices to anyone, and I definitely don't need to feel selfish for developing healthy boundaries I need for my recovery. I'm so grateful for every time my sponsor corrected me when I thought a resentment I had stemmed from some root of my selfishness. She taught me that what I was in fact finally doing was self-care—and she also reminded me how far I've come with this!

I'm a different person than I was six months ago. And this new person deserves every ounce of love and self-care I can receive. My greatest accomplishment has been my recovery. And as you can see, I don't tippytoe around that. I've been shouting out my accomplishments through my writing and will continue to do so for who knows how long.

It's not to say that I never received the encouragement or praise a child needs while growing up. Just like most parents, mine did the very best they could with the tools they had. Love was there, but there was also struggle and words that were mindlessly spoken. I am guilty of the same. But moving forward, I am all too happy to express my knowledge of the difference between selfishness and self-care in hope that someone out there afraid to set healthy boundaries may do so and feel the freedom of smiling whenever they want to.

~ THE POWER OF IMAGINATION

When I was young, the things I imagined appeared so real to me that I was often convinced they were my reality. I remember having such powerful daydreams of becoming a superhero who could fly and throw fireballs. Admit it, you imagined you were a super-hero too! It felt so real that I thought it would make perfect sense to attach myself to a helicopter and throw toys I had wrapped up in red construction paper at kids who bullied me. Then they would be in awe of my super powers! I also thought it made perfect sense to plan my marriage to Donnie Wahlberg from New Kids on the Block. (Insert eye roll.) I think it's fair to say my imagination had a broad spectrum.

But what has happened to that imagination I used as a child? Why is it that as we get older we often find it difficult to use the power of our imagination to the same level we did back then? Sure, busy days and busy lives may seem to only allow for daydreams at best, which include thoughts of how to get the kids to soccer, how to pay a bill, or how to plan for our retirement. And yes, these things need to be thought about. But why in our adult lives have we forgotten to use our imagination to truly inhabit the dreams and aspirations we have? Other cultures do it all the time. I would like to propose that we try to take back and use the power of our imaginations.

Yes, being a superhero who hangs from helicopters and throws fireballs isn't on the top of my to-do list anymore! But without genuine faith in my ability to succeed (a.k.a. use of my positive imagination), I am very capable of thinking that I can't be successful, that I can't attain a certain goal, and that I can't possibly be happy.

My Buddhist teacher has reminded me that when we use our imagination, we allow ourselves to go somewhere else at that very moment. You can experience your dreams through imagination. Every single human-made thing on this planet originated in our imaginations. If you can think it, you can do it! If you have an aspiration to be something, imagining your success in attaining that goal is so very important. Olympians deeply imagine what it would feel like to cross the finish line and win the gold medal in order to believe they can do so. Inventors deeply imagine their invention being used for its purpose in order to truly believe they can build it. Our imagination is the passageway to all possibility.

Now you may be asking yourselves, "When do I do this 'imagining,' Natalie?" My answer is, try to fall asleep imagining your positive goal instead of the busy day ahead of you. But just like meditation, this takes practice. Our busy minds are crammed full of stuff, and calming the storm long enough to imagine something positive may take a bit of getting used to. But make it part of your nightly routine and it will become just that—routine!

You may also be asking, "Isn't imagining a waste of time?" I can speak from experience that imagining happiness and the attainment of goals is not a waste of time. When I was sick, I actually found it silly to allow myself to imagine being happy. And by not even trying, I just became more angry and numb every day. Now I love the peacefulness I feel when I let my imagination guide me and my future goals. I also use this idea to keep my motives in check. If it feels right when I imagine myself following through with a certain task, I know I am on the right path. Furthermore, rather than embarking blindly on a life mission, imagining the mission can help me sort through the possible hurdles and begin to feel the rewards as I travel down that road.

So dust off that imagination cap and stop thinking that it makes you look silly. Use your dreams to calm your mind and see what possibilities arise. True, my imagination has matured, and I know that I won't be marrying Donnie Wahlberg or turning into a superhero— but through imagination, I sure do feel like I can fly!

~ THE WORLD ACCORDING TO MY DOG, WALTER

I bet that anyone who has kids has probably heard the following not-so-compelling argument:

Kid(s): "Can I *please* get a puppy! I promise I'll walk it and feed it and take care of it! *Please, please, please!*"

Parent(s): "No you won't. You will love it for a week and then I will be the one walking, feeding and taking care of it. No way. Not gonna happen. I will buy you a goldfish!"

Kid(s): "But *every* kid has a puppy! Goldfish are dumb!"

Parent(s): "Not *every* kid has one, and goldfish are lovely!"

Kid(s): "You can ground me forever if I don't take care of it! You can even take away my allowance!" …And then the clincher,

Kid(s): "You'll be the best mom/dad *ever*!

Then, at some point the begging wins out and you suddenly become the proud owner of a furry creature who pees in your house; chews your favourite boots; and eats dryer sheets, Nerf-gun bullets, roast string, and your underwear!

Well, that's my experience anyway. *Sigh*. Allow me to introduce you to Walter.

Of course everything I predicted came true. I walk, feed and take care of Walter ninety-eight percent of the time. I told ya, moms know these things. But what I didn't predict was that I would fall in love with him. This little creature has changed my life. He's my care-free shadow wherever I go. He follows me around the house, sleeps next to me, insists on laying on the bathroom floor whenever I am in there, and wakes me up every morning. We have a bond I never thought was possible. A loving, generous person once called him my therapy dog—and that he is!

~

The other day we (Walter and I) were cleaning the house and chatting about how, if he wasn't here, I wouldn't be chatting at all. Yes, I talk to my dog all the time. He keeps me company 24/7 and makes me laugh as I chase him when he attempts to eat things like granola bar wrappers and old, mouldy leaves. I can't help but think about how much he keeps me out of my bed and active as well. I understand his language, and miraculously, he understands mine. We just get each other, and I don't know what I would do without him—bad dog-breath and all!

He gets me out of myself and forces me to interact with the world. When we walk or go to the dog park, I find it easy to socialize with other dog owners because we have a common love. It's impossible not to smile when you see your dog happy and playing with other dogs. Furthermore, watching Walter run faster after a ball than any other dog at the park makes me a pretty proud dog mama! And the icing on the cake is watching those eyebrows blowing in the wind when he sticks his head out the car window—it induces laughter immediately! I'm even smiling right now writing about it.

Not only has Walter taught me so much about unconditional love, but our walks together have taught me to see things about the world itself that I never would have seen otherwise. While journeying around the neighbourhood, I have learned that lilac trees smell just as wonderful when they are wilting. That falling maple-tree helicopter seeds look just like snow when a big enough gust of wind blows. That crystal-clear nights sound as quiet as the sky looks. That rain puddles are super fun to splash in no matter how old you are. That fresh snow falling under the streetlights is as peaceful as a cool lake on a hot summer's day. That the smell of barbecued hamburgers and the sound of the ice-cream truck in the distance will never get old, and that no matter how hard Walter tries, he will never outrun a squirrel.

Being a depression survivor, I find it immensely comforting knowing that Walter knows when I'm sad. He can sense it. Even if I'm not crying, he will sit on my chest and kiss my face. And if I am crying, he lays his head on my leg and looks up at me as if to say, "You will be OK." He's a precious little creature who has helped me heal through many heartbroken, dark days. In fact, he's my best friend.

If I could write Walter a letter, this is what it would say:

Dear Walter,

If you only knew how much you have changed my life for the better. Your big brown eyes overflow with so much love, and I couldn't imagine not having you wake me up every morning. Thank you for the snuggles and laughs you give me every day, and for the bugs you eat in the house.

Sidebar: we have a king-sized bed, so it would be nice from time to time if you could give me some room to sleep, but I thank you for at least keeping your bones on the other side. I'm sorry that I've made you prone to begging because I share everything I eat with you, but your dog food looks super boring! I can't help but think that you love enjoying good food too. However, you do eat cat poo, so I'm fairly certain that we have exceptionally different taste buds. Thank you for letting me blame my farts on you and welcoming me home in the same enthusiastic like-you-haven't-seen-me-in-months way every time.

I know you miss your dad; I do too—very much. But he gave you to me because he knew without a doubt that you would continue to save my life. Just like you show me unconditional love, the gift of you is one of the greatest acts of unconditional love I have ever known! And if your dad reads this one day, he can see how much you have helped me to heal and grow and enjoy this amazing life.

You are the perfect dog for me, and I love you more than any super-expensive bone could say!

Please stop eating my underwear and bras. Love you so VERY MUCH FOREVER.

Natalie XO

~ SPARKLE PARTY

In my drinking days, I used to have what I called a "Sparkle Party" around Christmas. It was a night where people could come over wearing something sparkly (just because it's fun) and enjoy an evening of laughs—and a lot of alcohol! This year was the first time I didn't host one, and that makes me really sad. But no need for tears because last night I unexpectedly attended the biggest and best sparkle party I could ever imagine. I am fortunate to have been invited to Save-My-Life Boarding School's Twenty-Fifth Annual Spiritual Renewal Service, which is an event celebrating the gift of recovery. There are 400 pairs of healthy, sparkling eyes filled with hope, happiness, and gratitude who attend. Allow me to share my experience...

I haven't been back to Save-My-Life Boarding School since I was discharged six months ago, and I am very nervous about the emotions I am confident will bubble up throughout the night. *Buckle up, Natalie. This may be a bumpy ride!* As I sit in the car on the way there, my first emotion is good ol' anxiety. It isn't anything over the top, but I can definitely feel it rumbling through my whole body. Luckily, I am with two friends whose chatting distracts me from the anxiety and allows me to quietly reflect on what it feels like to drive the route to Save-My-Life Boarding School again, but healthy this time. I start to regret that I agreed to attend the event. Because I am now mindful of my emotions (insert sarcasm), I am pretty much guaranteed to have a lengthy self-analysis night. *Sigh.* Nevertheless, I tell myself that I will survive. I am going to kick my anxiety's butt, like the anxiety pro I am, and soak in every moment of the evening.

When we pull up to the treatment centre, my anxiety lessens and begins to mix with excitement as memories of the life-changing times that I experienced come rushing back—vividly. I feel as though I have suddenly jumped back on the emotional roller coaster of my seven-week stay—the one that scared me, twisted me in so many directions, made me sick, and made me cry. However, that same roller coaster also made me laugh and experience relief when the ride was finally over. I have no desire to ride that roller coaster again, but here I stand with another ticket for the ride and my proverbial vomit bag held tightly in hand. For a moment I wish this ride was out of order.

Save-My-Life Boarding School is beautifully decorated and displays obvious months of preparation. We are all given a pin that says "Recovery Means Freedom." As I examine it, I immediately bump into my first wonderful staff member. She tells me I look great, and I accept the compliment. She asks about my family and how we are doing. My family! *OK, hold on tight, Natalie, the roller coaster is clicking up the hill!* I tell her we are all doing great, and immediately I recognize my old friends "guilt" and "shame" as they flood my body. Rather than feeling gratitude, I feel sick as the memories of what I've put my family through are at the forefront of my mind—and they sting really bad. I know I should only be feeling happiness when speaking about my family now, but it quickly becomes apparent to me that guilt-ridden Natalie is still alive and kicking. Damn it. I take a quick bathroom break and try to tuck any negative emotions into my back pocket to deal with later. Then, one foot in front of the other, I continue to mingle among staff and friends, with what I'm sure is a timid look on my face.

Since leaving Save-My-Life Boarding School, I have had many people tell me that I have a sparkle in my eyes, and you know what, I can confidently say that I probably do with the amount of happiness and love I feel for life now. Being at the event tonight, I see firsthand what that sparkle looks like because I see it in so many of my friends' eyes. It is truly amazing. Positive physical transformations make my jaw drop, and their happy eyes make me smile from my soul! I can barely recognize some people, but that sparkle is impossible to miss. What a blessing it is to see this.

The night is filled with speeches of gratitude and wellness. At one point, we do what's called a "recovery countdown." A year, month, or day is called out, and people stand up and receive a round of applause when their correlating recovery day is announced. As the days of recovery get shorter and shorter, "three weeks," "two weeks," "one week," I can see the sparkle is not so prevalent in people's eyes. And as they continued to count, I can also increasingly see the physical demons of addiction that are still tightly grasping onto so many newcomers' lives. All I can think is, "WOW! That was me only six months ago!" I was the one who felt and looked hopeless and scared. I was the one who simply existed and nothing more. I was the one who had so much doubt in the program or any chance of living a happy life. And I was the one who still so desperately wanted to die because I saw death as the only way to end my suffering.

As a very sick lady who is only five days into her recovery is assisted onto the stage to receive her round of applause, I physically react to seeing her pain. I can clearly remember how every step felt like a mile in early recovery. I imagine how difficult it most likely is for her to even stay awake—as it was for me. I can imagine the shakes she probably battles, and the memory fog that probably makes it difficult for her to speak properly. And I imagine the darkness I can guarantee fills her entire body and soul—and the hopelessness she feels with every...single...breath. I want to tell her that her sparkle will one day return. But she will have to learn that for herself.

Who knew that I would be attending a sparkle party again?! Certainly not me. And who knew that I didn't need a fancy dress to have that sparkle radiating from me? Once again, certainly not me! I know that some days my sparkle won't be as bright as other days, but what a gift to know that it's there.

"I put my hand in yours and together we can do what we never could do alone. No longer is there a sense of hopelessness. No longer must we depend upon our own unsteady willpower. We are all together now, reaching out our hands for power and strength greater than ours, and as we join hands, we find love and understanding beyond our wildest dreams."

~ Closing Prayer

Happy sparkling!

~ APPRECIATION FOR LIFE

Through my personal journey as a paramedic, I have witnessed the unquestionable nearness of death and the hidden expansiveness of life. I've travelled through destitute darkness only to find the most radiantly beautiful light. I've trembled at evil and have rejoiced at true happiness. Simply put, throughout my career I have journeyed through the spectrum of life and death, touching each end, and am privileged to be able to share what I have learned along the way.

Knowledge of this "life-and-death spectrum" is obviously not reserved for just me. Throughout first responders' careers, they experience this spectrum on such a massive scale! I hear people say that first responders become *less* sensitive to the death end of this spectrum in order to last in their careers. But I worry that over the years, many first responder's sensitivity to the *life* end of the spectrum also lessens.

So how can first responders stay healthy among the tears we witness over the duration of our careers? When death is bound to stare us straight in the eyes more times than we can count, how can we continue helping people while maintaining our own healthy mind and body? My answer to this question is delivered to me through an enlightening conversation I have with my good friend Rob Theriault, and it's as simple, yet as profoundly complex, as this—continue to mindfully appreciate life. This rings so true with me. By remembering to also focus on the precious moments of life we experience as first responders, the spectrum of life and death balances out.

First responders impact the human race so profoundly! We are the last set of eyes many people look into. We offer the last hand many people hold. We leave the last encouraging voice they may hear and the last breath they will share with another human being. We are blessed with the privilege of being present for the "lasts" of their lives, and in these moments—rather than focusing on the inevitable death we know we are about to witness and very often can't control—we as first responders may be able to carry out longer, healthier, more fulfilling careers if we focus on our patients' joys of life as well.

Is this easier said than done? Most likely. And to be fair, many first responders may do this already. But for those who don't, I ask you to remember for a moment a time when you got to witness and experience the beauty of life amid inevitable death. When was there a time that you stood back after a call and felt like you had made such a difference in a patient's life? Or maybe in their family's life? What are the calls that changed your life for the better? When did you see a rainbow in the sky after the storm? When did you witness a thank you through a last breath? What is your paramedic life story? Well, allow me to share Rob's:

On one of my first shifts on the air ambulance helicopter in the 1980s, we flew up north to pick up an elderly male from a small hospital. He was involved in a house fire earlier in the morning and had sustained third- and fourth-degree burns to over eighty percent of his body. I was new to the air ambulance, and this was my first truly critically burned patient. I knew from the extent of his injury that he was dying and would likely die before the end of the day, or within the next couple of days. Did he know he was dying? I wondered. He was conscious and relatively pain free because the nerve endings are destroyed with deep burns. But he couldn't speak because he had a tube in his airway, and we had him connected to a ventilator. By the time we loaded him into the helicopter, the sun was just on the edge of the early morning horizon. Our helicopter, a Bell 212, was noisy and shook in flight. From the look in his eyes, I could see he was anxious. As we lifted off, I placed a headset over his ears so that I could tell him what was going on during the flight and try to give him some reassurances. He couldn't reply, but he would blink his eyes in acknowledgement. My partner was busy retaking vital signs, and I was monitoring his breathing and oxygen saturation. We flew just a hundred feet above the tree tops and when I could, I looked out the side window to see glistening lakes, tall trees, hills, and the rising sun. It was truly beautiful. The patient was lying on his back, and I told him that if he turned his head to the right, he could see out of the helicopter. He turned and stared for the next twenty minutes. I looked at him, a man who would inevitably die, and I looked at the rising sun—light illuminating some areas while others were cast in shades and shadows. It was breathtaking, and the contrast between this poor dying man and the sunrise ushering in a new day left an indelible memory.

The contrast between life's endings and new beginnings, the resilience and fragility of the human body, would be a part of my experience for many years to come. It's part of every paramedic's experience. We see things that are unimaginable for most. In an odd way, I am happy others don't see what we see. Their innocence makes me happy. I feel it's my duty to deal with life and death so others can be spared.

Years later when I was working back on the land ambulance, I recall a cold Sunday winter morning when we responded to a "jumper." He had jumped off a bridge and was lying on the frozen ground below. Resuscitation was futile, and when we left the scene, the image of his traumatized body lingered in my mind. Less than ten minutes later we stopped at a café. It might seem odd to stop at a public café for a coffee after just witnessing a death, but the job goes on. I went inside and as I waited for my coffee, I looked around to see customers sitting quietly, some conversing while others read the news or a book. They looked calm and peaceful. I took pleasure in the serene looks on their relaxed weekend faces. I smiled for them. I was genuinely happy for them. The contrast between the image of a dead body and the Sunday morning café reminded me of why I do what I do.

Rob Theriault has been a paramedic for thirty-one years and a professor for thirteen years. I am so grateful Rob shared his stories with me. They have the ability to take me out of what is left of my PTSD mind. They make me smile and remember some of my own beautiful life stories. In order to have a long and healthy career, maybe first responders don't have to become less sensitive to death; they just need to focus more on the beauty of life.

~ 12-STEP SPEAKER

I am asked to be the speaker at my dear friend's one-year recovery celebration. It's sort of a big deal. Being that I only have ten months of recovery, I am surprised when she asks me, but of course I excitedly said yes!

Like I have mentioned before, 12-step meetings are not what most people imagine. Movies and television portray their environment as glum and dreary. They make it seem like we don't want to be there and we are all unemployed and depressed. Now to be fair, there are some unemployed and depressed people who attend meetings, but there are unemployed, depressed people everywhere. Painting every 12-step member with that paintbrush is simply not even close to realistic. After following the steps and embracing the promises the program has to offer, we don't white-knuckle our way through a sad recovery life like many people may think. In fact many of us, if not most, enjoy happy and fulfilling lives without obsessing about our vices at all—lives that we never believed were possible! At Save-My-Life Boarding School I could have saved myself a whole lot of grief if I had clued in earlier to the fact that these 12-step programs actually work. Since then, I have learned that there are over 300 types of these programs around the world, addressing more addictions and emotional illnesses than you can imagine! Too bad that learning the hard way and I were BFFs back then. (Insert what-was-I-thinking head shake.)

What a night it is! I take the podium and am blessed to see a hundred sets of smiling eyes staring back at me. I didn't plan my speech, instead I decided to speak from my heart and allow the words to come to me naturally. I start to talk, and over the next thirty minutes I am able to share the story of my alcoholic childhood and the battles I conquered while being a teenage single mom. I share my love of being a paramedic and how sadly a double-murder call that I attended in 2012 caused me to develop PTSD. I talk of how mental illness and my disease of alcoholism wreaked havoc on my family and friends—and how I ended up with limited access to my son. I share with the audience that less than a year ago after multiple overdoses, my family had seriously discussed my funeral arrangements and planned what to do *when* I was gone...not *if*.

The purpose of being a speaker at a 12-step meeting isn't to glorify the bad that happened in our lives. On the contrary! It's by sharing our journey that we can take pride in the magnitude of our recovery and, even more importantly, hopefully inspire others to continue with theirs. Being a speaker doesn't involve puffing out your chest and showing how your struggle is worse than anyone else's. It goes without saying that each participant in the room has fought the fight of their life while suffocating under the darkness of their disease.

As a speaker, the main purpose of sharing life stories is to show that through the darkness there is light! And as a speaker it is my honour to shout from the depths of my heart that a happy life in recovery is possible! I share how waking up in the morning is a gift and how the feelings surrounding my heinous obsession with suicide are difficult to even remember now. I also talk about how I live my life mindfully with my higher power, God, leading the way. And how even though at times I still have nightmares, I know that my conscious wakefulness will be filled with new-found patience, peace, and love. In short, I share with so many surviving souls that their strength and perseverance is worth it and that hope and love are what will launch them into the fourth dimension of recovery. In short, I share what it is like to be free.

I am so happy that I don't need to hold a glass of wine up high to toast my success anymore. On this very special night, I am given the gift to celebrate my success by holding my head up high instead.

~ IS IT POSSIBLE TO VIEW TRAUMA IN A HEALTHIER WAY?

All feelings are universal, therefore no one (except a sociopath) is exempt from being hurt at some point in their lives. Trauma, abandonment, heartbreak, natural disasters, accidents, deaths (the list is endless) are all sources of terribly harrowing, seemingly unrecoverable events that cause us an unending cycle of torment. This torment can be so extreme that we may even turn to destructive choices, such as drugs and alcohol, to numb the pain they cause— but that numbness doesn't last forever (trust me), and we eventually experience the pain again—and sometimes we experience it even worse than before.

Our lives are often filled with so much agitation and angst. Whether we realize it or not, trauma can continue to harm us due to the negative outlook on life that it creates, causing us to stifle our healthy choices even years after the traumatic event(s) occurred. What can we do with these traumatic thoughts in order to live in peace, and is that even possible? No one wants to live with the resentment and anger these events cause us. In essence, they keep traumatizing us and make us very ill. If there was a way you could change your view of these traumatic events, would you consider trying it?

The mindfulness technique I want to share with you now is called "reframing." No, this doesn't mean literally reframing the pictures in your home, but it does mean reframing the pictures in your mind. This technique is based on accepting the premise that we can create (and therefore change) our emotions. We can be happy despite how much pain our past has caused us. Reframing moves us away from judging our experiences (without losing their reality) and changing the negative energy surrounding them to positive. By putting a new view or "frame" on our experiences, we change the way we see them. It involves giving yourself permission to take off the frame that other people (or an event) put on your memory and finally choose your own frame! It's like a redecorating of sorts—but of your life. We can't throw out our family trees or turn back the hands of time to avoid a trauma (even though God knows many of us try to), but we can choose to see our pasts through a different, more peaceful perspective.

Personally, I've had a lot of success with reframing when it comes to my painful childhood memories. When my mom sent me away against my will to a home for unwed mothers when I was eighteen, this experience caused me to carry anger, resentment, and guilt for the next twenty years of my life. And for those entire twenty years, my only means of recovery from this trauma was to numb the pain with alcohol, speak badly of my mother, and convince myself that I would be OK as long as I stayed mad at her. I thought that my anger would prove that I would never accept what she did to me; my daughter and her father; and my siblings. HA! That would teach her, right? Wrong. Sadly, an apology from her about ten years back didn't change the frame attached tightly around this traumatic event.

The shame-based messages I received growing up also affected my ability to set healthy boundaries. .

Through the lesson of reframing, I was eventually able to see my mother's choice to send me away differently. My new frame included truly understanding that my mom was doing the best she could at that time. It involved my acceptance that she was probably sick too. The lies she told became her truth—and yes they hurt me and so many other people deeply—but my frame comprehends that I will never be able to understand what was in her head or why she thought her actions were just. Scrutinizing them would only prolong my pain.

Some of you may be yelling at these words because you may be misinterpreting reframing as acceptance of her actions. But reframing couldn't be any different from that! I do not accept the pain and tears I witnessed my daughter experience when she didn't hear from her dad on her birthdays or any other holidays. I do not accept the pain Caroline's father and family experienced because we were removed from their lives. I do not accept lies. I do not accept manipulation. But in order for me to heal and grow in a peaceful way, I *do* accept giving myself permission to forgive and to understand that I am not my mom—I am not her choices. This new frame is much more beautiful! This new frame gives me peace. Yes, this new frame still allows me to see this traumatic experience as a part of my past, but more importantly, this new frame no longer allows it to be a detriment to my future.

Just like redecorating your home takes time and patience, so does redecorating your memories. My advice is to work on one room at a time. It will take some courage to dust off the ugly old photos you've been hiding in a drawer. But when you choose to, and after your tears have washed the dust away, put your new frame around them and place them wherever you see fit.

~ WHAT IS HANGING OVER MY HEAD?

During my most excruciating moments at Save-My-Life Boarding School, a certain nurse would always calmly tell me, "This too shall pass." She would say it when I was curled up in a ball on the floor when I knew my relationship with Leo was over. She would say it when I missed my kids and cried so hard that I couldn't breathe. She would say it when I shared my disappointment that I came back early on Christmas because I didn't feel safe being at home alone. She would say the words, and somehow they made sense—but in that moment they never took the pain away.

I am not feeling good today. I'm hovering between Layer 1 and Layer 2 of my depression, and I am hoping it will pass. I have a lot on my mind. I feel like big decisions need to be made soon—they are hanging over my head. Do I go back to work as a paramedic? Will that be healthy for me? I'm a lot more sensitive to little things these past few days. I feel like I'm putting up walls to protect myself from... something. But I don't actually know from what. Does that make sense? Maybe it's because the summer's nearing its end and the cold of winter is getting closer. Maybe it's a lot of things.

This too shall pass—but where will this uncomfortable feeling lead? A level of discomfort in life is still reasonable I suppose. I am human, even though I don't feel like it some days. I need to do some soul-searching. I need to listen to every gut instinct I have to try to decipher why I am building walls again. I need to continue to trust that the right path is in front of me and that the directions are visible if I keep my eyes on the road.

OK life, where are you taking me now? Why do I feel like my recovery is being tested? Why are certain things happening to me lately?

Leo has moved on, and rightly so—he deserves happiness. Why am I having such a hard time dealing with it? He has a new girlfriend and she is pregnant—and I just learned they live close by. What is life preparing me for? What is life strengthening in me? And why?

Please no nightmares tonight! I can't take them anymore. They hurt too much.

~ A DARK DAY

I am having a dark day. I feel the closest I have ever felt to wanting to die again. My suicidal mind pulls at me like an old familiar friend. The pain I feel is just too much! How am I going to get through this? Why is this happening to me? I suddenly want to drink and take as many sleeping pills as possible. I don't want to experience this pain.

I sit in my car in a parking lot and cry for three hours. I talk to my sponsor and sister-in-law on my phone, and they convince me to drive home. I hang up. Suddenly, like thick black smoke, the darkness of my depression enters into my body. Every breath I take suffocates any light that I have taught myself to see. Like a zombie, I leave the parking lot, and instead of going home I go to the drug store. I put my jacket hood up so no one will recognize me and go inside to purchase the over-the-counter drugs I need to take this pain away. I go to another parking lot with the boxes of pills in my lap. I cry and cry and cry. How I have any tears left, I don't know. I pop one of the pills out of its wrapper and swallow it. What am I doing? I snap into awareness and a different air enters the space around me. My mindset changes. The fog lifts. I'm making a huge mistake. I can't do this! I have tools now. I need to use them. I have to trust that I can handle life. I drop the pills and boxes in the parking lot and drive home. Nothing can make me go back to the darkness I fought so hard to get out of. My kids need me. I will never take my own life. I am going to be OK.

~ DON'T SWIM IN SHIT SOUP

This fast-paced world is brimming with agitation, angst, and impatience. These feelings rumble all around us, and I'm afraid we've become too accustomed to them. We sort of swim in shit soup on a daily basis and don't even realize it. Why? Well, because it's warm and oddly satisfies us—but it's still shit! Even when we notice that we're swimming in shit soup, we make excuses for why we haven't jumped out of the bowl yet. "It's such a steep climb out! I don't have time to find a different kind of soup! I can't leave this bowl—my family is in here with me!" Ugh. And so we swim and swim, get sicker and sicker, and we wonder why we smell bad. OK, that may have been a drastic analogy, but it's drastic for necessary effect. Now don't get me wrong; I do not profess to be a perfectly clean-life participant here. I am fully aware that my spiritual PPE (personal protective equipment) is still just fresh out of its box. I'm still cleaning off the shit I swam in for years. Heck, I was the shit soup president, lifeguard, and CEO for as long as I can remember—and that really stinks! But I'm out, and I don't want to go back.

We fill our days with so much stuff that we barely realize how out of control our lives are. Pedal to the metal—go, go, go! We collapse at the end of the day. Sadly, it often takes getting sick from the soup to finally realize how chaotic our lives are. When we are forced to take our foot off the gas, only then do we realize that the car still goes. How many experiences need to pass us by before we realize that driving fast only makes memories a forgotten plume of dust in the rearview mirror? And furthermore, without patience and time, love eventually becomes a four-letter word that gets thrown around just as often as the other popular four-letter words do.

When it comes to developing patience, we often avoid this sticky task because, well, we just don't have the patience for it! Have you ever noticed how many times you have worked really hard but ended up with a negative outcome anyway? If you had taken a moment to breathe along the way, you may have been able to reroute yourself. And have you ever beaten yourself up because you didn't even notice you were headed in the wrong direction just because you didn't take your foot off the gas? Just because the GPS in your car says turn left doesn't mean it's right—I mean correct. If you slow down and patiently read the directions, you may see that your gut tells you to turn an entirely different way. Maybe patience takes you off the beaten path—and it may get your car dirty. But I can guarantee it won't be as dirty as if you had crashed into a bowl of shit soup!

~ A NIGHT TO REMEMBER!

My sister-in-law Mandy and I have decided to create a mental health awareness and recovery celebration! I can't wait to announce it.

It will be a semi-formal evening that includes a presentation documenting my mental health journey of happiness, sorrow, and hope, followed by refreshments and mingling among fellow mental health advocates and organizations.

I've never planned an event like this before; wish me luck!

~ LIFE PYJAMAS

Change can be terrifying and very uncomfortable. So much so, many of us would rather live our lives in our "life pyjamas" day after day, snuggled up on the couch watching our lives pass us by like a movie. Don't get me wrong, life pyjamas are super awesome on those cold, rainy, dreary days we all have. But if we notice that our life laundry is piling up, and all it's filled with are pajamas, we may need to try on something different—for a change. Fear of the unknown can keep us from achieving so many successes—and also can keep us from those equally as important failures we so desperately need to learn from. When we are stagnant because of our fear of change, we block ourselves from getting dressed for life and from truly living.

What I'm trying to get at is I have been very afraid of a certain change in my life, but making this change (or not) has now become a matter of life or death. The change I am talking about is my codependent relationship with my daughter. I have known that our dependency on one another has always been extreme, but my guilt has overridden my ability to really wear the mom pants effectively. My rule-making sucks! And my follow-through is even worse. I am the Queen of Turning a Blind Eye to the dishes that were supposed to go in the sink. I'd rather not argue about the extra half hour of TV before bed. Laundry on the floor right beside the laundry basket takes me only two seconds to pick up. And the Xbox...what Xbox? What I thought was being a cool mom was actually not cool at all, and I've let my children run around in their life pyjamas way too long.

To be honest, I have parented out of guilt for all of my mothering years to some extent. But living with the guilt of making your children wonder when they would come home to find their mom dead is difficult. When I came home from Save-My-Life Boarding School as a guilt-riddled, barely-even-worthy-of-being-a-mom woman, our house became even more carefree. My son missed and worried about me so much that my guilt convinced me to let him watch *Full House* until the wee hours of the night and eventually to fall asleep in my bed. And when my daughter started to duplicate my depressive behaviours, rather than encourage healthy coping skills, my guilt told me to be at her beck and call and to simply watch her closely. I had offered her all the precious tools in the palm of my hands, but I rarely reinforced them. My guilt tricked me into thinking that any tough love would backfire on me. It told me that if I enforced house rules, they would rebel because how dare I suddenly start to act like a mother after what I had put them through?

I finally realized that what my kids needed was a mom who provided solid structure. I could *finally* stop sewing patches over the holes of our comfy life pyjamas. I know that change is good—I've been reaping the rewards of it for eleven months now. But it's time for me to lovingly enforce change in my children's habits and lackadaisical lifestyle. They may not like that I've remembered there's an Xbox in the house or that I deserve and need time to myself, but they will eventually get used to the change and appreciate it just like I do.

Our tattered and torn life pyjamas got blown away, never to be found again.

~ IT COULD HAVE BEEN ME

My daughter and I go to see the movie *South Paw*. I really enjoy it, as I normally enjoy movies about the challenges and triumphs fighters experience. It is nice being out, just the two of us, relaxing, laughing, and living. But just when it seems we can chalk the evening up to another normal movie night, the plot suddenly thickens. (Spoiler alert: there comes a point in the movie where the main mother character dies and leaves behind her husband and small daughter.) It rips me to shreds watching the actors grieve over their loss, and I am especially overwhelmed with tears when the daughter is driven away from the cemetery, looking out the limousine window, confused and alone. Then while wiping my eyes, a life-changing moment occurs. While watching this profoundly emotional scene, my daughter says something so candid that it shakes my world and heart almost to the point of collapse. She says, "I can't even imagine what that would feel like." Rewind to almost a year ago. She easily could have been that girl in the limousine driving away from her mother's funeral. She could have actually lived that scenario.

Hearing those words hits me with a wave of emotions. I feel the emptiness my daughter would have felt if I was successful with trying to end my life. I feel the sadness and pain she would have needed to battle for the rest of her life without a mother to guide her. I feel the guilt of being sick enough that I could have even thought about leaving my children behind. And while being very present in this poignant and sensitive moment, I feel gratitude and joy for how far I've come with my recovery to date.

Thank God I didn't die! How I didn't is simply a miracle. Thank God my daughter and son have me to help them heal from the agonizing memory of watching my lifeless body get taken away by the paramedics. Thank God they now have a mom who is striving to be healthy and an amazing role model for overall well-being. Thank God when my son wakes up from a nightmare and calls for me, I'm there to comfort him and reassure him that everything is OK. Thank God I am here for when my daughter has another heartbreak and so desperately just needs her mom to rub her hair and watch movies all day while she cries and heals. Thank God I am here to laugh. Thank God I am here to love. And thank God I am here to live!

Thank God!

~ NO EXPERIENCE IS EVER WASTED

Everything in the past and future has a relationship to now. Where I have been and what I have done in my life has brought me here, to this hour, this second, this moment. And what I will do and become tomorrow will dance before me like an intricate ballet designed by cause and effect. As I mark the passing of one-full-year sober and healthy, I can't help but reflect on all the experiences I've had along the way—all the ups and downs, which provide me with invaluable opportunities to change. I don't believe in coincidences anymore— now life is more like a platter of perfection masquerading as irony. At first, it appears to serve a dish of disappointment, but if you look closely enough, it's actually serving exactly what you need.

September 23, 2014, I drank copious amounts of wine and ingested a bottle of pills knowing full well that the possible consequence of this could be death. I didn't care. I didn't feel. I was so tired of thinking about suicide every day that having death "happen" would have been a gift to me. I didn't want to have another nightmare, I didn't want to watch my relationship fall to pieces, and I didn't want to feel guilty anymore for all of the inadequacies I believed whole-heartedly that I possessed. I don't remember that person anymore. She's gone. She somehow climbed out of the darkness that was suffocating her slowly, breath by breath. It feels like a hurricane of emotions and experiences has swept me up and finally spat me out. Leave it to me to need a hurricane as my healing vessel—I don't seem to do anything the easy way!

The transformation of my mind has changed all of me forever. I'm alive. I'm happy. I'm able to feel emotions in a healthy way. I am an amazing parent, modelling a life of hope and love for my children. I am beautiful. And I am free. I don't blame others for my feelings anymore, and I am not obsessively attached to the fulfillment of my dreams. I now prefer to live a life that maintains the passionate wish to prolong my health and well-being without harsh expectations. I let life guide me, rather than try to guide life. I've realized that when I thought I always had to be at the wheel, I continued to crash into resentment when things didn't go my way. Now I breathe. I walk. I smile. And I love.

I consciously try to build a mind of love every day now, which effectively eliminates my previous negative and deluded states of mind. I have learned lessons I never could have predicted in a million years, like how to reframe my experiences so that they remain congruent with my wish to be happy. I see difficult times as my teacher now, ever reminding me of the importance of humility. And I try to consciously abandon non-virtuous, toxic minds. Life is perfectly imperfect (I forget where I've heard that line before; I don't take credit for it), and one day at a time I experience its imperfections, never wasting what they are always trying to teach me.

~ TOMORROW IS MY BIG MENTAL HEALTH EVENT

I've never organized an event for 200 people before! My sister-in-law Mandy and I are just going with the flow and somehow things seem to fall into place, and now the event is tomorrow. Food, tickets, the venue, dishware rentals, flowers, and so much more needed to be arranged to make the event a success.

I am extremely lucky to have so many supportive people in my community who are willing to listen to my story and learn more about mental health. Local political leaders will be attending, and the chief of paramedic services, fire services, police services, and a representative from the Canadian military will all be speaking. A local radio celebrity will be hosting the night and my brother Ross will be introducing me. We also have an NHL referee as a guest speaker. I'm so excited!

My pink strapless dress is all steamed and ready to go. I'm going to get my makeup done professionally in the morning, and some family and friends are meeting me in the afternoon to help me set up the venue—I am so grateful for their help.

The best part of all is that the event is SOLD OUT! It feels like Christmas Eve. How will I sleep?

~ OVER $2600 RAISED

I am about to speak. I sit in a quiet room listening to a guided meditation through my earphones. I practise my deep breathing and feel confident in my ability to give a successful presentation. The night is in the universe's hands now. All of the months of preparation are about to unveil the efforts put in by so many amazing people.

My brother introduces me. As I walk towards the podium, I almost trip over my dress. *Phew, that was a near miss, Natalie.* I stand in front of the crowd, and strangely I am not nervous at all. I begin my presentation:

Imagine with me if you will, a world filled with fear and sadness that constantly undervalues your necessity to breathe. Imagine a world filled with permanent darkness, distorted thinking, and illogical reasoning. Imagine a world that constantly harbours powerful voices that tell you that you should hurt yourself because you are worthless and that everyone would be better off without you...

It is a great feeling being able to share my experiences through a forum other than writing. My heart pounds as I try not to mess up my words. Two hundred pairs of eyes, many with tears, are staring back at me as words tumble from my mouth, reflecting such a dark time in my life. It was a time that seems so far away now. My beautiful daughter, Caroline, sits in the front row, and I wonder what she is thinking as the night progresses. How amazing that she could be here with me. I continue:

Imagine feeling relentless exhaustion even while lying still in your bed and feeling completely alone in a crowd. Imagine walking down the street with a heavy, black cloud weighing your shoulders down and covering any glimmer of light that you could possibly see. Now imagine that this world has all become too much, and that you've decided to die...

There are tears and laughter all night, and The Paramedic Nat's Evening for Mental Health raises over $2600 for the Tema Conter Memorial Fund, which is a foundation created by paramedic Vince Savoia. He was diagnosed with PTSD over twenty years ago after attending to the murder of a woman named Tema Conter. When Vince was no longer able to work on the road as a paramedic, he made it his mission to educate people about the seriousness of PTSD and raise money for first responder and military mental health initiatives.

Other than the dress incident, the night goes off without a hitch! It is a night to always remember. I learn that maybe I can make a positive change to the mental health world by continuing my public speaking.

~ HOW CONFUSION GIVES BIRTH TO WISDOM

At the Buddhist centre, an amazing teacher once again shares a comment that puts a great deal of my past and present struggles into a positive perspective. While we are learning about the mind, she states, "Confusion must be present before wisdom can be born." I repeat it in my head a few times, but wow does it ever make sense. Suddenly this phrase allows me to recognize how much foresight I have gained by navigating through confusion—whether it be confusion in my life or confusion in my mind. Furthermore, as I ponder this "aha" moment, I realize my extreme circumstances of confusion actually launched me into a life filled with gratitude and love.

This lesson makes me recall how, when I was young, my parents tried to involve me in team sports, but I never really connected with the concept because I usually found the atmosphere confusing and overwhelming. Situations brimming with a lack of organization (like a sports field) required so much extra concentration in order for me to focus. Rather than having the physical action of the game bring me to exhaustion, my inner anxiety was what took my breath away. I preferred to do my own thing. I equally disliked group projects in school, because I would worry that my grade would suffer because of someone else's laziness, causing our group's less-than-exceptional performance to be perceived as a disappointment that I didn't deserve. Wow, I worried a lot!

So, like the rule-abiding child and student that I was, I would do as I was told, join the team or group with a smile (albeit fake) and get through the game or pick up the slack when needed without a complaint. But as I got older, something amazing happened. I started to see how necessary it was for me to learn how to thrive in confusion because the entire world is filled with confusion. I began to take small leaps of faith and see things beyond my narrow-minded view. I stopped believing that only my opinion was correct. Eventually, through my exposure to uncomfortable emotions, I gained the wisdom necessary to be able to excel in team environments. I learned the importance of professional delegation and embraced the opportunity to gather peer feedback. After all those hours I spent taping bubble letters to bristol board with a partner who had no concept of symmetry—and lacked any internal sense of urgency before a due date—I learned how to be an awesome team player. Who knew?

By being mindful in times of confusion, I gained a deeper insight into how I was projecting disappointment onto every team environment, rather than examining my lack of evidence. Luckily as years passed, I learned how to explore each individual experiences with teamwork and began to clearly see the positive outcomes they could produce.

Learning how to recognize the possibility of forthcoming wisdom is not an easy task—especially in a world permeated with confusion and chaos. But this insight all comes back to practising mindfulness. We sometimes think that certain people and circumstances cause us suffering. Instead, we could choose to perceive these people and events as opportunities to gain deeper insights in our own mind's misconceptions. Being able to do this is a precious gift. It may not be something we want to admit right away, but if we take the time to step back and reflect on the things that we perceive are causing us confusion, resentment, and eventually anger, we can learn that they are actually teaching us how to cultivate our happiness. Over time, I have learned how to consciously stop myself from quickly attaching an unpleasant emotion to a person or an event. Instead I examine where it is coming from inside myself. By doing so, I am no longer depriving myself of the opportunity to heal from any situation I am presented with.

May I suggest you try to be mindful when you are presented with a moment of confusion or frustration, and use it as an opportunity to gain inner wisdom. Ask yourself, "Why am I feeling this way?" You may not have a wise answer right away, but if you keep practising mindfulness in times of confusion, you will be amazed at what life lessons you will learn.

~ I AM STILL HUMAN

I share my lessons so you can learn;
that doesn't mean I'm not learning.

I share my joys so you can smile;
that doesn't mean I don't cry.

I share my victories so you can have hope;
that doesn't mean I don't struggle.

I share my visions so you can see too;
that doesn't mean I'm not doubtful.

I share my words from numerous friends;
that doesn't mean I don't have enemies.

I share my experiences so you don't feel alone;
that doesn't mean I'm not lonely.

I share my illnesses so you can relate;
that doesn't mean I don't feel stigma.

I share my love so you can feel loved;
that doesn't protect me from hate.

I share my recovery so you can believe;
that doesn't mean I'm cured.

I share how I breathe so you can too;
that doesn't mean I don't feel suffocated.

I share because that's who I am;
that doesn't mean all will agree.

I share my vulnerability so you can feel safe;
that doesn't mean I don't have insecurities.

I share my faith so you can find peace:
that doesn't mean I don't have demons.

I will continue to share as more work's to be done;
more people are clearly suffering.

The work I do will benefit you,
the ones who are living in darkness.

I know how you feel, I'll take it from here;
I'm not finished, I've only started.

~ A MIRACLE A DAY KEEPS THE DARKNESS AWAY

Guilt is a terrible feeling. After working with my sponsor to tackle my resentments and make amends where they need to be made, guilt still seems to be the tangled chain holding me back from complete peace. Forgiving myself for putting my family and friends through an attempted suicide isn't an overnight process. But I'm learning that there is no future in the past! I will always carry the lessons of my past experiences in a pocket close to my heart, but they don't have to drag me down and slow my progress forward. I'm also learning that as I extend forgiveness, I am able to forgive myself.

Forgiveness is a two-way street, and not in the way you may be thinking. Whether someone forgives me is completely out of my control. But I can't forgive others and not forgive myself. Different classes that I have participated in have taught me that forgiveness involves some aspect of self-forgiveness, and inner peace is the prized reward.

I have been doing a lot of serious contemplation about when I should return to work. Yes, that's right I said *when*. I have decided that I'm not finished being a paramedic. I'm not finished helping people or working alongside my colleagues. I still need to complete the groups and courses I am in now before being completely ready to tie up my black steel-toe boots again—but putting on my uniform doesn't seem so scary anymore. I have been blessed with the knowledge I have gained over the past seven months—knowledge I craved my whole life, and I'm ready to put it into action with my patients and peers.

It's still one day at a time—don't worry, I'm not rushing things that still need work. But I think that one day being able to continue to do the job I love so dearly will be the final step towards forgiving myself. I need to help people who live in darkness like I did. What a blessing it would be to shine more light on mental health by being a true example of hope myself as a paramedic again—but a healthy one.

I have forgiven the murderer for the illness and pain he caused me. He hasn't haunted my dreams for more nights than I can count now. And if I can do that, I can definitely learn to forgive myself. There is *always* hope.

~ TOUGH LOVE

I have been told by many people over the past year that I love to talk about love, and I suppose they are right. Unearthing the true meaning and sentiment of love after living a life where self-pity obscured its existence is like finding a sparkling jewel in the darkness that you thought you had no prospect of possessing. Once you find such a precious jewel, you make a necklace out of it and keep it as close to your heart as possible. You look at it often and hold it tight in your hands to ensure that finding it wasn't a dream. And you can't help but show it to everyone you meet! "Look at how magnificent this precious jewel is!" you say as people walk by, hopeful that sharing a glimpse of it will prove to them that they can find the same.

No wonder I am so fascinated by my discovery of the true meaning of love (to wish someone happiness and wellness without limitations or conditions) when it seems that its meaning is so distorted in our world these days. Love doesn't hurt even if the band Nazareth says so. Dating myself? Possibly…be quiet. It doesn't need anyone or anything else to complete it even if *Jerry Maguire* says so. Furthermore, love is never bitter, it is only ever sweet even if Kanye says so. Have I regained some of my youth now? In short, I don't blame anyone for thinking that love has a negative connotation with the way we refer to it in our society today.

We humans engage in actions that will inevitably lead to suffering because so many of our societal beliefs gain power without any true independent analysis. When did Taylor Swift's views on love's inevitable transformation to pain become the only data required to prove that when we feel pain it must mean that love is part of the equation? Love is never part of a painful equation. Pain that comes from the heart is more likely to come from attachment. But don't take my word for it—turn off Taylor's catchy tune for a bit and mindfully reflect on the difference between love and attachment, and how we often interchange them without thinking.

How can we expect to feel complete when we put so much pressure on someone else to complete us? This assumption alone weaves a level of self-grasping into our minds that has nothing to do with love at all. If we truly possessed the wish for everyone to be happy and well, we would never attach ourselves to them—it simply wouldn't be necessary. Furthermore, we would be happy with ourselves and see clearly how attachment can only lead to jealousy, envy, and anger. And how jealousy, envy and anger are what actually lead to pain.

In order to find the transformative jewel of love, we must deliberately take a stand to reverse negative tendencies of attachment and exchange them for new, positive, selfless habits. Luckily, the more we explore a topic, regardless of how difficult it may be, the more we come to understand it. And I certainly can't think of a better topic to explore than the topic of love.

~ WINGS OF CHANGE—PEER SUPPORT

As my journey expands through social media, I make many connections with first responders and healthcare providers around the world. Sadly, through these connections, I learn that mental illness is running rampant in these professions. The fear of being stigmatized is causing so many of these amazing people to secretly suffer until their bodies and minds can no longer bear the toxic silence they believe is necessary to keep their jobs—jobs that deep down most still dearly love. I learn there are lots of heroes who believe that asking for help equals weakness, and I vow to myself that when I am healthy enough, I will work hard to change this belief.

While adjusting to life back home after Save-My-Life Boarding School, I realize how much I miss the peer support from others who are recovering just like me. Their presence and strength played such a huge role in my successful recovery.

Through conversations with fellow paramedics and mental health associations, I find there is a lack of regular peer support available in communities for those concerned with operational stress and associated mental illnesses—this sparks my desire to research peer support groups in other fields. I obtain expert advice from Syd Gravel (retired Ottawa staff sergeant, member of the Order of Merit for police and author of *56 Seconds*), Vince Savoia (founder of the Tema Conter Memorial Trust) and Bill Rusk (director of Badge of Life Canada) and work on developing a peer support model that I think will be well received. This model is an adaptation of Syd Gravel's Police peer support group, Robin's Blue Circle. I then form a focus group with peers who have just as much passion about seeing an improvement in peer support, and their valuable feedback is used to create Wings of Change—Peer Support.

Wings of Change offers structured meetings where anonymous, solution-based discussion and education can occur regarding any operational stress. All first responder, military members, communications officers, healthcare providers, funeral services workers, and corrections and parole officers are welcome—be they professional or volunteer. While an employer may provide the group's contact and location information as a resource they sanction, they are not directly affiliated with the group.

These informal meetings are only facilitated by peers experiencing similar struggles and concerns with operational stress. Professional assessment and care is not provided at the meetings, and the diagnosis of a mental illness, such as PTSD, is not required in order to attend. However, we advise that all members seek professional medical help concurrently and do not rely on the meetings as their sole means of support.

For the comfort of all participants, anonymity is a fundamental component of Wings of Change. However, we encourage individual discussion outside the meetings in order to combat the mental health stigma. After a meeting if anyone feels they require further immediate support, we encourage them to talk to the chairperson or other participants—and crisis-line information is always made available.

Wings of Change offers a safe and caring place for our dedicated community heroes to heal through talk, fellowship, and education. It is my personal experience that whether an individual chooses to attend to simply listen, learn, or interact with peers, they can obtain the understanding, support, and respect necessary to heal from trauma—thus improving career longevity as well as overall health.

It is my sincerest wish that this model will provide the framework needed to implement peer support groups around the world and complement programs already in place. Through non-stigmatized fellowship and education, Wings of Change—Peer Support encourages a new outlook where the need to be comfortable with uncomfortable no longer exists.

~ DUSTING OFF MY UNIFORM

Well, ladies and gentlemen, the universe opened up and sent me the most suitable job at my paramedic service—training coordinator. This role is made for me—figuratively, not literally. I have years of teaching and curriculum development experience, so this job is right up my alley! But (there's always a but), according to my contract, I have to go back on the road as a paramedic for three months before I can begin. I'm very nervous about how I will react to the sights and sounds of paramedic-land after being off for a year, but I will try to tough my way through it because there is a light at the end of the tunnel—an opportunity to teach my peers and, drum roll… not work night shifts! Woo hoo! All right, now where did I put those steel-toe boots?

~ BACK TO PARAMEDIC-LAND

It's like the night before the first day back to school. My stomach is queasy, and I am wide awake. I haven't put my uniform on for over a year and doubted for a very long time that I ever would again. I have talked with Mandy lots over the last few weeks, and she has assured me that if I need to call her for some positive reinforcement while I'm at work, I can. Well, here goes nothing…

~ A LOVELY UNDERTONE OF VOMIT

It's snowing out. Ugh, I don't miss driving in the snow. I make my way to the paramedic station for the first time since testifying at the double-murder trial that sent me into the darkest places my mind had ever been to. I walk into the ambulance garage—it still smells the same. Diesel mixed with stale air—I love it. I mean, I don't love the *actual* smell, but I love what it represents—being a paramedic. My boots squeak on the painted garage floor, and the sound echoes off the high ceilings just like it always did. I don't even have to step into the back of the ambulance (a.k.a. my office) to know what it will smell like: three parts plastic, one part disinfectant wipes (if you're lucky), a pinch of the sweet smell of the IV tourniquets, with a lovely undertone of…vomit. *Ahhh, home sweet home.*

I walk into the living room area, and my partner that I've had for nine years greets me. I will be working with him for the next three months, so it's nice knowing that I will at least be comfortable with that part of my return. God, we've had some fun times together! As paramedics we get to glimpse into people's lives and experience their behaviours multiple times in a day, and boy are human beings entertaining! Patients have called my partner the silliest names (a monkey's uncle; President Lincoln); we've slipped into ditches on our asses while trying so hard not to laugh at each other because we know that someone's emergency is in that very ditch. If I had a dime for every time he or I bashed our heads off the roof of a car while trying to look professional in our helmets as we checked on patients inside, I would be a millionaire!

It's not long before we get a call. Nothing serious, a standard generally ill. As I'm driving to the hospital with the patient and my partner in the back, I hear another crew's call on the radio. A supervisor is going to a possible suicide. My stomach flips over. I have heard and attended so many possible suicide calls in my career, but now they mean something very different to me.

I think about the patient and their family, and suddenly I feel even sicker as my self-stigmatization starts to figuratively turn my strong paramedic uniform into a hospital gown. To me, this represents that I will forever be one of those "possible suicide" patients. I can't escape it. I can't hide from the fact that everyone in my service knows about what happened to me. My brain rushes back to a time when I was petrified of anyone knowing I had mental illnesses. My body feels the sensation of how afraid I was that people could hear my voice through the phone when I used to call Leo in the middle of a panic attack. In that moment while driving to the hospital, I feel weak.

I call Mandy as soon as I can and tell her about the painful coincidence that the first call I hear on the radio is a possible suicide. Her wisdom washes over me like warm water when she says, "Maybe it wasn't a coincidence at all. Maybe you needed to *hear* that call before you would be able to *attend* that call." It was like exposure therapy—listen before you see.

I manage to get through the shift. But I'm not so excited about what lies ahead over the next three months on the road. I'm happy I can still bang off a chest-pain call like nobody's business, but those aren't the calls I am worried about. *Deep breath. You can do this, Natalie, somehow.*

~ MENTAL HEALTH DAYS

I manage to use up all my sick days for the year in a short period of time. I'm not coping well. My PTSD symptoms are appearing at work (something that never happened before). The siren is way too loud. My anxiety pulls me away from socializing with anyone. I sit in the ambulance alone as much as possible. I *dread* putting my uniform on. I'm afraid—*really* afraid—of ever getting pulled back into the darkness I fought so hard to get out of. I'm still completely confident in my skills and my intellectual ability to be a paramedic—thank God. But I have zero faith in being able to stay clean, sober, and healthy if I ever walk into a murder call again. Every call is a possible murder call. That's just the nature of our job. I always knew that, and before the "very bad call," I welcomed *any* call that would challenge my ability to del-egate, manage a scene, prioritize my medical directives, and per-form advanced life-saving skills—including calls that involved violence. I used to jump at those calls and loved having students, which always added another dynamic angle for me to navigate. The bigger the call, the better. To non-first-responders this must sound dark and twisted. I'm not saying I wanted people to get sick or injured. The fact of the matter is people were going to get sick or injured anyway, and when they did I wanted to be the paramedic on the call to get shit done.

I am a different person now. In so many ways. I want to pro-tect my health so badly. My heart is telling me that no matter how much satisfaction being the paramedic at a big call would bring me, it wouldn't outweigh even the potential of how sick it could make me too.

~ MERRY CHRISTMAS FROM THE ROAD

Well, with the promise of my dream job waiting for me at the end of three months on the road (just a few weeks to go), I have managed to make it to Christmas and haven't turned in my uniform yet. It hasn't been easy, but by the grace of God I have been spared any serious calls so far.

I have so much to be grateful for on this Christmas Day! Last year, after only being able to stay home for a few hours on my Christmas pass from Save-My-Life Boarding School, I went back to a barren building where at least I knew I would be safe, feeling defeated and wondering how I would make it through another year.

Who knew that this year I would be back to work and surrounded by people I love. God is good. Merry Christmas to all!

~ A SECOND CHANCE TO ENJOY LIFE'S OPERA

I have a pretty big case of the winter blahs. I'm not yet ready to call them blues, because overall I'm still loving life—but some sun would be nice! So, while under the influence of rain clouds (better than alcohol), my sister-in-law and I decide to inject (too many addict puns?) some fun into our winter days until the earth decides to tilt a little more toward the sun to provide some desperately needed vitamin D. So, the other night we, along with my niece and her friend, travel to Toronto to see *The Phantom of the Opera*—it is amazing!

I had never seen it before, and from beginning to end I am on the edge of my seat in awe of the imagination necessary to create such a masterpiece. There is so much beauty evolving on the stage at any given moment that I feel I can't move my eyes around enough to see it all. The costumes, the sets, the characters, all take my creative heart to a mesmerizing world, and I love every gasp and tear along the way. But as I am watching, I realize—while I'm sure that most of the audience is wrapped up in the drama of the story and in the voices bearing a gift that prove to me that there is a heaven—I can't help but to notice other things on stage. Like how complex the lighting is, and how every angle and every colour must have been envisioned before even turning on a switch; how brilliant the minds are behind the scenes! When it finishes, I turn to my sister-in-law and tell her that I want to see it again so I can have a second chance to see what I missed—there's just so much to experience.

I want to see it again so that I can have a second chance to see what I missed. Well, isn't that a perfect line in the *Opera of My Life?*! True second chances are presented to me every day, and I love them all. I love all the angles of new light, the evolution of my imagination, and the beauty this earth envelops me in—the beauty of patience and acceptance. Day after day, my trust in the script set before me helps me to stop worrying about the small set-malfunctions and most importantly teaches me to stop continuously rewriting it. It's already wonderful the way it is. The actors change along the way, but that's normal—and good! They leave their mark on the legacy of this production and go forward to other experiences in order for them to continue to grow and develop their craft, their own masterpieces.

What a gift it is to learn how to be present in the now and to experience every aspect of life. My sister-in-law taught me a very important mantra that reminds me how to stay in the now and not get too ahead of myself, which is very easy for me to do! She says, "Today, you are already enough." How profound! Saying this to myself when my mind is racing into the next millennium of ideas or recounting things of the past reminds me to stop and continue to enjoy the all the angles of light I would miss if I were the old me. This simple sentence allows me to experience my second chances, and I highly recommend everyone try it out for themselves!

Before you race into a new year with a list of resolutions that you will want to burn faster than the speed of the New Year's countdown, take a moment to admire the second chances all around you and let your life opera sing the words that are already written—because today, you are already enough.

~ EMOTIONS AND ANGELS

Well, this new year starts off with a bang—bang of water shoes, laughs, and tan lines to be specific! Instead of spending money on Christmas presents that get used once and then forgotten about the day after, this year my family and I decide to spend money on memories. I travel to Cozumel, Mexico, with my son, brother, sister-in-law, niece, and nephew to enjoy seven days of blissful sunshine and well-deserved relaxation. If you asked me last January, while I was adapting to my new sober, post-Save-My-Life Boarding School lifestyle, if I thought I would have (a) been sitting on a beach in Mexico in a year, and especially, (b) been there with the family members who I thought I had lost after they desperately and necessarily removed themselves from the road of destruction that I was barreling down, I would have said, "No way! Impossible." But, here I am, sitting on my bed with a kick-ass tan and a beach bag full of memories and a sober smile on my face.

Along this journey of life, we are blessed with meeting people who impact our growth on very profound levels. In fact, under the right non-coincidental (in my opinion) conditions, strangers can turn into friends in all of a heartbeat—really. Yes, people can connect when they find that they have experiences in common or mutual friends. But I am learning that the strongest bonds are formed through the realization that two people have experienced the same emotions—universal emotions, if you will. And further to my very non-scientific observations, I find the emotion that connects two people faster and stronger than any other is grief. The moment when a heart feels the pain of another person's loss is, in my opinion, the bond of humanity.

While sitting around the pool in Mexico, we meet a family from Edmonton, Alberta. Striking up a conversation about whose driveway had the most snow when we left home is a given when you are both from Canada, but more pool time together reveals a much greater connection—that of the mutual experience of grieving over a loved one's death. They are also on a family vacation, but their reason for such a vacation is much different from ours. They are away together to support one another while they grieve the sudden heartbreaking loss of a young lady. Megan was the wife of one of the Edmonton family members and the sister of another. She was only twenty-nine when she tragically died this past October. Seeing and feeling the emotion of loss in this family's eyes is excruciating. While the family member who lost his wife eats breakfast alone or tries his best to relax by the pool, I can barely contain my tears. I keep thinking how hard it must be to try to just "be." And I keep thinking of how close my family came to experiencing the same thing when I tried to take my own life last year. I feel selfish and embarrassed recalling this time in my life, but I accept that I was very sick then. I need to live in the now and continue to heal. I need to allow these experiences to increase my gratitude rather than increase my guilt. Easier said than done.

My sister-in-law Mandy experiences her own connection with our new friends. Their story reminds her of her father, Rudy, who died several years ago. The universal emotion of grief may lessen over time, but it never fully leaves, and she can't help but feel an overwhelming amount of compassion for this family, immediately identifying with their pain.

A wonderful part of this story is that this family realized that by acknowledging their emotions of loss and grief through a charity they have created called A Circle of Angels, they are able to heal together. Amazing! And by doing so, they are helping so many around the world do the same. A jewellery designer in the family created a beautiful angel accessory that a grieving family can assemble together while they remembering their lost loved one.

On our last day in Mexico, my sister-in-law, brother, and I are each generously given one of these angels. I want to once again thank our Alberta friends not only for the gift of these beautiful angels but for the gift of friendship and healing. See you next year.

~ FROM MY ROCK, MANDY

My sister-in-law Mandy is my rock. But she's not like any rock! She is the kind of rock you find while you're alone on a beach and the sun reflects off it just the right way for you to be able to find it. She's beautiful and doesn't ever push her way onto the shore. She is content with shining in the background, compassionately allowing the other rocks to enjoy the view too. Peacefully glistening on a path less travelled, she blesses the earth wherever she lands. She's a tiny rock, but she is strong! And I am so lucky to have her in my life.

Today Mandy drops off a birthday gift and card for me. I open it and read:

Natalie, Natalie, what a year 2015 was! In hindsight it was, I think, your best year ever. You packed a lot into those twelve months—you learned a lifetime's worth of lessons, you ran (and won) more "mental marathons" than any Olympian, you forgave and were forgiven, you set boundaries and stood your ground, you rekindled a love for your profession, you made plans and released them to God, you saved countless, faceless lives and also a few you knew too...But most importantly, you saved yourself, your family, and your future. All the best for 2016, Nat! Namaste.

~ WINGS OF CHANGE AND PTSD BILL 163

February is going to be busy! I am settling into my role as training coordinator now, and I have a lot on the go. Wings of Change—Peer

Support is being launched on February 1, and the Ontario PTSD Bill 163 will have another reading at Queen's Park in Toronto, on February 16.

I've been asked to speak about my mental health journey and Wings of Change at quite a few upcoming events, which I am very happy about.

On a side note, the photocopier beside my desk is so loud! I'm sure it's really just normal photocopier loud, but my sensitivity to noise is really apparent lately. I asked if I could move into an empty office but was told I couldn't because it was eventually going to be used by a supervisor. I don't feel like my old I-can-deal-with-anything self anymore. I'm frustrated that something as simple as a photocopier can disrupt my ability to focus. *Sigh.* I have all the confidence in the world in my ability to perform the tasks I am given, but my body just isn't the same. I feel like I literally have super-human hearing power! I don't want to wear earplugs at my desk, but I may have to.

~ NOT YET

People are asking me for advice on coping with sadness a lot lately. What techniques do I use when I'm really upset? How do I manage really bad days? Well, I have a tip that may help some of you.

Let me preface this tip with the disclaimer that people who have *not* been burned in the depths of depression hell to the point where death or self-harm is what they believe to be their only form of solace may disagree with the advice I am about to give. But for those of you who *have* been there, I am sure you will find that this technique can help you to get through those days of hell, like it recently helped me.

I had a horrid day a few weeks ago. So much so that for the first time in a long time, I felt the petrifying feeling of numbness that came with my old suicidal ideations, and I started to reflexively dissociate. When this feeling crept in, I fought to ignore it with all my might! I didn't want to admit to myself that it was even possible for me to still feel that way. Logically, having this reaction appear made sense to me. Since thoughts of suicide have been my automatic response to traumatic emotions for so long, it's no surprise to me that my brain tries to rationalize the option of permanently removing myself from experiencing those painful emotions by killing myself. Death was my way out for so long! And just like a smell can trigger a memory in a second, feelings can trigger emotional responses just as quickly.

So on this day, I sobbed uncontrollably and wanted to vomit. I cried and cried, and out of nowhere the thought of suicide appeared—in a very different form—but nevertheless, it appeared. I knew I was *not* going to kill myself. But that still didn't take away the battle that ensued between a devil and an angel on each of my shoulders, tugging me back and forth from familiar thoughts of destruction to reminders of how far I've come.

Then something amazing happened. Something simple, but so powerful! While the devil was winning and my mind was spinning, the angel whispered, "Not yet." The devil reminded me how easy it would be to stop the pain, and the angel again whispered, "Not yet." The devil pulled me so deeply into my sorrow that I believed I was sick enough to hurt myself, then the angel whispered, "Not yet." The devil tried to convince me that one drink would be OK, and that no one would know, and the angel whispered, "Not yet." Minute by excruciating minute, I told myself, "Not yet," and minute by minute, the pain lessened, until I was strong enough to turn to the devil and scream, "No!"

When immersed in the torturous, helpless depths of hell, saying "no" to death is impossible because it takes away my only (albeit toxic and quite possibly lethal) possibility to cope with the pain. But "not yet" gives me the time I need to calm down and still feel like I am in control.

Having yes as an option does not mean I suggest the implementation of it—it's just simply an option. To you, saying "no" to suicide may be the immediate and only possible option—but luckily, you've never been to hell.

"Not yet" allows me to remain on earth until my deluded irrational thinking subsides. "Not yet" lets me play the tape to the end and remind myself how amazing life is now. In short, "not yet" gives me the time I need with my angel.

~ AND THEN LISTEN

There are many people and organizations in Canada who help to promote mental health awareness—such as six-time Canadian Olympian Clara Hughes. We are learning how talking is the key to the initiation of mental illness diagnosis and treatment and how tremendously important that awareness is! But what happens when a loved one or friend *does* talk to you? What do you do? Take it from this mental illness survivor—the answer may be simpler than you think. It goes like this…LISTEN!

Family and friends are well intentioned and hate to see their loved one in pain—of any kind. But when it comes to mental illness, the often stigma-filled invisible pain that is associated with it makes for an uncomfortable conversation between people because of two factors. First, the person talking about their personal concern is afraid of being judged. Second, the person being told about the concern doesn't know how to help. If you are on the receiving end of the talk, you don't need to know how to *fix* the person at all; you just need to listen!

From my perspective, I wish people would refrain from saying, "You just need to do this or that"—the person suffering would if they could, *believe me*; refrain from saying, "Don't worry, it will pass"— the person suffering probably won't believe you; refrain from changing the subject because *you* are uncomfortable—the person suffering may not open up to you again if you do; and refrain from diagnosing or turning the conversation to something about you—the person talking has probably rehearsed what to say to you a million times and has finally mustered the courage to talk—so just *listen*!

You don't need to have the answers right away. The person talking doesn't expect you to—they are just as confused as you are, and I can tell you from experience that at the point of first conversation, the *only* thing on the sufferer's mind is hope that they will be listened to! Be open and really listen with your full attention.

~ ONTARIO STEPS UP

A day we have been fighting for finally arrives! Even though it has yet to be passed, the Supporting Ontario's First Responders Act is introduced in Ontario today.

How can I put into words the emotions of this day? I will use a phrase: "Bittersweet gratitude and hope—*finally!*"

First of all, I want to take a moment to remember every life we as first responders have lost before this landmark day. I want to pay respect to every tear that has fallen from a loved one's eyes. I want to let every peer who is not feeling the overwhelming emotion of happiness that this day should bring because they are still battling their darkness know that they are not alone. I'm with you. I have been in that darkness too.

~ COMPASSION FATIGUE, HMM

I am fortunate to participate in a resiliency course today. The day is educational and inspiring, filled with amazing fellow paramedics from across Canada. We discuss topics such as primary and secondary trauma, organizational stress, involuntary emotions, and stigma reduction. I am always excited to learn about different mental illness recovery techniques and the latest evidence-based findings with regard to diagnosing mental illnesses. Today, as expected, we chat about all of these things. But I must confess, for all of my love of medicine and research, I am even more intrigued to listen to other people's non-scientific thoughts about "compassion fatigue."

Why does this interest me so much? Well, because I thought I suffered severely from this condition a year and a half ago to the point of not ever wanting to put a paramedic uniform on again because it reminded me of how "caring hurt me." Luckily, one fateful day I learned what the true definition of compassion is and realized that I never really had a problem with caring at all!

According to a very wise teacher, compassion can never hurt. Compassion is the act of wishing the best for someone—that's it, that's all. And when I really think about this, being a paramedic never made me have a problem with that, ever. What did hurt me was my attachment to what happened beyond that wish. Allow me to elaborate...

As a paramedic, I became sad when the wish I had for people to be well often wasn't fulfilled, and subconsciously this made me feel like my compassion was wasted. What fatigued me was that no matter how strong my wish was, the result of my best efforts to help was never in my hands in the first place. And what hurt me the most was not realizing how attached I was to those wishes that didn't come true.

All the compassion that I could provide would never alter the universe's ultimate outcome in particular situation. This realization not only renewed my love of being a paramedic, but also changed the way I look at life! I'm a caring person, I always try my best to help regardless of the circumstances I'm presented with—and when things don't go according to my wish for them to go well, it's out of my hands.

So leave it to me to politely challenge a name given to a condition that was created by many highly educated and accomplished psychological experts! (My sister-in-law Mandy wouldn't be surprised.) But I feel that by renaming this condition "attachment fatigue," compassion will once again be allowed to represent all of the light and joy it is intended to.

~ PATIENCE AND TOLERANCE *TESTED*!

Regardless of how much I practise patience and tolerance, there are always days that push me over the edge! So to prove that I am nowhere close to being a Buddha or a perfectly compassionate soul, get ready for a solid ride on this roller coaster of a rant!

February, you sort of suck! You make my dog's feet super muddy, and your visual temperature cues are completely out of whack! Snow usually means cold—but NO! When you are around, I bundle up only to find myself squirming in the car like an overheated jellyfish trying to get my jacket off on the only day I do not have a red light to do so calmly!

To the guy sitting beside me for a half an hour while smacking your lips and burping uncontrollably in a setting where getting up to move away from you was impossible. ARE YOU KIDDING ME?! DO YOU NOT HEAR YOURSELF?! Congratulations, you tested my patience to a whole other level. *Natalie, you can so do this! Stay! Sit and breathe!* I don't want to breathe in his burp-air. And he is *not* seeing my eye rolls! Ugh! I can't take this. *OK, relax—it's not that bad.* Ugh! It is *so* bad. I'm OUT of here!

Healthy boundaries are in full effect today in the form of me sleeping for eighty percent of the day. To-do lists can kiss my butt! I wake up only to make sure Walter and the cats are fed and healthy. But don't worry—they were having a wonderfully fun day despite my laziness. And FYI, the roll of toilet paper chewed and scattered all over my house like confetti on New Year's Eve still remains where I found it!

Rant over. I'm going to watch TED Talks and eat oatmeal.

~ POST-ACUTE WITHDRAWAL

I found a picture that was taken December 31, 2014—New Year's Eve while I was at Save-My-Life Boarding School. What I'm sure may appear to be a normal picture to many is actually a picture filled with memories of struggles, sadness, and fear that I felt behind the forced smile I was wearing.

As I sat on blankets that covered the floor because I hate germs (and still do), I muscled my way through probably the worst New Year's Eve I had ever experienced. I was unwillingly sober, living in the fog of withdrawal. I hated that I could only sit on a floor and eat chips and drink ginger ale before our eleven o'clock curfew, which was a "treat." (Our curfew was normally ten.) Bitter and lonely, I actually remember being very frustrated. My friend and I calculated how long it would take for alcohol to metabolize in our body— because we were actually considering finding a bar, numbing the pain, and coming back in the right amount of time to still have a clean urine test! WOW! This "brilliant" idea was wrong on so many levels. But that is how sick I was. In the moment it was exactly what I thought I needed to do, and thank God I didn't.

Overall, the symptoms of withdrawal are so vast and compli-cated. I am grateful once again for my stay at Save-My-Life Boarding School because while I was in my last few weeks there, we learned about post-acute withdrawal. According to the experts, addicts will most likely feel symptoms of their withdrawal for up to two years! *Sigh*. And one of the landmark times to experience this is at eighteen months.

I am happy to say that I am approaching the eighteen-month landmark very soon, and just as predicted, I got hit with what I'm pretty sure is post-acute withdrawal over the past few weeks—and mostly over the past few days. I was transported back in time to the world I experienced when I was in that New Year's Eve picture. I was mad, irritable, physically sick (vomiting), anxious, tired, apathetic, couldn't sleep properly, craved sugar big-time, had dreams about drinking again, and even woke myself up with a night terror. Could I have had a touch of a gastrointestinal virus? Possibly. But when I thought back to how the doctors at Save-My-Life Boarding School explained post-acute withdrawal, I would bet money that that's what I had been experiencing. I don't recommend that anyone diagnose themselves without seeing a doctor first, but knowing that this even existed allowed me to find peace faster and took away some of the fear I would have experienced if I had not known.

Frustrating—yes. End of the world—far from it! Even though my body brought me back to a time and feeling I had for the most part forgotten, I once again used my tools, talked to friends and family, told my kids straight up that I wasn't feeling good instead of hiding, focused on the successful recovery I was blessed with (when I was awake), and allowed it to pass. No thoughts of self-harm in any way. No depression demons appeared. No hope was lost! I was educated and knew that what I was experiencing was quite normal and may even happen again. Overall, it served as a reminder of how far I've come and how strong I am.

Happy almost eighteen months clean and sober to me!

~ ANSWERING OUR KIDS' QUESTIONS HONESTLY

I am getting ready to go to a gala and my son asks me a question that makes me realize how much my behaviour when I was drinking still affects him deeply. While doing my makeup, I am not thinking anything about the topic of alcohol because I am no longer obsessed with it due to a lot of hard work and dedication. So the words, "Mom, what would you do if someone gave you a drink?" shock me. I look at him and I can see the seriousness in his eyes.

I realize I have two ways of answering the question. I can (a) laugh and say, "Oh don't be silly that won't happen," or (b) take the time to answer his question honestly and clearly. I feel it is important to choose option (b).

One of the biggest lessons I've learned over the past year and a half of recovery is that my old belief that I should hide my emotions from my kids and avoid answering serious questions never helped them at all. In fact it hurt them.

When I came home from Save-My-Life Boarding School, my daughter was still very hurt, afraid, and distant. Thankfully, I learned how important honesty was when I was away, and I slowly put that into practice when my kids became comfortable enough to ask me questions.

Now I look at my son and reply, "I would say no thank you to the person and get a Perrier." That is all he needs to hear. He knows this is the truth because he knows how I *do* love my Perrier!

~ LET OUR BOYS CRY TOO

As if speaking up about emotions isn't difficult enough, I will strongly agree with anyone who says that it's even more difficult to do so if you are a male. We still live in a society where boys are told to suck it up and stop crying more often than girls are, which is largely due to the fact that for years, boys have been bombarded with the task of maintaining pop culture's mostly unrealistic image of super heroes. Let's face it, on the big screen, being strong and brave rarely factors in an acceptable level of sensitivity that includes tears.

My son has experienced his fair share of struggles in his short life. That's not to say that he doesn't have a happy life—because he does. But I think it's safe to say that the ups and downs his precious mind and soul have experienced are already greater than many adults have experienced. Seeing stressful relationship breakups, and witnessing the effects of mental illnesses that caused his mom to be taken away in an ambulance are all too much for anyone's eyes, let alone a small boy's.

But by the grace of God, our lives have done a turnaround, resulting in a home life that is peaceful (for the most part—as long as we aren't chasing Walter while he tries to eat dryer sheets or making sure that he isn't cornering the cats and eating their food). We laugh a lot now. Adam is doing better in school, and he has that sparkle back in his eyes that I missed for so long! But no matter how much better life is, there are still times when I can tell that he is feeling sad and worried. He is very conscious of not hurting my feelings and tries to make sure I am always happy. That must be very tiring for a little guy, and I get it because I used to try to make my mom happy all the time too. No matter how hard I try to show him that I am healthy and already very happy, he gets overwhelmed and afraid at times, and just needs a good cry.

I have learned a lot of amazing things about the power of accepting our feelings. I am so grateful for this, and I now do my best to share these strategies with my kids. And to reiterate the theme of this entry, I am mindful that I allow my son to express his feelings as freely as my daughter does.

The old me often got frustrated when my kids cried, and looking back now, I realize that the frustration came from a lack of knowledge of how to deal with their emotions in a healthy way. I feel sick to my stomach when I remember the times I sent my kids to their room until they stopped crying or for telling them that they were OK when clearly they were not.

Here are some emotion-accepting tips I now implement with my kids and equally with my son. These may seem pretty basic to most parents, but to me they were not.

When my son is sad I console him and tell him it's OK to cry, and I don't give him a time limit on when that should be done. No more "OK, that's enough crying," because who am I to judge that it's enough? I would be pissed if someone said that to *me*, so why is it OK to say that to our kids?

I validate his fears and concerns. I don't say, "That's nothing to cry about" or "That's a silly thing to be afraid of" because once again, I am not in his mind and have no right to choose how he feels.

I take the time to listen to why he is upset. I am the first to admit that I usually have my phone in my hand, but when he is sad, I put it down. Granted, I may need to actively remind myself to keep doing so—but I do. Nothing is more important in that moment than giving my full attention to him.

And last but certainly not least, I show my sadness too! When I was sick I thought that hiding my emotions protected my kids from pain, but in fact it caused it. They are so in tune with our personalities, including our nonverbal language, that they can tell when we are sad. Denying this only confuses them and in makes them worry more. To my surprise, when I started telling my kids the truth about my emotions, they accepted it and went on with their day.

Crying isn't easy for most of us. But I challenge you to remember a time when you didn't feel better after you cried! I can actually compare the feeling of calm after a good cry to that of the feeling of relief and happiness when a run is done. Let's make sure that we don't hold those opportunities for happiness and relief hostage from our sons.

~ ONE-OF-A-KIND ADAM

Hello, my name is Adam. I am the son of a great woman who I call Mom. I want to share with you how I felt when my mother was sick. Hopefully it will help kids my age to know that they are not alone.

Of course I was sad when my mother got sick—as all kids would be. I even had to go to therapy for a little bit. Now here's the thing—I did not feel the same way when my mom was ill. I felt "off" at school, and I could not focus because I was worried about my mom. Slowly I realized my mom would be OK. Through all the good and bad days in my life, I learned that you either give something up or go through hard times to be successful at even the little things.

Things are a lot better now, and of course I feel amazing. I have met awesome people—and I live with one too. Some-

times when I was sad, I would be really funny on purpose to hide my feelings. I needed to talk about things. When my mom and I are sad, we talk to each other. If you don't talk, then things will slowly get worse. It will really hurt—not physically, but mentally. Always remember to please talk to someone if you are sad. Remember you're beautiful. You're one of a kind.

~ GIVING'S ULTERIOR MOTIVE

I'm a fan of a good egg salad sandwich. And I'm willing to bet that the best egg salad sandwiches are found at a baby shower. You know the kind—cut into triangles, often crustless, made with real mayo. Yup! Those are the ones. So in the interest of enjoying said sandwiches, I am often willing to shell out an average of a hundred bucks at a baby store to fit into the baby shower crowd. You know the kind—often early thirties, moms themselves, happy to have several hours set aside to drink wine without their own kids crying in the background. Yup! Those are the ones.

Where am I going with this, you may ask. No, I'm not about to share a Pinterest board of sandwich recipes and photos of the cute little cake-kabobs in the shape of a baby's bum. I'm actually raising a point or two about how so much of our society has giving and generosity confused with receiving and subconscious expectations.

If I were truly going to attend a baby shower to *only* see the baby and share in the excitement of their birth, (a) I wouldn't print off the registry list and after scouring the store for a practical gift, end up choosing my item by the awesome-gift-giver price tag anyway, (b) I wouldn't secretly judge fellow gift-givers when I recognize that some of the gifts are from the dollar store (especially when I am a huge fan of the dollar store!), and (c) I wouldn't need to walk away feeling confident that my gift represented my exceptional friendship status with the new mom. *Sigh.*

It's going to take time to change a culture that grew up on needing positive acknowledgement for almost everything, including any act of giving. I can clearly remember that the paintings I made with my kindergarten hands were given to my parents not only to make them happy to have received them, but equally for the satisfaction I got from watching them get stuck to the fridge with the banana magnet. It's not easy to remove our faulty sense of what giving should feel like when we are accustomed to being acknowledged for it. Many of us have even been taught that it's necessary to return the giving gesture, rather than just be thankful—am I right? So with that being said, I'm pretty sure that Hallmark won't be discontinuing their "thank you card" line any time soon when they make millions on how we inherently have difficulty in trusting that the root of giving comes from love—not from the need for acknowledgement.

I challenge you to check your motives next time you are out buying a gift for someone. Honestly check to see if a need for something in return is there (whether in the form of social acknowledgement or a thank you card). I bet you an egg salad sandwich that your gift isn't truly rooted in love.

~ BILL 163 IS PASSED

I sit on the edge of my seat in the spectator's gallery of Queen's Park with colleagues from Waterloo, Ottawa, and Elgin County (to name a few) and hope and pray for Bill 163: The Supporting Ontario's First Responders Bill, to pass.

As we wait and talk among ourselves, the consensus is that we are excited—but equally nervous—to hear the party leader's decision. Ontario has been in a "PTSD Bill holding pattern" for years. Educated through experience, we have learned quite well about the numerous steps it takes for a Bill to be granted Royal Assent. In fact, before Bill 163, several PTSD Bills had been presented in the Legislative Assembly, only to have their progress halted for one reason or another.

So here we are on a chilly April afternoon, with Bill 163 needing a majority vote to be passed (this is the furthest any Bill of its kind in Ontario has made it). As the vote takes place, I hold my breath and the hand of a colleague who has become my friend throughout this fight. Then, one by one, every...single...member of the Liberal, Progressive Conservative, and New Democratic parties stand up to unanimously vote in favour for the passing of Bill 163. It is a surreal and amazing feeling.

Bittersweet tears fill the eyes of many. Too many lives have been lost and families destroyed while waiting for a PTSD Bill to be passed. Too many night terrors, divorces, and bankruptcies occurred while heroes waited for the financial help they desperately needed to get well. Yes, we leave Queen's Park triumphant, but we also leave with heavy hearts as we remember those who never had the chance to celebrate with us.

~ CAPITAL MEMORIES AND MOTIVATIONS

While I sit on the train, returning home from our nation's capital, Ottawa, I can't help but think that the noise of sandwich wrappers opening, washroom doors slamming, and people sneezing shouldn't be bothering me (because believe me, those noises are bothering me). Why? Well, because I am on a comfortable train while many of my colleagues from across Canada and the U.S. are riding bikes from Ottawa to Washington. They are willing to brave bad weather, exhaustion, and homesickness in order to promote remarkable changes! So what the heck do I really have to complain about?

First responders have been preparing to embark on a 1538 km, fifteen-day journey for quite some time now, and they officially took their first pedal toward Washington, DC, yesterday. With Canada's Parliament Buildings as the back drop of their pre-race group photo, riders cheered as they prepared for the road ahead. Dignitaries were on hand to show support and pride for both the participants and those who had worked behind the scenes.

The Capital to Capital Ride was founded by Ottawa paramedic Norm Robillard and New York State EMT Ken Martin after they met at other fundraising and awareness events. The ride's goal is to raise awareness about the mental health of first responders across both countries. I was so fortunate to have participated as a guest speaker in the pre-ride symposium held at the Ottawa Police Association yesterday.

I had never been to Ottawa before. Every person I talked to said it was beautiful. They were right. Not only did I enjoy the perfect spring weather on Parliament Hill, but I was also given a personal tour of the spectacular Parliament Buildings by my local member of Parliament and fellow mental health advocate, John Brassard. I think he was just as excited to give me the tour as I was to partake in it, and I can't blame him for a second. The magical energy of the history of our country that radiates through every room is palpable! The pin on MP Brassard's suit lapel signifies that he is a member of Parliament and allows him twenty-four-hour access to the building. Having the opportunity to go behind the scenes with him raised the experience to a whole other level.

I learned about the history of the Red Chamber and saw the bullet holes in the wall from the shooting that took place a few years back. The artwork and architecture was breathtaking! I could have spent an entire week admiring the work that must have taken countless hours to create.

My favourite room by far was the Parliament Library. Being a book lover myself, I had goosebumps when I walked into the sunbeam-filled room of pure history and craftsmanship. Every wooden carving that lined the circular walls was handmade and different from the next. Even more remarkable was learning that this room was the only room that survived the 1916 fire because its iron doors were closed. Can you even imagine the devastation if all of Canada's historical documents were destroyed? How powerfully symbolic it is that regardless of whether the fire was arson or not (they still do not know to this day), nothing could destroy our county's heritage. Like I said—goosebumps!

To top it all off, I was finally able to meet the representative from Caribou-Prince George, MP Todd Doherty, who has created the Federal PTSD Bill C-211, which I support and look forward to helping move through to law. He's a genuinely amazing person and advocate for first responders!

My presentation for the Ottawa Police Association went very well, and even though I travelled alone, a "friend" showed up while I was speaking. While I stood there and shared my story of hope and recovery, a little spider crawled across the podium. Spiders are everywhere I go. They remind me to stay strong and remember how far I've come from the times I spent staring out a hospital window, watching them spin their webs—allowing me to take my mind off the pain and guilt that filled my body while I was hospitalized. Looking back now, I can see how they were my first "mindfulness" friends, and seeing one yesterday grounded me quite well as I looked away from my speech and shared that part of my story. Life is good.

~ DAY IN THE LIFE OF MY MILD DEPRESSION

I know I have written about the healing power of mindfulness and living in the moment a lot, but I just want to share how difficult it is to do such things when depression rears its ugly head. When depression engulfs me in its cloud, I *need* to sleep all day or be bombarded by reminders of (a) things I am not doing and should do, (b) things I have done in the past that I shouldn't have done, or (c) things in the future that I want to do but don't know how to. *Sigh.*

For those of you who are fortunate enough to not live with depression, let me share what it's like to live inside my head when I experience it. And keep in mind, the following daily routine example is one during my mildest form of depression.

9:00 a.m.—What I want to do: Clean the backyard. Get a coffee. Get caught up on paying bills. What I do: Nothing.

10:00 a.m.—What I want to do: Get dressed in a nice outfit and drive to get a coffee from Tim's. What I do: Flop out of bed (which is an accomplishment in itself), throw on some shoes and a sweater even though it's thirty degrees outside because putting on a bra is *way* too much energy; I'd rather sweat like a track runner while I drive than make an effort to look good.

11:00 a.m.—What I want to do: Go outside with my neighbour who invites me to have a Perrier. What I do: Ignore the invitation until my guilt takes over, then text him from my bed telling him that I can't today.

Noon—What I want to do: Make lunch, walk my dog, and put together my new rowing machine. What I do: Eat ice cream out of the carton, let my dog go for a quick pee in the backyard, and walk past the rowing machine that is by the door still in its box that the cats have torn apart.

1:00 p.m.—What I want to do: Not sleep. What I do: Sleep.

2:00 p.m.—What I want to do: Not sleep. What I do: Sleep.

3:00 p.m.—What I want to do: Get out of bed because I have a headache from not doing anything all day. What I do: Convince myself to stay in bed, because I have a headache from not doing anything all day. I proceed to wallow in self-pity because this time of the day is the danger-zone part of the day, meaning that if I don't force myself to get out of bed, there is *no* turning back, and I will remain in bed all day.

4:00 p.m.—What I want to do: Some stretches on the floor to get my blood circulating and hopefully relieve my headache. What I do: Touch my toes. Once.

5:00 p.m.—What I want to do: Laundry. What I do: Kick the pile of dirty clothes into a taller, smaller-looking pile and return to bed.

6:00 p.m.—What I want to do: Brush my teeth. What I do: Remind myself that I am well into the danger zone, so it is not even practical to do such a thing when I will be asleep very soon.

7:00 p.m.—What I want to do: Nothing. What I do: Nothing. Success!

8:00 p.m.—What I want to do: Anything but sit in bed! What I do: Not even change positions in bed.

9:00 p.m.—What I want to do: Write. What I do: Write. The only way I can live in the moment—my healthy source of serenity.

There you go, folks. As I sit here and type from the same spot I woke up in twelve hours before, I am actually happy that to me I had a relatively productive day!

Now I'm off to bed—I'm exhausted.

~ DISAPPOINTMENT AND CONFUSION

Being the training coordinator at work isn't what I thought it would be. Not even close. The excitement I went into this role with has faded and has been replaced with disappointment and confusion. I will be resigning tomorrow. I'm not sure what the next step will be for me, but I do know that it will include my continued successful recovery. If I remain in this role, I feel I will be pulled down a deep, negative path that will most certainly jeopardize my health. I didn't see this coming…

~ HEALING POWER OF VULNERABILITY

I'm nearly forty years old but have amazingly done most of my personal growth in just one year. Crazy right? *Whoa, Natalie! Back up. Are you really going to use the word "crazy" when you're a mental health advocate? What impression will people get of you?* So there it is—a perfect example of how a lifetime of depression-guided, self-appraisal can to this day influence how I think about (or over-think) the impression I'm making on people.

Even though recovering from the dark world of depression, PTSD, and addiction has undoubtedly strengthened my confidence and inner peace, there is still a side of me (the tattoo-free side I suppose) that deeply safeguards my (albeit false) perpetually smiling image. But why does this side of me still care what image I am portraying? I really have nothing to hide. I have already very publicly written and illustrated to thousands of readers who the Natalie is behind a fragile bubble of incessant laughter. People already know that I have travelled from the relentless hell of suicidal ideation to the heaven of self-acceptance and love. So why would I still worry about whether or not I make a good impression when I know that I am a good person and when I'm pretty candid about, well—everything?

I think the answer lies in the fact that I am still a woman who battles mental illness in a world that often smiles and nods in the limelight of mental health awareness, but quickly closes the blinds when the cameras are off to retreat to the comfortable world of com-placency—a fact that can make even me feel like I should retract certain impressions that I've made.

Promoting a stigma-free world is somewhat of a social hot topic these days, but hot-topic talk is cheap when lives are still being lost. Many people simply give the impression that they maintain a stigma-free view of people who battle mental illnesses when really they would rather gargle hornets than speak out about the stigma-filled acts they still witness. So no wonder depression still makes an impression on even me.

But alas, my doubts about speaking up and fighting for the sup-pression of mental health stigma always subside, and I soon feel the need to strip down to my core beliefs again.

I finally feel comfortable in my own skin, and the world remains a much better place when I don't have to hide.

~ VERY AFRAID

I've spoken with my Human Resources Department, and we have come to the conclusion that the only full-time position available to me if I resign from the training coordinator role is to go back to being an advanced care paramedic on the road. I'm not so sure how I feel about this. At the very least, I'm afraid.

I will be part-time for a short while to fulfill my contract requirements, and then I will be back full-time, night shifts included. It already hurts my brain just thinking about it.

Regardless of my limited choices for employment, I send the resignation email and give hugs to the girls in my corner (literally—we sit in a square and all have a corner). I love these girls. They have really helped me get through the last three months. I give one of them my baby plant and another an "I will miss you" note. I pack up my stuff and leave the building. I know I won't ever be back there again.

~ NO LIGHT AT THE END OF THE TUNNEL THIS TIME

I've done lots of positive self-talk. I have a family to feed, and I don't want to seem like a failure. Without a light at the end of the tunnel this time, I drive to the paramedic station and accept the fact that I really don't know what will come of this.

First shift back: I'm almost late because I get lost (I hate that). I'm going to a station I haven't been to before, and I'm working with a partner I've never worked with. No comfort-zone buffer this time. "Thrown into the fire" is a suitable phrase to describe how I feel. I don't want to psych myself out, but the three months on the road before moving into the training coordinator role was hard enough to get through.

My out-of-control thoughts are bouncing around in my brain like a tennis ball. Noise is still difficult for me to cope with, and I'm not as able to make small talk as fluidly or willingly as before. I think this happens because I just don't have the space left in my brain to coordinate my words—especially not for very long. This difficulty with small talk doesn't just apply to my partners; it also applies to my patients. Lots of small talk happens in the county I work in because most drives to the hospital are over fifteen minutes and most patients are wide awake and chatting fine.

I get home irritable and exhausted. We weren't even busy, nor did we do any dynamic calls, and yet I feel like I just ran a multi-casualty incident all day long. I'm bitter, angry, and can barely fall asleep.

~ SHIFT NUMBER SIX

Shift number six is my last as a paramedic. The darkness is back.

~ MY STRETCH OF THE HIGHWAY

I just finished recording a video after my therapy session about PTSD, and in it I mentioned how I have so many memories of working on the highway as a paramedic. There is a stretch of highway that I often worked on, which is nicknamed the "Bermuda Triangle." Coincidentally, I am on my way home, and I am stuck in traffic in that very Bermuda Triangle. It's a beautiful sunny day (which is when some of the worst accidents happen). A lot of people don't know that beautiful sunny days can bring horrific accidents. Sometimes, when people are happy, on their way to the cottage, or singing and smiling, they don't pay as much attention to the road as they should. So, as I am not moving an inch, I thought I would use this nostalgic location to do some of my own personal talk-therapy. I turn on my voice recorder and record this while waiting for traffic to clear:

I realize there are still so many emotions that I can carry with me that don't necessarily trigger nightmares and are a time of personal pride that I share with my first responder family.

Some sensations I will never forget, like the heaviness in the air right now. It's a hot August day, and I can remember going to the motor vehicle collisions on days like today that I knew were going to be bad because the traffic was backed up forever. Dispatch would get multiple 911 calls, and I would have a gut feeling that I should start the air ambulance early. I was in my full black uniform so I knew I was going to be sweating my butt off. However, that was OK because I also knew that I was going to be helping quite a few people. I would arrive and find my own spot among the wreckage. Usually the highway was already shut down, but if it wasn't, I would tell the police officer to shut it down because we needed room to work safely as well as a place for the air ambulance to land. And then I would get to work.

I will never forget the feeling of the crunching glass underneath my workboots. Or the smell of oil and rubber and hot asphalt on those really hot days. They were just noises and smells I knew. They were familiar. I can probably tell you how tall a guardrail is because I can't even count how many times I've climbed over one in my career. These are things that most people never experience. Pulling up to the call and getting that first look at what condition the car is in and where it is. What will you have to be traipsing or crawling through? It's just an amazing career.

I remember having butterflies in my stomach when I could finally hear the air ambulance overhead and thinking, "OK, they're here. Perfect. We gave them an accurate extrication time, and we have the patient packaged and ready to go. They will be going where they need to go to get the best care." But still thinking, "Did I miss anything? Will I give the report right?" You want to get this patient moving as quickly as possible. And then feeling that elation and pride when the helicopter takes off while every bystander in their car watches in awe and wonders what has happened.

It's funny because I'm right beside the highway exit I would take to get to my former station, barely moving because most likely there is an accident ahead.

Then there are the patients that you don't have to send by air ambulance who you finally get into the back of your ambulance. You close the door and have quiet. The noise from the extrication machines and sirens and people suddenly goes away.

I can also remember the nights when it's minus forty and you know you're going to have the calls on the highway where you won't feel your hands after two minutes of being outside. You will have to fumble with your frozen hands to put a patient on a backboard as fast as possible. You won't be able to feel your face because there is nothing to cover it from the wind that whips across the road—but you love it! You just love it. And it's dark and the lights are flashing, and you're worried about patients in cars getting hypothermia because you haven't gotten to them yet. I always loved the feeling of finally getting into the back of the ambulance and taking off my winter coat and having more room to move around without it.

I don't need to be sad that I don't experience these things anymore. I'm grateful that I had so many opportunities to help people in those situations. I'm grateful for the partners I've laughed with while driving the wrong way on the highway (when it's closed) because that was the only way to get to a scene. I'm grateful for all of those times in my life and for everyone I've been able to share those moments with.

You're my family. You get what I'm saying when I describe all of those things. You know what it feels like to crawl through a broken window to hold a patient's hand. You know what it's like to try to balance an unconscious patient's head upright so that you can get a cervical collar on them. You know how to figure out how to do eight things at once. That's what we are so good at doing!

To all of you out there who are still doing these incredible things, I've got your back. I'm going to keep fighting to make sure that you get through the hard times you may experience when dealing with all those sights and sounds and smells. I'm fighting to make sure that one day you are hanging up your uniform because you choose to, not because you have to.

~ BOTH WILL MAKE ME SHIT, I'M SURE

This damn darkness. Why is it back? Not nearly to the extent it used to be (don't worry, I am safe), but it's here nonetheless—close enough to make me feel like a fraud and dark enough to make me want to hide from all the positive advice I have given over the last however long it's been.

I've been wanting to write about it because, as you know, writing is therapy to me. But no matter how hard the magnetic pull has been between my fingertips and these keys, before right now, I have filled my time with sleep in order to avoid how honest this entry may end up being. So as you may be reading this and thinking, "That's courageous of her to share this," I promise you that all I can feel are figurative fingers pointing at me and hear skeptics yelling, "We knew that you weren't better," when I say that I am depressed because I can't be a paramedic anymore.

I'm torn and uncomfortable. I have finally closed the pages of a figurative old book, but not before reading the last few chapters over and over again because I didn't want to admit that this book was done. It sucks. I had finally settled into the comfy corner of pillows in my reading spot, had finally chosen my favourite coffee mug, and had gotten so comfortable with the feel and smell of the pages—and now, that book is done. I'm not getting anything else out of reading it over and over again. The comfy pillows are making my back hurt. The coffee mug is suddenly just a coffee mug. And the pages feel cold and smell boring.

Today, unable to stop the force to write, as my mind and soul know how necessary writing is for me to grow, I have finally accepted that a new book, chapter, page, whichever you choose, has come to be— and this first edition really sucks for me.

Days are boring, long, and filled with my old alien brain lately. Nights are sleepless. Thoughts are dark and incessant. This makes me mad! I will get through this. I have the tools. But man, oh man, it feels like a punch in the throat having to share that I feel like shit again. I am not looking for sympathy. I am not looking for anything really. Selfishly, this post is for me. The honesty, vulnerability, and egoless peace I feel from writing this are what I need right now.

I'm doing a juice cleanse today. I think it will suck, but I can tell you that this writing cleanse is worse. Both will make me shit, I'm sure.

~ FIVE FACTS ABOUT MY PTSD SYMPTOMS

Living with PTSD sucks. Living with addiction and depression sucks. Let me highlight some reasons why:

First, I often can't remember who you are. I know that it's common to forget a name when we meet an individual again, but I forget I have ever even met you at all! This doesn't happen all the time, but it's common enough that I avoid large gatherings for fear that the person I'm talking to is expecting that I remember them. I try so hard to practise name association, but that memory technique is completely useless when I can't remember that we've ever met. It's an embarrassing fact about my life now.

Second, I rarely leave my house. I've become somewhat of a hermit. I try to get out and enjoy the nice weather, but there is not a single bone in my body that wants to do so. Noises like motorcycles, loud mufflers, chainsaws, and buses put me into full anxiety mode. I try to plug my ears fast enough, but it's usually too late. When the noise comes at me, all I want to do is sit in my room with my fan on, which provides enough white noise to block out the world.

Third, I can be very apathetic. Don't get me wrong, I'm a caring person; buried deep down is my desire to help people all the time—which makes sense as I had been a paramedic for so long. But allowing strong emotions such as love to bubble to the surface as much as I allowed it to before is very scary to me. My ability to logically match an appropriate reaction to an emotion has changed, often causing me to worry and overreact to something quite minor. So I avoid feeling all together. Love for my kids is a different story. I love them so much I could explode. However, as for any intimate relationship in the future, I am doubtful any will last. So, I imagine myself living alone on a mountain, and somehow I'm completely OK with that.

Fourth, I constantly fear that you don't believe me. There is a liar in my head that tells me that anyone who has not experienced PTSD, depression, or addiction doesn't believe me. It tells me that people are just nice to my face but that behind closed doors they roll their eyes and laugh at me. I suppose that's why almost all of my friends have changed to ones who get it, and that's OK. I know for the most part people support me, but the liar convinces me from time to time that even my closest friends and family think I'm putting on somewhat of an act—that I can just pull up my socks and stop being so glum and useless. It's funny how I think that people think that I want to be sad.

Finally, I forget really important things. Not only do I forget that I've met you, I forget things that are super important, such as medical appointments or to pick people up—heck I even forget what I've forgotten! Eff!

The struggle is real.

~ I WAS A PARAMEDIC

I remember telling people over the years that being a paramedic was not the be all and end all of my identity. Yes, I loved my profession (and still do), but I was positive that I could take the good memories that I had and move on to a different profession if need be. Wow, was I wrong! I am learning now how being a paramedic is deeply rooted in my psyche. For over eleven years, it allowed me to feel like I was making a difference in the world every day. It gave me purpose and filled me with a passion for education. It allowed me to provide financially for my family. I was proud, happy, and accomplished. I WAS A PARAMEDIC. Now...well, I don't know what I am.

I have come to the conclusion that I am without a doubt grieving the loss of part of my identity. Many people would give anything to stop doing their job, but I was never one of those people. Not to be insensitive to other professions, but being a first responder is more than just a profession; it's a passion, and now having to accept that I may for the rest of my life be doing a job that I am not passionate about because I have a mental injury (yes, I am now accurately calling what I suffer from a "post-traumatic stress *injury*" or PTSI) is very difficult for me. Allow me to elaborate:

~

I went from closing down highways so that helicopters could land to closing the fridge on a good day if I chose to eat. I went from phoning base-hospital physicians to get permission to pronounce a death to being suffocated by anxiety and not being able to phone anyone at all. I went from performing life-saving skills such as chest needles and intubations to only being able to perform the life-saving skill of taking my own breath. I went from teaching others how to run a dynamic cardiac arrest to teaching others how to leave me alone so that I don't get triggered. I went from feeling pride when I put on my uniform to not being able to look at my uniform at all without bawling my eyes out. I went from racing to calls with the lights and sirens on to the racing of my heart even while I'm alone in my house. I went from having friends at work to laugh with every day to barely seeing those friends at all. I went from feeling successful to feeling like a failure.

Don't get me wrong, any job is a blessing, but being a paramedic is more than just a job; it's part of who I am, and rewiring that part of my conscious and subconscious world is exhausting, confusing, and very difficult.

If I somewhat sound like a complaining, ungrateful person, it is because changing a part of me that I loved SO MUCH is not easy.

~ LITTLE LIGHTNING

So there's this cat...

I agree to help a friend in the form of becoming a cat sitter. He is in need of a home for his cat for three to four weeks, and although hesitant (as I already have two cats and a dog of my own), I oblige. I have learned that so much of successful addiction recovery is linked to my ability to selflessly help others. So, my friend drops off Little Lightning (a.k.a. LL Kool Kitty) and what ensues is terrifying—but also a hidden gift of enlightenment.

LL seems to be quite calm and accepting of her new home-away-from-home when we first open up the crate she arrives in. Caroline and I introduce our two cats, Olly and Pepsi to our feline guest. OMG, it is horrible! We hear noises come out of all three cats' mouths unlike anything we have heard before. It sounds like a combination of children screaming and a siren stuck in the "on" position! Caroline and I freeze! Then we do the only natural thing to do—we scream ourselves! Everyone is screaming and frozen on the stairs. We are all pretty much ready to call the visit quits.

The traumatic cat introduction causes poor little LL to run into Caroline's room and hide in the corner. Due to fear, her bowels let go and she proceeds to poop on the floor, dresser, bed, and, well—everywhere. Olly and Pepsi need to be kept in a separate room down the hall because they are hissing at Caroline's door so loudly that I am sure their vocal cords will dislodge and land on the floor in front of them!

We don't know what to do. Caroline and I stare at each other with our jaws on the ground while we let what we have just experienced sink in. Then we recruit some help from our friends who are over visiting.

LL finally hides *inside* Caroline's box spring mattress. She is scared and ready to scratch anyone who comes near her (totally understandable). So the following attempts to get LL out from the box spring go a little like this:

Attempt: With an oven mitt on, Jorden tries to scoop LL out of the box spring. Result: LL quickly takes the oven mitt. Jorden retreats.

Attempt: With cat treats in hand, Jackson and I try to lure LL out. Result: LL starts to *bark* at us. Jackson and I retreat.

Attempt: With laundry baskets and me in full riot gear (snow pants and uniform jacket on and shin pads on my arms), Trevor and I attempt to coax LL into the laundry basket. Result: Trevor catches LL and sustains some claw injuries while I scream uselessly with sweat dripping down my ridiculous Arctic attire. LL *snuggles* Trevor immediately!

The poor thing. LL is just scared and lost, and is looking to be comforted. But isn't that the case with *all* beings?

During the following three weeks, LL occupies Adam's room. She transforms from a hide-in-the-corner, hissing kitty to a loving, affectionate, and sweet cat. Patience, love, and hope is what she required in order to start trusting again. What started out as a scary set of circumstances turned into an example of how over time, post-traumatic growth can occur.

We really miss LL, but witnessing the reunion of her with her dad (owner) was *priceless*!

Healing from any trauma takes time, and just like LL, we all need patience, love, and hope along the way in order to do so. Lucky for LL and me, we have no shortage of these things in our lives.

~ GOD'S FILTER

I absolutely love the mountains! I swear they are where I am supposed to live one day. So, I am over the moon to have a speaking engagement in Alberta. I fly out alone, and I'm excited to do so. What an amazing opportunity to reflect on my journey so far. It feels symbolic to physically travel so many miles to share my story when I have mentally travelled a great distance with my recovery to get to where I am today.

As I get comfortable at my window seat on the plane, I mindfully celebrate my growth. The plane breaks through the clouds, and the light from the sun shines through my window. The blueness of the vast sky is breathtaking. This is a feeling and a memory I want to capture—I take a selfie with my phone. Right now in this moment, I feel like my life is soaring higher than the clouds we are flying above. I look at the photo; I am smiling as I look out the window. The image shows the sunbeams streaming across my face as if I had planned it that way—but I didn't. It was like God decided to apply His own filter to my picture! I will call it "happiness."

As we lower and break through the clouds, I can see the Rocky Mountains in the distance. I am at peace, and I think to myself, "The only thing that could make this trip any better is if David Beckham is waiting for me in the airport." OK, I won't push my luck!

~ HEALTHY PERSPECTIVES. HOW?

Today I wake up to horribly loud noises outside. They are noises I was expecting to eventually hear but didn't want to.

I live in an older neighbourhood with the most beautiful, mature trees. Now that it's fall, the leaves are bright orange, yellow, and red, and one of my most favourite things to do is to sit on my bed, write, drink coffee, and look out my window to see the most spectacular tree in my front yard.

The noise that wakes me up today means that this spectacular tree will soon be gone.

Today is the day that a wood chipper and some chainsaws will destroy my gorgeous view. Today my forty-plus-year-old ash tree will be cut down. I dread looking out the window to *not* see what

I loved so much. Sadly, the beautiful tree is diseased, and my city mandated the removal of it and some others on the street—three are to be cut down on the small section of my road alone.

So why am I sharing this story? Why am I boo-hooing about losing a tree when I am lucky to have a lawn for the trees to grow on in the first place? I'm also lucky that the sick tree didn't come down in a storm and land on my roof or car—or family member. I'm sharing it to remind myself (and anyone who chooses to read this) about the importance of somehow finding a healthy perspective after a loss. Easier said than done, I know.

I finally look out my window when the horrendous noises cease and pull my earplugs out. My first reaction is, "I'm moving! That's it! I'm calling my real estate agent brother and moving somewhere else! Get me the 'FOR SALE' sign!" At this moment, all I see is my sad, broken tree. I have forgotten how to have a healthy perspective (or gratitude for that matter) and am ready to start packing *today*!

I simmer down, keep the packing tape in the garage, and find a meaning in this experience. I start to change my perspective and now see how the process of this tree being cut down greatly resembles my own journey with coming to terms with my PTSI and not being a practising paramedic anymore.

The tree was strong on the outside, capable of providing many good things to the people who came around it. Shade, oxygen, beautiful scenery—a place for Walter to pee. All great things! But over time it got sick on the inside. I did notice that there were a lot of dead branches underneath it when I would mow the lawn, but I would simply move them and carry on. I never for a minute thought that this enormous tree could actually be *very* sick. Years went by and the tree seemed to still be OK, but no one knew how much it was actually struggling. Then one day, the tree doctors came by and let me know that this tree was so sick that it actually had to be taken down.

I couldn't believe it. How could that be? It had been such a good tree for so long!

So from then on I enjoyed the tree every day knowing that it wouldn't be there for much longer. Its usefulness was now questionable, and I could somehow relate to how this experienced tree must have felt if it had feelings, learning that it wasn't able to do the thing it loved the most anymore—it couldn't be a tree.

Time went by and I hoped that the tree doctors had forgotten about my sick tree. I hoped that all of its beauty and experience had fooled them into believing it was OK again. I also hoped that the tree itself had forgotten it was sick, or that there was some kind of miracle that fixed the inside of it and made it strong and capable again. But alas, as the tree kept trying to be what it wasn't anymore, it got sicker and sicker. At some point the tree and I both needed to accept that big changes were inevitable—and that they weren't going to be easy.

During the tree's removal, I knew that its transformation was going to get ugly. Branches that used to be there would be gone and would leave an empty space that would take some time to be filled. It would hurt hearing the wood chipper take my tree away—but it had to be done.

Next spring a new tree will be planted. One that will grow into a very different tree. In the meantime I will miss seeing my old tree's beauty, and it will take some time for the new tree to feel as capable and important as the old tree was—but it will happen. Change happens, and that's OK.

I wonder what the new tree will look like. I wonder how well it will hold up a swing or provide shade on a sunny day. On a positive note, I won't have to rake up the thousands of leaves the old tree was about to let go of. And now that it's gone I get to use the time it would have taken to rake the leaves to instead imagine how great the new one will be. I bet it will be *beautiful*.

~

AFTERWORD

~

Much more still needs to be done to help first responders cope with PTSI. The Supporting First Responders Ontario provincial Bill 163 has made obtaining support from the Workplace Safety and Insurance Board much easier and significantly less traumatic, but we are now at a crossroads with how to effectively and compassionately help this group of individuals beyond solely providing financial support.

It is my experience that returning to the profession that caused a traumatic stress injury is not always the best decision for the long-term health of some individuals. I know this to be true because after a brief return to the road, I relapsed.

I am back on track, and with the support of many other first responders, my family and friends, I have been grieving the loss of my career in a healthy way—but it's anything but easy.

Through personal stories, I've learned that because of the uniqueness of our careers, being first responders becomes a large portion of our identity and is deeply rooted in our psyches—so it's not surprising that it's difficult to permanently hang up our uniforms even when we are injured. Being a first responder is a complex job, and PTSI can cause an individual to have difficulty with even the most basic tasks. Quite simply, I went from feeling successful to feeling like a failure.

Because of this, it is my goal to prompt all insurance companies, such as the Workplace Safety and Insurance Board, to employ clinical psychologists who specialize in first responder therapy *and* first responders who have experienced similar injuries as consultants for these cases. After reading dozens of testimonials, I know that many first responders believe that returning to their previous profession is the *only* return to work option they have, and many have been pressured by workplace claims specialists to do just that—and this needs to change.

A good friend and paramedic chief once asked me why I introduce myself as a "paramedic" and then always add "but I'm off the road." I told him that I felt like a fraud if I didn't include that I wasn't a practising paramedic. He replied that he didn't agree and that I would *always* be a paramedic. He said that just because I didn't wear the uniform anymore didn't mean that the values I have and my desire to help people had changed. This advice has been a gift to me. First and foremost I'm Natalie, but I'm still a paramedic, and a damn good one, and I hope to be able to inspire the realization within other first responders who feel they have lost their identity because they are off the road.

We are moving in the right direction, folks! But there is still a lot of work to be done. It's imperative that we keep this positive mental health momentum moving forward.

I believe that surviving PTSI, suicide attempts, and addiction has bestowed upon me the responsibility to help others who are still suffering. Let's reset the tone of mental health culture in the first responder's world to one where our core belief isn't that talking equates to weakness, but rather that it equates to strength and leadership. We need to keep asking questions and sharing recovery stories. We need to combat the fear that holds us back from taking the steps necessary to heal and help.

~

As students of life, it is my hope that you take the incredible lessons I was fortunate to learn at all the Save-My-Life Schools and implement them into your day-to-day lives. Whether or not you live with a mental injury or illness (or have a loved one who does), we need to support each other to the best of our ability.

Life school isn't easy—recess will always be my favourite class. But no matter what, the lessons are always worth learning.

Until next time—class dismissed!